ALSO BY CARLOS LOZADA

WHAT WERE WE THINKING:
A BRIEF INTELLECTUAL HISTORY OF THE TRUMP ERA

THE WASHINGTON BOOK

HOW TO READ POLITICS AND POLITICIANS

CARLOS LOZADA

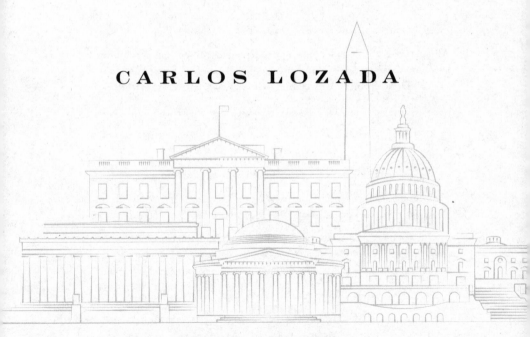

SIMON & SCHUSTER
NEW YORK   LONDON   TORONTO   SYDNEY   NEW DELHI

100 YEARS
SIMON &
SCHUSTER

1230 Avenue of the Americas
New York, NY 10020

Copyright © 2024 by Carlos Lozada

First Simon & Schuster hardcover edition February 2024

SIMON & SCHUSTER and colophon are registered trademarks of Simon & Schuster, LLC

Simon & Schuster: Celebrating 100 Years of Publishing in 2024

For information about special discounts for bulk purchases, please contact Simon & Schuster Special Sales at 1-866-506-1949 or business@simonandschuster.com.

The Simon & Schuster Speakers Bureau can bring authors to your live event. For more information or to book an event, contact the Simon & Schuster Speakers Bureau at 1-866-248-3049 or visit our website at www.simonspeakers.com.

Interior design by Erika R. Genova

Manufactured in the United States of America

1   3   5   7   9   10   8   6   4   2

Library of Congress Cataloging-in-Publication Data has been applied for.

ISBN 978-1-6680-5073-6
ISBN 978-1-6680-5075-0 (ebook)

For Kathleen

CONTENTS

THE
WASHINGTON
BOOK

AUTHOR'S NOTE

IN MY WORK AS A critic and columnist, I often attempt to absorb the major books by a single author, or the vital books on a single subject, and tease out unexpected themes and insights. It never occurred to me that one day I would take a similar approach to my own writings. But when I was invited to deliver the Red Smith Lecture in Journalism at the University of Notre Dame, I decided to revisit a decade's worth of my essays on politics and reviews of political books to find what might be worth resurfacing and reconsidering. *The Washington Book*, which gathers fifty pieces that first appeared in the *Washington Post* and the *New York Times* between 2013 and 2023, is the result of that effort.

There is something both egotistical and humbling about assembling an essay collection. The ego is in assuming that you've produced a body of work worth dressing up in hard covers; the humility in realizing that the sum of the parts adds up to something far different from what you might have anticipated. You never really know what you've written until you read it again or, better yet, until someone else reads it for you.

The introduction to this book is adapted from my Red Smith lecture, "How to Read Washington," delivered on February 9, 2023. The rest of the book is divided into six sections, and each focuses on a recurring activity in the nation's capital. "Leading" covers books by and about major political figures, especially presidents, vice presidents, and candidates for the throne. "Fighting" explores Washington at war, from the 9/11 era to the current standoff between liberalism and authoritarianism. "Belonging" touches on political debates over citizenship, race, gun violence, and identity. "Enduring" centers on the challenges to democracy and community in America, moving from the musings of Tocqueville to the menace of January 6. "Posing" lingers on the obfuscation and posturing inherent in Washington life. "Imagining" considers how history, politics, and thought come together, and often clash.

The pieces in *The Washington Book* appear almost exactly as originally published in the *Post* and the *Times*. I have taken the occasional liberty of eliminating some redundancies across essays that were not originally meant to appear together; omitting a few references that, removed from the moment in which they were published, are too obscure years later; and tweaking some transitions and awkward phrasing that, in the rush of newspaper deadlines, I settled for rather than embraced. Any of the wisdom and all the folly found in the originals remain here.

INTRODUCTION:
HOW TO READ WASHINGTON

I'M A WASHINGTON JOURNALIST, BUT I don't interview politicians or cover foreign policy. I don't report on Congress or break news about government agencies. I don't dig up classified documents, and I certainly don't meet secret sources in parking garages.

Instead, I read.

I read histories and manifestos. I peruse centuries-old essays and decades-old commission reports. I scour Supreme Court decisions and the texts of the latest congressional investigations. I read many books about American politics, and, I must confess, I also read books *by* politicians and government officials. I read the campaign biographies candidates write when they're dreaming of high office, and the revisionist memoirs they publish when they leave office. I read the tell-all books by mid-level administration staffers, and the tell-some books by presidents, vice presidents, senators, chiefs of staff, and FBI directors.

I've spent nearly a decade devoted to this work, first as a book critic at the *Washington Post* and now as an opinion columnist at the *New York Times*. And when people learn that I've spent so much time reading and writing about political books—rather than, say, discovering the next Great American Novel—they typically have one response:

You read those books so we don't have to!

The assumption behind this reaction is that these books are simply terrible. They're self-serving, ghostwritten propaganda, so there's no need to take them seriously. "Does Anyone Actually Read Presidential Campaign Books?" the *Washington Post* asked in a 2022 op-ed essay. The question was rhetorical, of course, because the author concluded that such books range from "mediocre" to "spectacularly bad," and that there's no reason to publish, buy, or read them. And when I wrote a book of my own in 2020 that drew on some 150 volumes about the Trump era in American politics, the reviewer in the *New York Times* suggested that my reading all those other works was "an act of transcendent masochism."

Not just masochism—*transcendent* masochism. That's what people think it is like to read political books.

The pundit Chris Matthews wrote an essay some years ago admitting that a lot of Washingtonians don't really read these books; instead, they give them what he calls the "Washington Read." Rather than reading the full book, you can just "go through it"—give it a quick skim and hope to absorb it that way. Another kind of Washington Read is to read one chapter and pretend you've read the whole book. Or, if you're a serious power player, you scan the index for your own name, examine the relevant pages, and, based on how well you're treated, decide whether to keep reading. In 2013, the journalist Mark Leibovich published a classic Washington book called *This Town*, and he omitted an index because he wanted to force boldface Washingtonians to read the book if they wanted to find their names. (I had our interns at the *Washington Post* build an index of the prominent figures in *This Town*, which we published along with my review.)

Yes, there are some wretched political books. I've encountered plenty. But I am here to make the case for the Washington book. I believe in the Washington book. The relentless negativity about political books misses the point of reading them.

First, this critique is hypocritical. These supposedly serious readers would never lower themselves to read the memoir by, say, Donald Trump's third White House press secretary, but they still want to know what is in such books. They want to know whom these authors criticize or praise, and the scores they settle. When people ask me about one of these books, they don't ask me if it's good. They ask: *What's the news? What's the takeaway?* They want the Washington Read. Even worse, they want me to do the Washington Read for them.

These readers also love nothing more than a brutal takedown of a book written by a politician they despise, or rapturous praise of a book authored by a politician they admire. They treat these books as sources of partisan ammunition. They rarely come to them with an open mind.

And that's a shame—because here's the real reason to read these books: no matter how carefully these politicians sanitize their experiences and positions and records, no matter how diligently they present themselves in the best and safest and most electable or confirmable light—they almost always end up revealing themselves. Whether they mean to or not, in their books, they tell us who they really are.

They can't help it. Politicians can't stop talking about themselves, and in their own pages, they eventually admit or reveal something that helps us see them in a new light. They expose their true fears, their unresolved contradictions, their unspoken ambitions. They tell on themselves. And when you read enough of these books, you don't just learn something about this or that political figure. You also glean something about the state of our civic life.

It is rarely the sexy or newsy material that proves most revelatory. It might be a throwaway line here, a recurring phrase there, maybe something a politician casually said to a low-level aide. It might even be a line in the acknowledgments section of a book. But it's in there somewhere. And that means that even these presumably bad books can be enormously illuminating.

You don't need to rely on the Washington Read. You just need to know how to read the Washington book.

One politician who probably could have made his living as a writer—and now he does, to some extent—is Barack Obama. His 1995 memoir, *Dreams from My Father*, may be his best book, so much so that I think all his subsequent works suffer by comparison.

There is a moment in that memoir when Obama, early in his post-college years, considers his aspirations for community organizing in Chicago. "Because this community I imagined was still in the making, built on the promise that the larger American community, black, white, and brown, could somehow redefine itself—I believed that it might, over time, admit the uniqueness of my own life." He's talking about the challenge of fitting into the African American community, and how the country might evolve, so that he—a young man bringing together Hawaii, Kansas, Kenya, Indonesia, Chicago—could feel a greater sense of belonging.

You might forget about that line until you revisit his keynote address at the 2004 Democratic National Convention in Boston, the speech that affirmed Obama's broad national appeal, the speech in which he hailed the promise of an America that was not red or blue but united, a place so unique that, as he put it, "in no other country on Earth is my story even possible." That is less about struggling to fit in than about embracing a country that enabled him, that made his life a reality. It's a celebratory line in a celebratory speech.

And you might forget about *that* line until you read his 2006 campaign book, *The Audacity of Hope*, where Obama writes that, as a black man of "mixed heritage," sometimes he feels like "a prisoner of my own biography." Obama's view of his own life story has changed again—rather than celebratory, it is now confining.

When I pull these lines together, I start to understand why Obama, throughout his presidency, constantly defaulted to discussing his own life as a symbol—whether of national aspiration, collective self-improvement, or unfulfilled promise. This most self-referential presidency was fully outlined, in his own words, long before he ever sat in the Oval Office.

Obama also tried to manage and refine public perceptions of that story. One place I see that is in *Power Forward*, the memoir by Reggie Love, Obama's former personal aide. Love recalls the time he forgot Obama's briefcase before a flight when they were headed to a Democratic primary debate in 2007. He worried he might be fired, but Obama gave him another chance. It's a passing anecdote in the book, but then Love mentions one reason Obama was annoyed about the missing bag. It turns out, he liked to be seen carrying something when he got off a plane. Here's how Obama explained it to Love: "JFK carried his own bags."

That one moment, that one line—"JFK carried his own bags"—is what I remember best from *Power Forward*. It says so much about how carefully Obama cultivated his public image, how he wanted people to think about his story, and maybe how he thought about it himself. You wouldn't know it unless you read Reggie Love's book.

Sometimes politicians are less subtle when they tell on themselves. If you had read Trump's books—*The Art of the Deal* and *Surviving at the Top* and *The Art of the Comeback* and the rest—you would not have been surprised by the presidency that followed. Shocked, yes, but not surprised.

Here is what I concluded when I read eight of his books in July of 2015: "Sitting down with the collected works of Donald J. Trump is unlike any literary experience I've ever had or could ever imagine . . . Over the course of 2,212 pages, I encountered a world where bragging is breathing and insulting is talking, where repetition and contradiction come standard, where vengefulness and insecurity erupt at random. Elsewhere, such qualities might get in the way of the story. With Trump, they *are* the story."

Although these books are far from truthful—even the ghostwriter of *The Art of the Deal* has disowned that book and regrets ever working on it—they still reveal Trump. For instance, he wrote a book in 2004 called *How to Get Rich*, where he drops a bizarre passage that says much about him. It's about his hair.

"The reason my hair looks so neat all the time is because I don't have to deal with the elements. I live in the building where I work. I take an elevator from my bedroom to my office. The rest of the time, I'm either in my stretch limousine, my private jet, my helicopter, or my private club in Palm Beach, Florida. . . . If I happen to be outside, I'm probably on one of my golf courses, where I protect my hair from overexposure by wearing a golf hat."

Now, what does this show, aside from Trump's vanity? Political reporters often say that the White House traps the president in a bubble, but, judging from that passage, Trump lived in a bubble of his own making long before he came to Washington. In a soliloquy about his hair, Trump reveals his complete and deliberately constructed isolation—the kind of isolation that lets you spin whatever story you've created for yourself.

Sometimes a book reveals the central tension of a politician's ambitions. Here I'm thinking of Hillary Clinton's 1996 manifesto, *It Takes a Village*, published during her tenure as first lady. In this book, two Hillary Clintons are doing battle: she combines progressive tendencies on big policy debates such as health care with a surprisingly moderate to conservative streak on cultural issues including sex and family. Throughout *It Takes a Village*, you see Clinton weaving a line through the center, calling on Americans to stop pitting government against the individual, "and recognize that each must be part of the solution." She even writes that "most of us would describe ourselves as 'middle of the road'—liberal in some areas, conservative in others, moderate in most."

It was a tension Clinton never resolved. Do you remember that 2016 Democratic primary debate with Sen. Bernie Sanders, when CNN's Anderson Cooper asked her if she was a progressive or a moderate? "I'm a progressive," she answered, "but I'm a progressive who likes to get things done." There are many reasons Clinton did not become president of the United States, and lots of them have nothing to do with her politics, qualifications, or values. But that combination of principle and expediency, that semi-reluctant centrism, helps explain why she was perceived as far too cautious and establishment for the left, and far too much of a big-government progressive for the right. If you want to see that in her own words, you can find it in *It Takes a Village*.

Sometimes politicians' books are notable not for the words they include but for those they omit. In his 2022 memoir, *So Help Me God*, Mike Pence covers the drama of January 6, of course, when the vice president, as presiding officer of the Senate, refused to go along with the effort to decertify the results of the 2020 election. Yet when Pence describes the events of that day—a day when rioters were calling for his hanging, and when Trump did nothing to protect him—Pence still obscures the president's transgressions.

He quotes Trump's video message that afternoon, in which the president finally calls for the rioters to leave the Capitol. Here is how Pence quotes Trump: "I know your pain, I know your hurt . . . but you have to go home now, we have to have peace."

Trump did say those words, but that's not all he said. What did Pence cut out of the quote with that ellipsis? If you watch the video, here is what Trump said in the middle of that passage: "We had an election that was stolen from us. It was a landslide election, and everyone knows it, especially the other side." Only then does he go on to say, "but you have to go home now, we have to have peace."

Even when telling his supporters to stand down, Trump was still lying about the election. And in his memoir, where Pence is making his case to history, he still covers for the boss.

When you're reading a Washington book, you must look for the go-to lines, the rhetorical crutches that politicians lean on. In her 2019 memoir, *The Truths We Hold*, Kamala Harris, then a US senator from California, repeatedly brings up the notion of false choices. For instance, she writes that "it is a false choice to suggest that you must either be for the police or for police accountability. I am for both." And she recalls a town hall meeting in Sacramento during which a constituent complained that Harris cared more about undocumented immigrants than about American citizens. She said that was another "false choice," and that she "care[d] deeply about them both."

Now, it sounds very thoughtful to say that something is a false choice. But politics is all about making difficult choices, about picking among competing priorities. Harris's eagerness to stay on both sides of difficult questions is captured in her frequent invocation of false choices—and it may explain why she has had some trouble carving out a distinctive role as vice president. Her memoir helps me understand that; Harris doesn't like zero-sum choices, so she says they aren't real.

As I mentioned earlier, when you're reading a Washington book, always read the acknowledgments section. That is where politicians disclose their debts, scratch backs, suck up, and snub. (For instance, Pence does not thank Trump by name in the acknowledgments of *So Help Me God*.) By far my favorite acknowledgments moment in a political book comes in *American Dreams*, the 2015 memoir by Sen. Marco Rubio. The first person that Rubio thanks by name is "my Lord, Jesus Christ, whose willingness to suffer and die for my sins will allow me to enjoy eternal life."

The second person Rubio thanks? "My very wise lawyer, Bob Barnett."

Bob Barnett is an influential lawyer for the Washington political set—he helps candidates prepare for presidential debates, for instance, and his clients include major politicians and media figures, for whom he negotiates lucrative book deals. It does not get more establishment than Bob Barnett, which is why I just love that Rubio wrote this. It tells you so much about the inside/outside game that politicians play, beating their chests about God in one sentence and hiring a DC power broker in the other. It's the Washington addendum to Pascal's wager: believe in God, but just in case things go wrong, hire a big-time lawyer.

There is another kind of Washington book, written not by individuals shaping their own stories but by institutions telling our collective story. These are studies by high-level panels, reports by congressional committees and special counsel investigations, even Supreme Court decisions. Reading Washington also means reading these documents.

The Supreme Court's 2022 decision in *Dobbs v. Jackson Women's Health Organization*, which overturned the constitutional right to abortion established in *Roe v. Wade*, was a monumental event and news story, and the leak of the decision to the press some weeks in advance had Washington debating the politicizing of the high court. Since then, the justices have been the subject of news coverage regarding their outside incomes and outside influences. But if you want to see how the court has grown politicized over the past fifty years, you can also just read the justices' decisions.

Examining the *Dobbs* decision alongside the original *Roe* ruling in 1973 and the *Planned Parenthood v. Casey* decision on abortion in 1992 reveals an institution that was becoming politicized long before anyone leaked anything to *Politico*. The accusations and recriminations the justices fling at each other grow more contentious across the decades. In his dissent from the majority opinion in *Roe v. Wade*, Justice William Rehnquist acknowledged the historical inquiry and legal scholarship of the majority ruling; despite his disagreement with it, he wrote, the opinion "commands my respect." That politeness disappears from the subsequent two decisions. The opinion that decided the *Casey* case warned that overruling *Roe* could constitute a "surrender to political pressure"; one justice even wrote of his "fear for the darkness" if his four colleagues who opposed *Roe* ever found one more vote. Of course, one of those four justices disparaged the other side's "almost czarist arrogance." In *Dobbs*, different factions of the high court accuse one another of incompetence, duplicity, and hypocrisy. The majority in *Dobbs* dismisses the *Roe* ruling as an "elaborate scheme" that was "concocted" to make up a constitutional right, while the dissenters denounce the majority for letting personal preferences get in the way of their duty; they say that with *Dobbs*, "the Court departs from its obligation to faithfully and impartially apply the law."

When some justices accuse others of succumbing to insidious political impulses—whereas they alone remain uncorrupted—they sound much like the rest of our political class, robes notwithstanding.

Landmark documents such as the 9/11 Commission report, the Kerner Commission report on urban riots in the late 1960s, and the January 6 committee report on the assault on the Capitol, among so many others, are also essential Washington texts. Together, they form an unofficial historical record, snapshots of America at its most traumatic moments. They deserve to be read, not just discussed.

After the terrorist attacks of September 11, 2001, the CIA embarked on a program of "enhanced interrogation"—that is, of torture against terrorism suspects in clandestine sites around the world. And to do this, the Office of Legal Counsel of the Justice Department issued a series of memos, between 2002 and 2005, approving of the techniques. These memos were revealed in the press, and were later published as a book, titled *The Torture Memos*. Reading them is excruciating; it is also vital. They show what our government can do in our name, and in the name of our security. They show how, in moments of great fear, it is tempting to abuse both law and language. No Washington documents have seared themselves in my memory like the torture memos, with their dry, clinical prose.

And yet part of the reason we know so much about what the CIA did—how it used the interrogation methods that the Justice Department initially endorsed in these memos—is because of another Washington document that appeared years later: the Senate Intelligence Committee's massive investigation into the CIA's post-9/11 interrogation programs. The executive summary, published as a 549-page book in 2014, found that torture did not generate useful intelligence, that the interrogation sessions were even harsher than the CIA ever acknowledged, and that the spy agency impeded oversight of its actions. The brutality permitted in one series of documents is exposed and condemned in another. The story of these Washington books is the story of how we fail, and then how we attempt to atone for those failures.

I read the House's January 6 report, another effort to understand the vulnerabilities of our political and constitutional system. It offers a damning assessment of President Trump's actions on that day and in the weeks leading to it. And there is one passage I can't stop thinking about.

You may recall the testimony before the special committee by Cassidy Hutchinson, a former aide in the Trump White House, describing the president's behavior on the morning of January 6. She said Trump was upset that the magnetometers (weapons detectors) were inhibiting some armed supporters from entering the area where the president would deliver his speech. Trump wanted a bigger crowd, and Hutchinson said she heard the president say something like this:

"I don't f—ing care that they have weapons. They're not here to hurt me. Taking the f—ing mags away. Let my people in."

Think about that second sentence: *They're not here to hurt me.* Which word might the president have emphasized when speaking out loud? If it's the verb "hurt," the sentiment would be somewhat innocent. They are not here to hurt me, but perhaps to praise or cheer me. If the stress falls on "me," the meaning becomes more sinister. They're not here to hurt me, but to hurt someone else. That could be Mike Pence, Nancy Pelosi, Capitol Police officers, or any of the lawmakers gathering to fulfill their duty and certify the election.

So, which was it? The January 6 report doesn't exactly clarify matters: it cites the passage twice, italicizing the word "me" in the final chapter but leaving it unitalicized in the executive summary. The video of Hutchinson's testimony shows her reciting the line somewhat neutrally, with perhaps a slight stress on "hurt" rather than "me." (You can watch for yourself.)

It may seem odd to linger on how a single two-letter pronoun is rendered in print. But these accounts purport to serve as historical records. Every word and every quote, every framing and every implication, merits scrutiny. And if the result is sometimes ambiguous, sometimes unclear, that is okay. Because history can be murky, too—even with a written transcript.

In *The Speechwriter* (2015), Barton Swaim described his time working for a southern governor, drafting speeches and statements and letters, and channeling the ideas and ambitions of a boss he didn't respect. Swaim reached an intriguing conclusion about political rhetoric. "One hears very few proper lies in politics," he wrote. "Using vague, slippery, or just meaningless language is not the same as lying: it's not intended to deceive so much as to preserve options, buy time, distance oneself from others, or just to sound like you're saying something instead of nothing."

To sound like you're saying something instead of nothing. That is a politician's specialty. "Words are useful," Swaim wrote, "but often their meanings are not." If the art of politics can be to subtract meaning from language, to produce more and more words that say less and less, then it is my purpose as a journalist to try to find that meaning and put it back.

I realize this kind of journalism may seem a bit passive. After all, I'm just reading. But by digging through the books that politicians write, I can help explain, reveal, and understand them. I may not have found that next Great American Novel, but I hope that reading these texts helps me fill in a little bit more of the great American story.

Consider the range of human experience found in just the few books and documents I've covered here. Personal identity and the construction of one's self-image. Isolation and delusion. Principles and expectations, the lowest kind of subservience and the highest of ambitions. Posturing, ambiguity, conflict, deception, revelation. These are some of the great themes of literature, and the great struggles of life—whether of individuals or of nations.

So when people tell me that I read these books so that they don't have to, I just smile to myself. They're missing so much. The more I read Washington, the more intricate the connections I find among different books and ideas and visions of our politics. I embarked on this path almost accidentally, and now I cannot stop. There is so much more to read.

Please read along with me. I assure you the experience is rarely masochistic, and even occasionally transcendent.

Red Smith Lecture, University of Notre Dame,
February 2023

I. LEADING

THE MEMOIR GEORGE H. W. BUSH
COULD HAVE WRITTEN

GEORGE HERBERT WALKER BUSH NEVER wrote a real memoir. In fact, he seemed to avoid it.

Leading up to his 1988 presidential campaign, Bush published *Looking Forward*, a ghostwritten affair he later dismissed as "the kind of book that comes out about the candidate during an election year." The 1998 volume on his foreign policy, *A World Transformed*, is coauthored with Brent Scowcroft and features alternating passages by the two men. (Scowcroft's are better.) A decade later, Bush's diary from his time as China envoy in the mid-1970s morphed into a book only after a historian pitched the idea and did all the work. And a lifetime of letters came together in *All the Best, George Bush*, a 2013 collection that the former president stresses was "not meant to be an autobiography."

Loved ones have written about him—his late wife, Barbara, in her 1994 memoir; George W. in the loyal *41*—and historians and former aides have taken their turns. But not Bush himself. "I was unpersuaded," he explained simply.

It's our loss. George H. W. Bush had the experiences, insights, revelations, and blind spots that could have made for a terrific memoir. The raw material is scattered throughout these various works. Individually, they are snapshots of a life. Together, they could have redefined it.

In these pages, Bush—so often labeled the speedboating, fly-fishing scion of Kennebunkport—grapples with his advantages, early and late in life. He is aware of his rhetorical limitations but, even as a younger man, treats higher office as a certainty. He is indignant at the suggestion that he cared more for foreign than domestic policy yet privately admits the truth of the charge. A decorated navy pilot who fought a world war and closed out a cold one, he is thoughtful about the horrors of armed conflict but lets slip a moralizing militarism that feels more 43 than 41. Remembered as awkward and out of touch, here Bush can be emotional, self-aware, even funny.

Most revealing, the candidate and president who couldn't nail down the "vision thing" displays in his writing a clearer worldview than he gets credit for—one in which leadership, America's and his own, is not a means but its own end. Bush, who passed away Friday, at ninety-four, had a vision. He just had to look in a mirror to find it.

When Bush was preparing to accept the Republican presidential nomination in 1988, he sent his speechwriter a list of notions that he believed best represented him. "Words I like: family, loyalty, kids, freedom, grandkids, caring, love, heart, decency, faith, honor, service to country, pride, fair (fair play), tolerance, strength, hope, healing kindness, excellence ... I like people; I'm proud of USA; I like sports; I'm experienced; I love kids." Yes, he likes kids so much he mentions them twice.

This jumble exemplifies Bush's difficulty in conveying his personal values and political project, a condition he both disputes and acknowledges in his writings. "The criticism was off-base," Bush complains of the coverage he received during his 1980 presidential bid. But even as vice president, he couldn't really explain, beyond banalities, why he sought the top job. "I want to see an educated America," he writes in a November 1986 diary entry. He also wanted to see an America that was literate, drug-free, employed, peaceful, and focused on family values. "But, how do you say all these things and get it into a slogan or a formula—a catch-all. I don't know."

Bush received frequent letters from voters complaining about his speaking style, and when his phrases proved memorable—"voodoo economics" or "read my lips"—he wishes they hadn't. What is mushy on the stump, however, becomes sharper with Bush in action. In *A World Transformed*, Bush and Scowcroft explain their thinking during the end of the Cold War, the Tiananmen crisis, Desert Storm, and the Soviet collapse. "While there were dramatic moments, epitomized by the opening of the Berlin Wall, perhaps the most important story is that they came largely *without* great drama," they write. The framework for Bush's foreign policy "was very deliberate: encouraging, guiding, and managing change without provoking backlash and crackdown." Bush was "no drama" before Obama.

As president, Bush was most concerned with affirming American strength. "My own thoughts were focused on putting the United States back out in front, leading the West as we tackled the challenges in Eastern Europe and the Soviet Union," Bush writes of the earliest days of his presidency. And though he had difficulty making the public case for military action in the Persian Gulf—"I am not good at that," he said when people encouraged him to deliver FDR-style fireside chats on the war—in private he stated it forthrightly. "Saddam Hussein will get out of Kuwait, and the United States will have been the catalyst and the key in getting this done, and that is important," he dictates to his diary. "Our role as a world leader will once again be reaffirmed."

Bush's sense of leadership was wrapped up in the presidency. Though he served in the House of Representatives and twice ran for the Senate, he didn't much like the legislative branch, where "there are a lot of weirdos who have all sorts of crazy ideas," as he confided to Margaret Thatcher. The fall of 1990, when Bush dueled with a Democratic majority over his Mideast military buildup and the federal budget, "became one of the most frustrating periods of my presidency," he writes. "I knew that there were some areas of genuine disagreement with members of Congress over policy, but I thought the budget and the Persian Gulf should not be among them."

Consider that. Lawmakers can disagree with the president—just not on matters of federal spending or military force.

This mix of duty and arrogance surfaces throughout his career. Bush's posts are so brief—two terms as a congressman from Texas, two years as ambassador to the United Nations, less than two years as Republican National Committee chairman, fourteen months as China envoy, one year as CIA director—that they feel like bullet points on a predestined presidential résumé. He goes to China to nail down foreign policy credentials "that not many Republican politicians will have." While in Beijing, he plots a possible campaign for governor of Texas in between tennis matches and stomach viruses. "If the Texas Gov thing in '78 makes any sense at all I'd maybe take a look at it hard," he writes to a Washington friend, ". . . keeping in mind that I wouldn't do it unless there was a possibility of taking a shot at something bigger in '80." And when President Gerald Ford offers him the CIA director job, Bush worries he is being frozen out of veep consideration in 1976. "Could *that* be what was happening?" he wonders in his diary. "Bury Bush at the CIA?" His top suspect, White House chief of staff Donald Rumsfeld, denied any scheming, Bush recalls, and "I accepted his word." (Reminder: "I accepted his word" is Washington-speak for "I can't prove he's lying.")

But when Jimmy Carter defeated Ford in 1976, even the president-elect foresaw Bush's continued ascent. Among his final acts as CIA chief, Bush briefed Carter. In *Looking Forward*, Bush recalls that when a colleague began outlining national security challenges that could arise by the mid-1980s, Carter held up his hand. "I don't need to worry about that," he said with a smile. "By then George will be president and he can take care of it."

Bush has the grace—or false modesty—to express bewilderment. "*George will be president?* It was an odd statement, coming from Jimmy Carter," he writes. "I wondered what he meant."

I'm pretty sure Bush knew.

At key moments, Bush's progress came thanks to the wealth and connections of his family—from his uncle Herbie Walker, who provided money and expertise to help young George start an oil-lease business in Texas, to his father, Prescott Bush, a Wall Street executive who served for a decade as a US senator from Connecticut. George Bush availed himself of these advantages, though with some ambivalence. "I am not sure I want to capitalize completely on the benefits I received at birth," he writes to a friend shortly before graduating from Yale University. "Doing well merely because I have had the opportunity to attend the same debut parties as some of my customers, does not appeal to me."

Who knew privilege-checking was around in 1948?

Yet using public service to ease a wealthy conscience is a Bush family tradition. "I knew what motivated him," Bush writes of his father's decision to run for the Senate. "He'd made his mark in the business world. Now he felt he had a debt to pay." Speaking at a 1997 alumni reunion of the Greenwich Country Day School, which Bush had attended during the Great Depression, he decried the "elite editorialists" who had argued that a man like him couldn't relate to ordinary Americans. "You know what the critics missed? They missed 'values' ... Our parents taught us to care—and the faculty here seemed to be intent on inculcating into us the fact that we had an obligation to care."

At times, Bush struggled to balance another obligation—political self-preservation—against these more civic-minded imperatives. As GOP party chairman during the final months of Watergate (a "political nightmare," he calls it), Bush was torn between loyalty to his president and the pangs of his conscience, though it is hard to miss more political considerations. Eight days before President Richard Nixon announced his departure, Bush was strategizing with White House Chief of Staff Alexander Haig about the best timing for the move, suggesting that Nixon should leave before the midterms, thus avoiding a "bigger bath" for Republican candidates. "I told Haig I didn't feel that political expediency should be a consideration for resignation," Bush assures in his diary, adding: "But it was hard to discount politics."

Only on the eve of Nixon's resignation speech did Bush send a letter urging the president to step down—a missive directed as much to the history books as to the White House. He relied on it later when he became CIA director under Ford. "I am confident the record will reveal I spoke out over and over again against Watergate," he writes to a *Time* magazine reporter. "I did, however, stop short of condemning the President until the final tape proved to me that he had been lying. At that point I urged him to resign."

Always take the high road, Bush admonishes. "Jugular politics—going for the opposition's throat—wasn't my style," he writes. After going negative against Sen. Bob Dole in the 1988 Republican primary, Bush insists that he did so "against my better judgment." He congratulates himself for refraining from "red meat" speeches against Massachusetts governor Michael Dukakis, omitting mention of the attempts to link the Democratic nominee to Willie

Horton, a convicted murderer who committed further violent crimes while on a Massachusetts weekend furlough. "By the time we're finished, they're going to wonder whether Willie Horton is Dukakis's running mate," Bush campaign manager Lee Atwater said. Bush's only admission of anything untoward appears in a footnote describing Atwater's tactics: "He was young, aggressive (some people would say ruthless), and brilliant at politics."

And Bush brilliantly, some would say ruthlessly, averted his eyes.

Bush is less self-serving, more circumspect, when it comes to war. As a young naval aviator, he was shot down on a bombing run against Japanese installations in the Pacific; his two crewmates died. "I still don't understand the 'logic' of war—why some survive and others are lost in their prime," Bush reflects in a letter to his parents written aboard the USS *Finback*, the submarine that rescued him from his lifeboat.

Bush's careful attitude toward foreign policy and national security became evident when the Berlin Wall fell and reporters wondered why the new president's mood was not more celebratory. "Of course, I was thankful about the events in Berlin," he later writes, "but as I answered questions my mind kept racing over a possible Soviet crackdown, turning all the happiness to tragedy." Much, too, has been made of Bush's restraint at the end of the Persian Gulf War, when he did not march toward Baghdad because, as he explains in *A World Transformed*, he worried about embarking upon "an unwinnable urban guerrilla war [that] could only plunge that part of the world into even greater instability." In a diary entry from the fall of 1990, Bush notes that "my wartime experience does condition me as commander-in-chief and makes me cautious."

The contrast with George W. Bush, who invaded Iraq a dozen years later, is stark, and distinctions are easy to draw between the levelheaded father and reckless son. But as the elder Bush built the coalition to oust Iraq from Kuwait, his case also became more strident than sober. "I began to move from viewing Saddam's aggression exclusively as a dangerous strategic threat and an injustice to its reversal as a moral crusade," he wrote. "It was good versus evil, right versus wrong." When Soviet premier Mikhail Gorbachev suggested that the international community should not back Hussein into a corner, Bush replied, "If we had offered Hitler some way out, would it have succeeded?" In *A World Transformed*, Scowcroft recalls worrying that Bush was becoming "emotionally involved" in the crisis and that the president risked making it seem like a vendetta against Iraq's leader.

It wasn't quite axis-of-evil stuff, but it was close.

What grounded Bush's foreign policy, in part, was the president's ability to forge close relationships with other heads of state. "I had known many of the current foreign leaders for years, often before they took office, and that would help strengthen trust." He admires the forthrightness of French president François Mitterrand—"when I would call him about difficult problems, he would give me a straight answer"—whom he had buttered up during a visit to Kennebunkport. He regrets that he was never as close to Thatcher as Ronald Reagan had been. And his most significant connection was with Gorbachev. "I liked the personal contact with Mikhail—I liked *him*," Bush writes in his foreign policy volume. "I thought I had a feel for his heartbeat." (It was not the final time a President Bush would attempt to glimpse the soul of a Russian leader, a family tradition with uneven consequences.)

At times Bush grew defensive about his personalistic approach to foreign policy. "Some feel emphasis on personal relationships between leaders is unimportant or unnecessary," he writes. "Henry Kissinger once argued to me that these are no substitutes for deep national interests ... For me, personal diplomacy and leadership went hand in hand." Of course, this disagreement may have been personal, too. In his China diary, Bush unloads on Kissinger, calling him "intolerable," "nasty," "regal," and "dictatorial." Three decades later, in the preface to the published version of the diary, Bush tries to take it back. "When I finally did reread the diary, I was amused by some of my frustrations with then-Secretary of State Henry Kissinger, a man whom I greatly respect and consider a friend."

On this, let's accept Bush's word.

So effective on the international stage, Bush's personal touch faltered at home. He knew it, and it annoyed him.

"The Libs charge that I am not interested in Domestic Policy," he writes in a 1991 letter to a friend in Texas. "Wrong!!" But in Bush's diary, his preferences are clear. In the early days of Operation Desert Shield, for example, he felt "fully engrossed in this international crisis, and I must say I enjoy working on all the parts of it and I get into much more detail than I do on the domestic scene."

Bush expresses contempt for Washington politicking, for "the posturing on both sides . . . [people] putting their own selves ahead of the overall good." He was confident that he embodied that overall good and that voters would recognize that. When he ran for reelection in 1992, Bush thought he would defeat Bill Clinton because he was a better person than the Arkansas governor. "He's better at facts-figures than I am," he writes to Peggy Noonan. "I'm better at life." No surprise, he resented the charge that he was aloof or disconnected—"that I never stood for anything, that I didn't care about people," Bush writes to one of his brothers after the loss to Clinton. "I stood for a lot of things on issues . . . but what I want to have people know I stood for were 'Duty, Honor, Country' and yes, as Dad taught us, 'service.' That's not all bad."

His empathy emerged in small, forgotten moments and in dramatic ones, too. As a congressman from Texas, Bush voted for the Fair Housing Act in 1968, essentially reversing his earlier position on civil rights. He suffered through boos at a rally back home but insisted that "a man should not have a door slammed in his face because he is a Negro or speaks with a Latin American accent." At the end of the event, he received a standing ovation, and nearly two decades later, he wrote that nothing else he'd experienced in public life matched the feeling from that evening. Bush also recalls skipping Nixon's 1969 inauguration parade to attend President Lyndon Johnson's farewell at Andrews Air Force Base. "This was a President who not many years before had moved through crowds with outstretched hands," Bush writes. "But because of Vietnam, the cheering had stopped, and he was going back to Texas a defeated man. I shook his hand and wished him a safe journey. He nodded, took a few steps toward the ramp, then turned, looked back at me, and said, 'Thanks for coming.'"

And Bush had been vice president only a couple of months when John Hinckley Jr. shot Reagan. A military aide wanted to helicopter the vice president straight to the White House, but Bush insisted that they stop at his residence and then drive to 1600 Pennsylvania Avenue. As he explained to the perplexed aide, "only the president lands on the South Lawn."

Symbols and gestures, perhaps, but they matter. Bush's leadership was less about achieving specific goals than about having the United States in charge when such goals were established. "So much of the world depends on the United States," he writes in his China diary. "So much depends on our own self-confidence in our ability to cope." And not just anyone could project that confidence. "America needed someone in the Oval Office who could restore the people's faith in our institutions, a leader who could revitalize the national spirit," Bush writes in his 1987 campaign book, leaving little doubt who he thinks that leader should be.

In *A World Transformed*, Bush expresses awe and reverence for the Oval Office. Two decades later, he was hardly enthralled by its latest occupant. "He's a blowhard," Bush told Mark K. Updegrove, author of a 2017 book on the two Bush presidents. Indeed, with his mix of private insecurity and public bluster, President Trump is an inversion of Bush's inward confidence and outward diffidence.

So many of the things Bush said and wrote may seem quaint, but today they also represent something vital and increasingly fragile. "It is not fashionable in these days of tearing down our institutions to say 'trust me,'" he said in a 1976 speech as CIA director. "Yet Americans have to have faith and trust in some degree or none of our governmental systems will work." Bush was also alert to the risks of intolerance. After the 9/11 attacks, his first thoughts were for his son in the White House, but "a second immediate thought," he wrote in a letter the next day, "was that Muslims in this country were going to be abused." And he insisted on listening: "I have tried to keep not only my door but my mind open to what other people think, even if I disagree," he wrote. "It gets both sides seeing each other as human beings."

Even in his patrician way, Bush could be disarmingly reflective, emotional, and sentimental. A few years after his three-year-old daughter, Robin, died of leukemia in 1953, Bush wrote his mother a lengthy, poignant letter about the longing he and Barbara felt for her and their wish that the feeling would always remain. "We need her and yet we have her. We can't touch her, and yet we can feel her. We hope she'll stay in our house for a long, long time." When he won a House seat in 1966, Bush began a fifteen-month correspondence with a cranky Houston constituent named Paul Dorsey, who had voted for his opponent. The two men bonded via their missives, which continued through Dorsey's cancer diagnosis and treatment. Shortly before Dorsey passed away, Bush visited him in the hospital.

Bush was a leader who could laugh at himself. The balloon drop at his 1987 presidential campaign announcement looked more like a "condom drop," he quips, because several of the balloons coming down had popped overnight. As president, he established the White House's Scowcroft Award for Somnolent Excellence, a spoof prize honoring the official who could best doze off in a meeting yet still perk up when needed. (Dick Cheney was the second recipient.) And for all his rhetorical missteps, Bush finds solace in Al Gore's speeches. "Poor guy's in real trouble if he's worse than I," he deadpans in his diary.

The forty-fifth and forty-first presidents are also contrasts in their intellectual lives. Trump proudly declares that he has no time for reading, whereas Bush reveled in works of politics, history, and world affairs. During his year in China alone, he devoured *Thunder Out of China*, by Theodore H. White and Annalee Jacoby; *China After Mao*, by Doak Barnett; *The Good Earth*, by Pearl Buck; and *Stilwell and the American Experience in China*, by Barbara Tuchman, among several other China-related works. (Ever the politico, he also took in *Before the Fall*, William Safire's 1975 memoir on the pre-Watergate Nixon White House.)

Maybe Bush didn't have time to write a lengthy autobiography, or perhaps he feared that his difficulties articulating a vision in speeches would recur on the page. But it's a shame that he never quite captured, in a single volume of his own, that vanishing era of political leaders who mixed duty, entitlement, and a sense of destiny to serve the nation. American voters rejected that formula in 1992, perhaps with good reason. But, more than a quarter-century later, it seems like a presidency, for all its faults, and a life, for all its advantages, that would be worth reading, and worth reevaluating.

Of course, who knows what kind of book Bush would have written if inspiration had struck? On only one occasion in these works does he explicitly consider writing a book, and his subject is surprising: "Someday I will write a book on massages I have had, ranging all the way from Bobby Moore and Harry Carmen at the UN to the steambaths of Egypt and Tokyo. I must confess the Tokyo treatment is the best. Walking on the back, total use of the knees, combination of knees and oil, the back becoming a giant slope does wonders for the sacroiliac, and a little something for the morale, too. Massage parlors in the U.S. have ruined the image of real massage. It is a crying shame."

I would have read that book. (Suggested title: *Read My Hips*.)

December 2018

THE SELF-REFERENTIAL
PRESIDENCY OF BARACK OBAMA

BARACK OBAMA'S SPEECH AT THE 2004 Democratic National Convention was an astonishing piece of oratory. It was also a bit of sleight of hand.

Then a US Senate candidate from Illinois, Obama wove his personal ancestry and biography—black and white, Kenya and Kansas, Hawaii and Harvard—into the American story of opportunity, multiplicity, and solidarity. Not red versus blue, but out of many, one. David Axelrod calls the address a love letter to America. "In no other country on Earth is my story even possible," Obama declared, his most poignant line of the night.

Two words in that sentence would matter most. Throughout Obama's time in the White House, his touchstone would not be that singular country whose politics he was never able to bind together. Rather, it would be the man himself. *My story.* This was a presidency preoccupied with Obama's exceptionalism as much as with America's.

Modern presidents have often become conflated with the challenges and aspirations of their times. We speak of Richard Nixon's silent majority, Jimmy Carter's malaise, Ronald Reagan's morning in America, and George W. Bush's wars. But with Obama, this personal identification has been unceasing, compulsive as well as strategic. In *The Audacity of Hope*, Obama called himself "a prisoner of my own biography," yet throughout his presidency, biography would also empower him. Whether in foreign policy, race relations, electoral politics, or even in the meaning of the hope and change he promised, Obama has turned to his life and its symbolism as a default reference and all-purpose governing tool.

The personalized presidency can be inspiring. It can also feel arrogant. And it can bypass some of the very norms and institutions Obama rhapsodizes about so frequently—a dangerous proposition as the country braces for an unpredictable, unmoored successor.

Biography plays a central role in all political campaigns, with candidates deploying their life stories to buttress their messages. During Obama's first presidential run, however, the story did not just strengthen his pitch—it became interchangeable with it. This was not by accident but by design. "Barack is the personification of his own message for this country, that we get past the things that divide us and focus on the things that unite us," Axelrod, the campaign's chief strategist, told the *New York Times* in 2007. "He is his own vision."

So much so, in fact, that when President-elect Obama endured criticism for recycling Clinton-era officials into top posts, he argued that it didn't matter, that he was enough. "I was never of the belief that the way you bring about change is to not hire anybody who knows how things work, and to start from scratch and completely reinvent the wheel," Obama said to the *Washington Post* in January 2009. "I'm the one who brings change. It is my vision. It is my agenda."

Turns out he was the change we had been waiting for.

His effort to improve US ties with the Muslim world, for instance, was premised on the notion that his personal story could make a difference. In his speech at Cairo University in June 2009, the president said that a "new beginning" was possible in the troubled relationship. "Part of this conviction is rooted in my own experience," he explained. He invoked his Kenyan family, with its generations of Muslims; recalled his childhood in Indonesia; and cited his work with Muslim communities in Chicago. His story was supposed to dispel foreign stereotypes of a self-interested, imperial United States and show that not all Americans shared apocalyptic visions of Islam.

Obama's personal narrative is so flexible that he has cited it as proof of his empathy for Israel, too. As the president told the *Atlantic*'s Jeffrey Goldberg, he once interrupted Benjamin Netanyahu when he felt the Israeli prime minister was being condescending, lecturing him about the dangers Israel faced. "Bibi, you have to understand something," the president said. "I'm the

African American son of a single mother, and I live here, in this house. I live in the White House. I managed to get elected president of the United States. You think I don't understand what you're talking about, but I do."

Everyone was supposed to fall under the sway of the Obamaness. As a candidate, Obama explained the logic. "I think that if you can tell people, 'We have a president in the White House who still has a grandmother living in a hut on the shores of Lake Victoria and has a sister who's half-Indonesian, married to a Chinese Canadian,' then they're going to think that he may have a better sense of what's going on in our lives and in our country," Obama told journalist James Traub in 2007. "And they'd be right."

The Obama story would also surface around sensitive matters of national security. In a 2009 speech at the National Archives, the president stressed the importance of keeping America safe while upholding our laws and values, noting that the documents preserved in that building—the Declaration of Independence, the Constitution, the Bill of Rights—were the foundation of liberty in America and a light for the world. And then, it came back to him.

"I stand here today as someone whose own life was made possible by these documents. My father came to these shores in search of the promise that they offered. My mother made me rise before dawn to learn their truths when I lived as a child in a foreign land. My own American journey was paved by generations of citizens who gave meaning to those simple words—'to form a more perfect union.' I've studied the Constitution as a student, I've taught it as a teacher, I've been bound by it as a lawyer and a legislator. I took an oath to preserve, protect and defend the Constitution as commander in chief, and as a citizen, I know that we must never, ever, turn our back on its enduring principles for expedience sake."

Over time, Obama would rely on that lawyerly background to render lofty principles more malleable, with a "don't worry, it's me" approach to national security powers. When the *New York Times* described the president's personal role in selecting terrorists to target for attack, for example, it noted how "the control he exercises also appears to reflect Mr. Obama's striking self-confidence: he believes, according to several people who have worked closely with him, that his own judgment should be brought to bear on strikes." After not fully establishing the limits on such powers, Obama is turning them over to a new commander in chief with no less self-confidence and much less self-control.

Obama drew on the personal to address the revelations in 2013 about the National Security Agency's electronic surveillance. After reassuring Americans on the extent of NSA oversight, he offered some unusual comfort. "I will leave this office at some point, sometime in the ... next three and a half years, and after that, I will be a private citizen," Obama said. "And I suspect that, on a list of people who might be targeted so that somebody could read their emails or listen to their phone calls, I'd probably be pretty high on that list. It's not as if I don't have a personal interest in making sure my privacy is protected."

So, because Obama worried about his own future privacy, we should trust that he would never violate ours? That argument required a generous helping of self-regard. Then again, as Henry Kissinger has suggested, "Obama seems to think of himself not as a part of a political process, but as sui generis, a unique phenomenon with a unique capacity." (And Kissinger seems like a guy who knows the feeling.)

It is with race that Obama's story as the first black president has taken on the most salience. His political ascent prompted dreams of a post-racial America as well as incessant racist attacks, and it turned Obama into an African American studies professor for the nation during what would become the Black Lives Matter era. In that role, his lectures leaned heavily on his biography.

When videos of the Rev. Jeremiah Wright's sermons denouncing America threatened Obama's presidential bid, the candidate drew upon his story to deliver the most memorable speech of the 2008 race. "I believe deeply that we cannot solve the challenges of our time . . . unless we perfect our union by understanding that we may have different stories, but we hold common hopes; that we may not look the same and we may not have come from the same place, but we all want to move in the same direction," he said at Philadelphia's National Constitution Center. ". . . This belief comes from my unyielding faith in the decency and generosity of the American people. But it also comes from my own American story."

Such faith may have been misplaced. Throughout his presidency, Obama staked much on "a goodwill that his own personal history tells him exists in the larger country," journalist Ta-Nehisi Coates argues in the *Atlantic*, adding that "only a black man with that same biography could underestimate his opposition's resolve to destroy him." Obama's frequent calls for African American communities to take greater personal responsibility for their conditions, his preference for universal efforts to improve education and opportunity for all over targeted programs to help minority populations—these attitudes reflect a sincere trust in white America, Coates argues, one that has been forged through Obama's particular experience.

The controversy surrounding Wright involved Obama's faith and relationship with his former pastor, so the personal emphasis there was inevitable. But when Trayvon Martin was killed by George Zimmerman in central Florida in February 2012, Obama, evocatively yet unmistakably, brought the discussion back to himself. "If I had a son, he would look like Trayvon," the president remarked. After Zimmerman's acquittal, Obama detailed the indignities and injustices black men face in America, explaining that such experiences informed how African Americans viewed that verdict. Then, as he often has, the president concluded by stressing the strides the country has made.

"Each successive generation seems to be making progress in changing attitudes when it comes to race," Obama said. "It doesn't mean we're in a post-racial society. It doesn't mean that racism is eliminated. But when I talk to Malia and Sasha, and I listen to their friends and I see them interact, they're better than we are—they're better than we were—on these issues." It is noteworthy that he cited his family as evidence, an individualized benchmark of national self-improvement.

Similarly, when he spoke in 2014 about a grand jury's decision to not indict police officer Darren Wilson for killing Michael Brown in Ferguson, Missouri, Obama reiterated that the nation was moving forward. "We have made enormous progress in race relations over the course of the past several decades," he said. "I've witnessed that in my own life."

In *The Black Presidency* (2016), Michael Eric Dyson lingers over that moment. "Obama lauded the racial progress that he said he had witnessed 'in my own life,' substituting his body for our black bodies, his life for ours, and signaled again how his story of advancement was ours." The problem, Dyson argues, is that despite his enormous symbolic power, Obama is an imperfect stand-in. "The ordinary black person possesses neither Obama's protections against peril nor his triumphant trajectory that will continue long after he leaves office," Dyson writes. "And Obama's narrative does not answer a haunting question: If America can treat him as badly as it does … what will it do to the masses of Michael Browns in black communities?"

In multiple speeches, Obama has offered a distinct vision of American exceptionalism—that of a country constantly striving, sometimes struggling, to perfect itself. It is a process he interprets through his own story. In *Dreams from My Father*, Obama tells of his hope that "the larger American community, black, white, and brown, could somehow redefine itself—I believed that it might, over time, admit the uniqueness of my own life."

Perhaps, as president, Obama has turned so often to his story because of this belief that America was validating it. Or maybe because the inner circle of his 2008 campaign, the truest of true believers in the Obama story, exerted inordinate influence over his White House. Or perhaps Obama's tendency fits our era of oversharing, self-obsession, and first-person arguments. Or it could be simply that he believes, as he argued in a 2006 speech on faith and politics, that Americans are missing "a narrative arc to their lives," and he is supplying us with his own.

Whatever the motivation, it certainly worked with voters when he was on the ballot. In both the 2008 and 2012 elections, Obama bested his opponents on the "cares about people like me" question in exit polls. But it was an appeal that remained with him alone. Indeed, one result of Obama's personalized presidency is that his electoral fortunes far outshined those of the party overall. After his two presidential victories, Democrats suffered sharp reversals in both midterms, and the party has seen its power diminished at all levels under Obama.

"Washington Democrats hated the White House for believing that the Obama brand and the Democratic Party brand were distinct, and that one was paramount over the other," NBC's Chuck Todd writes in *The Stranger: Barack Obama in the White House*, published in 2014. "The White House did little to dispel the notion that Obama came first, over and above the party."

When Obama did inject himself into his party's contests, he often emphasized his legacy. "I am not on the ballot this fall," he stated in a speech on the economy delivered one month before the 2014 elections. "... But make no mistake: These policies are on the ballot. Every single one of them." At the time, the president was deeply unpopular in key states, and his personalization of the race did his party no favors.

In the 2016 presidential contest, Obama campaigned with more vigor and, at times, with no less self-regard. "I will consider it a personal insult, an insult to my legacy, if this community lets down its guard and fails to activate itself in this election," he urged a Congressional Black Caucus gathering. "You want to give me a good send-off? Go vote."

That vote is now in, and the presidential candidate promising to dismantle the Obama legacy has won, even while Obama still enjoys high approval ratings. Some voters who had cast their ballots for Obama, perhaps even twice, threw their support behind Donald Trump. "I don't have an explanation for that, to put it bluntly," White House press secretary Josh Earnest admitted.

The answer may not be that mysterious. Even in his party's most crushing defeat, Obama remains popular because this presidency was less about particular federal programs, or the Democratic Party, or certainly Hillary Clinton, than about Obama himself.

They fall low, he goes high.

The man soon supplanting Obama in the Oval Office is even more enamored with his own story and more dismissive of his own party, and promises to remake the nation on the strength of his personality. "Nobody knows the system better than me," Trump asserted at the Republican National Conven-

tion, "which is why I alone can fix it." It is a more concentrated and insidious
iteration of the personalized presidency.

Trump came to national political prominence on the back of "birther"
lies—in essence, an effort to retroactively erase Obama's story—and now
seeks to unmake Obama's legacy, too. A president who used his story in the
attempt to uplift and empower is giving way to a leader for whom the office
seems an exercise in personal brand extension.

It is a far different ending than the one a captivating Illinois state senator
may have imagined twelve years before. The failure to fulfill that vision of a
united America, or bring us closer to it, is now part of the Obama story, too.

"The spirit of national conciliation was more than the rhetorical pixie
dust of Obama's 2004 speech to the Democratic National Convention, in
Boston, which had brought him to delirious national attention," *New Yorker*
editor and Obama biographer David Remnick wrote in 2014. "It was also an
elemental component of his self-conception, his sense that he was uniquely
suited to transcend ideology and the grubby battles of the day. Obama is
defensive about this now."

But a new battle is coming, and that defensiveness may prove useful.
Trump's vision for America threatens to make stories such as Obama's less
likely. Will this most self-referential of presidents retreat to speeches and
memoirs, or will he fight to preserve the country that indeed made his story
possible? What if that's next—the Obama legacy no one saw coming, more
about the nation than the man?

It would make for a great epilogue.

December 2016

THE CHOICES OF BARACK OBAMA

OF THE BOOKS THAT JOURNALISTS and historians have written on the life of Barack Obama, three stand out so far. In *Barack Obama: The Story*, David Maraniss shows us who Obama is. In *Reading Obama*, James T. Kloppenberg explains how Obama thinks. In *The Bridge*, David Remnick tells us what Obama means.

Now, in a probing new biography, *Rising Star*, David J. Garrow attempts to tell us how Obama lived, and explores the calculations he made in the decades leading up to his presidency. Garrow portrays Obama as a man who ruthlessly compartmentalized his existence; who believed early on that he was fated for greatness; and who made emotional sacrifices in the pursuit of a goal that must have seemed unlikely to everyone but him. Every step— whether his foray into community organizing, Harvard Law School, even his choice of whom to love—was not just about living a life but about fulfilling a destiny.

It is in the personal realm that Garrow's account is particularly revealing. He shares for the first time the story of a woman Obama lived with and loved in Chicago, in the years before he met Michelle, and whom he asked to marry him. Sheila Miyoshi Jager, now a professor at Oberlin College, is a significant presence in *Rising Star*, and her pained, drawn-out relationship with Obama informs both his will to rise in politics and the trade-offs he deemed necessary to do so. Garrow, who received a Pulitzer Prize for his biography of Martin Luther King Jr., concludes this massive new work with a damning verdict on Obama's determination: "While the crucible of self-creation had produced an ironclad will, the vessel was hollow at its core."

By now the broad contours of the Obama story are well known, not least because Obama has repeated them so often. With Kansas and Kenya in his veins, he carries Indonesia in his memory, Hawaii in his smile, Harvard in his brain, and, most of all, Chicago in his soul. "It wasn't until I moved to Chicago and became a community organizer that I think I really grew into myself in terms of my identity," he said in an interview about *Dreams from My Father*. "I connected in a very direct way with the African American community in Chicago" and was able to "walk away with a sense of self-understanding and empowerment."

Inspired by Harold Washington, the city's first black mayor, Obama began to discuss his political ambitions with a few colleagues and friends during his early time in the city. He wanted to be mayor of Chicago. Or a US senator. Or governor of Illinois. Or perhaps he would enter the ministry. Or, as he confided to very few, including Jager, he would become president of the United States. Lofty stuff for a twenty-something community organizer who struggled to write fiction on the side.

Jager, who in *Dreams from My Father* was virtually written out, compressed into a single character along with two prior Obama girlfriends, may have evoked something of Obama's distant mother, Stanley Ann Dunham. Like Dunham, Jager studied anthropology, and while Dunham focused on Indonesia, Jager developed a deep expertise in the Korean Peninsula. She was of Dutch and Japanese ancestry, fitting the multicultural world Obama was only starting to leave behind. They were a natural pair. Jager soon came to realize, she told Garrow, that Obama had "a deep-seated need to be loved and admired."

She describes their time together as an isolating experience, "an island unto ourselves" in which Obama would "compartmentalize his work and home life." She did not meet Jeremiah Wright, the pastor with a growing influence on Obama, and they rarely saw his professional colleagues socially. The friends they saw were often graduate students at the University of Chicago, where Jager was pursuing her doctorate. They traveled together to meet her family, as well as his. Soon they began speaking of marriage.

"In the winter of '86, when we visited my parents, he asked me to marry him," she told Garrow. Her parents were opposed, less for any racial reasons (Obama came across to them like "a white, middle-class kid," a close family friend said) than out of concern about Obama's professional prospects, and because her mother thought Jager, two years Obama's junior, was too young. "Not yet," Sheila told Barack. But they stayed together.

She sensed a change in early 1987, when Obama was twenty-five. "He became . . . so very ambitious" quite suddenly, she told Garrow. "I remember very clearly when this transformation happened, and I remember very specifically that by 1987, about a year into our relationship, he already had his sights on becoming president."

The sense of destiny is not unusual among those who become president. (See Clinton, Bill.) But it created complications. Obama believed that he had a "calling," Garrow writes, and in his case it was "coupled with a heightened awareness that to pursue it he had to fully identify as African American."

Maraniss's 2012 biography deftly describes Obama's conscious evolution from a multicultural, internationalist self-perception toward a distinctly African American one, and Garrow puts this transition into an explicitly political context. For black politicians in Chicago, he writes, a non–African American spouse could be a liability. He cites the example of Richard H. Newhouse Jr., a legendary African American state senator in Illinois, who was married to a white woman and endured whispers that he "talks black but sleeps white." And Carol Moseley Braun, who during the 1990s served Illinois as the first female African American US senator and whose ex-husband was white, admitted that "an interracial marriage really restricts your political options."

Discussions of race and politics suddenly overwhelmed Sheila and Barack's relationship. "The marriage discussions dragged on and on," but now they were clouded by Obama's "torment over this central issue of his life . . . race and identity," Jager recalls. The "resolution of his black identity was directly linked to his decision to pursue a political career," she said.

In Garrow's telling, Obama made emotional judgments on political grounds. A close mutual friend of the couple recalls Obama explaining that "the lines are very clearly drawn. . . . If I am going out with a white woman, I have no standing here." And friends remember an awkward gathering at a summer house, where Obama and Jager engaged in a loud, messy fight on the subject for an entire afternoon. ("That's wrong! That's wrong! That's not a reason," they heard Jager yell from their guest room, their arguments punctuated by bouts of makeup sex.) Obama cared for her, Garrow writes, "yet he felt trapped between the woman he loved and the destiny he knew was his."

Just days before he would depart for Harvard Law School—and when the relationship was already coming apart—Obama asked her to come with him and get married, "mostly, I think, out of a sense of desperation over our eventual parting and not in any real faith in our future," Sheila explained to Garrow. At the time, she was heading to Seoul for dissertation research, and she resented his assumption that she would automatically postpone her career for his. More arguments ensued, and each went their way, although not for good.

At Harvard, the Obama the world has come to know took clearer form. In his late twenties and slightly older than most classmates, he had a tendency to orate in class and summarize other people's arguments for them. "In law school the only thing I would have voted for Obama to do would have been to shut up," one student told Garrow. Classmates created a Obamanometer, ranking "how pretentious someone's remarks are in class."

Such complaints aside, he was generally admired, including by his professors, one of whom wrote a final exam question around comments Obama had made in class. And his election to the presidency of the *Harvard Law Review*, the first time for an African American, signaled the respect the school's elite students had for him—even if some liberal classmates later regretted their choice, finding Obama too conciliatory toward conservatives in their midst. Garrow re-creates the drama around the election, with *Law Review* colleagues debating the candidates' legal acumen and leadership skills, as well as the possible history-making aspect of the selection. It is an unexpectedly riveting part of the book. The black editors on the staff began "crying and running and hugging" when the final choice was made—and with the national news coverage that followed, Obama's star was on the rise.

Law school also provided Obama one of his most important intellectual interlocutors: classmate and economist Rob Fisher. They took multiple classes together and cowrote a never-published book on public policy, titled "Transformative Politics" or "Promises of Democracy: Hopeful Critiques of

American Ideology." The manuscript explored the political failures of the left and right and expounded on markets, race, and democratic dialogue, showing glimmers of the political philosophy and rhetoric that Obama would come to embrace. A few years later, Fisher helped Obama rethink *Dreams from My Father* (originally titled "Journeys in Black and White"), making it less a policy book and more a personal one.

Obama met Michelle Robinson at the Chicago law firm where she worked—and where he was a summer associate—after his first year of law school, and the couple quickly became serious. However, Jager, who soon arrived at Harvard on a teaching fellowship, was not entirely out of his life. "Barack and Sheila had continued to see each other irregularly throughout the 1990–91 academic year, notwithstanding the deepening of Barack's relationship with Michelle Robinson," Garrow writes. ("I always felt bad about it," Jager told the author more than two decades later.) Once Barack and Michelle were married, his personal ties to Sheila were reduced to the occasional letter (such as after the 9/11 attacks) and phone call (when he reached out to ask whether a biographer had contacted her).

If Garrow is correct in concluding that Obama's romantic choices were influenced by his political ambitions, it is no small irony that Michelle Obama became one of those most skeptical about his political prospects, and most dubious about his will to rise. She constantly discouraged his efforts toward elective office and resented the time he spent away from her and their two young daughters. Barack vented to a friend how often Michelle would talk about money. "Why don't you go out and get a good job? You're a lawyer—you can make all the money we need," she would tell him, as the couple struggled with student loans and the demands of family and political life. (Garrow sides with Michelle, highlighting how, on the day after Sasha was born, Barack went downtown for a meeting.)

As he considered a US Senate bid, Obama's team commissioned a poll that covered, among other questions, his name. "Barry," as he was known from childhood into his early college years, polled better than "Barack," but Obama never considered resurrecting the old name. He had made his choice, of identity and image, long ago. Jager recalls that one of the few times

Obama became genuinely angry with her was in Hawaii, when she heard relatives calling him Barry, and she did so as well, just for fun. He became "irrationally furious," she said. "He told me that under no circumstances was I ever to use that name with him."

There was no going back.

Rising Star is exhaustive, but only occasionally exhausting. Garrow zooms his lens out far, for instance when he recounts the evisceration of Chicago's steel industry in the early 1980s, providing useful context for Obama's subsequent work. And he goes deliciously small-bore, too, delving into the culture of the Illinois statehouse, where poker was intense and infidelity was rampant. "There's a lot of people who f—ed in Springfield," a female lobbyist tells Garrow. "What else is there to do?" Obama, however, did not. "Michelle would kick my butt," he told a colleague there. At times Garrow delivers information simply because he has it; I did not need a detailed readout of all of Obama's course evaluations from his years teaching at the University of Chicago Law School. (Turns out his students liked him.)

The book's title seems chosen with a sense of irony. Garrow shows how media organizations invariably described Obama as a "rising star," in almost self-fulfilling fashion. Yet after nine years of research and reporting, Garrow does not appear too impressed by his subject, even if he recognizes Obama's historical importance.

The author is harsh but persuasive in his reading of *Dreams from My Father*, for instance, calling it not a memoir but a work of "historical fiction," in which the "most important composite character was the narrator himself." (Reviewers were impressed by it, but few who knew Obama well seemed to recognize the man in its pages.) He points out that Obama's cocaine use extended into his post-college years, longer than he had acknowledged. And he suggests Obama deployed religion for political purposes; while campaigning for the US Senate, Garrow notes, Obama began toting around a Bible and exhibited "a greater religious faith than close acquaintances had ever previously sensed."

Throughout the book, Obama displays an almost petulant dissatisfaction with each step he takes to reach the Oval Office. Community organizing is not ambitious enough, he decides, so he goes to law school. But then he moves into politics because "I saw the law as being inadequate to the task" of achieving social change, Obama explains. In Springfield, he is again disillusioned by "the realization that politics is a business . . . an activity that's designed to advance one's career, accumulate resources and help one's friends," as "opposed to a mission." And upon reaching the Senate, he tells *National Journal* that he is "surprised by the lack of deliberation in the world's greatest deliberative body." Nothing measures up.

Rising Star concludes with Obama announcing his presidential campaign, and Garrow speeds through his presidency in a clunky and tacky epilogue, in which he recaps the growing media disenchantment with Obama and goes out of his way to cite unfavorable reviews of earlier biographies. (Come on, David. Other books can be good.) In his acknowledgments, Garrow says Obama granted him eight hours of off-the-record conversations and even read the bulk of the manuscript. "His understandable remaining disagreements— some strong indeed—with multiple characterizations and interpretations contained herein do not lessen my deep thankfulness for his appreciation of the scholarly seriousness with which I have pursued this project," Garrow writes.

That is Obama now: a scholarly project, a figure of history. After the eight years of his presidency, it is odd to consider him in the past tense. Yet he is not going away, certainly not with a post-presidential memoir still coming. But now he is fighting for history and legacy, and one of those battles is against another figure whose ascent is even more bizarre, yet perhaps no less personally preordained.

Obama had considered Donald Trump long before either man won the presidency, and brushed off his appeal as a national fantasy. Americans have a "continuing normative commitment to the ideals of individual freedom and mobility," Obama wrote in the old Harvard book manuscript, now more than twenty-five years old. "The depth of this commitment may be summarily dismissed as the unfounded optimism of the average American—I may not be Donald Trump now, but just you wait; if I don't make it, my children will."

May 2017

THE EXAMINED LIFE
OF BARACK OBAMA

I'VE LONG BEEN IMAGINING BARACK Obama's presidential memoir. Would it be an extension of the life and mind found in *Dreams from My Father* and *The Audacity of Hope*, part three of a most introspective trilogy? Would it see itself in conversation—or competition—with the memoirs and reflections of presidents past? Or might it somehow complement Michelle Obama's blockbuster 2018 memoir, *Becoming*, on the struggle to articulate one's purpose while shifting from private to public life?

The answer is yes. Obama's lengthy and still partial account of his presidency is some version of all of these books; its strength, like that of its author, is in the ability to be many things to many people.

But the deeper one wades through it, the clearer it becomes that *A Promised Land* is less a personal memoir than an unusual sort of history, one recounted by the man at the center of it, a man who seems always to be observing himself in action, always wondering if he is guiding the currents or is driven by them. There is chronology here, from childhood to schooling to community organizing to law to marriage to politics and finally to the White House, and then from financial crisis to health-care battles, from endless war in distant lands to an endless spill at the bottom of the ocean. Yet Obama himself remains at a distance, immersed more in thought than action, always on the lookout for contradictions and symbolism, unveiling himself only in select moments. If there is a narrative here, it concerns what happens inside the writer's own head.

The book's main revelation concerns that, too. Obama says he wrote *A Promised Land* to invite young people "to once again remake the world, and to bring about ... an America that finally aligns with all that is best in us." Implicit in such an invitation is an admission of his failure to bring about

that alignment in his time. Part of it is due to obstructionism by congressional Republicans, who turned opposition to the first black president from a
means of politics to its end. Part of it stems from the impossible expectations
with which Obama imbued his politics and his speeches, which, as he puts
it, "tapped into some collective spirit, a thing we all know and wish for—a
sense of connection that overrides our differences and replaces them with a
giant swell of possibility." Yet it is also a function of Obama's innate caution,
of his skepticism—hopeful slogans notwithstanding—of dramatic change.

In domestic policy and foreign affairs, in debates over culture and race,
Obama splits differences, clings to the middle ground, and trusts in process
as much as principle. The first few months of his presidency "revealed a basic
strand of my political character," he writes. It turns out he is not a "revolutionary soul" but a reformist one, "conservative in temperament if not in
vision." Behind those dreams, the audacity and all that promise is a stubborn
streak of moderation.

Obama says he wants to give readers "a sense of what it's like to *be* the president . . . to pull back the curtain" on the day-to-day, and he succeeds in small
and big ways. Readers witness a twenty-minute tutorial he receives on proper
military salute etiquette ("Elbow a little farther out, sir . . . Fingers tighter,
sir"), learn Obama's tips for surviving international summits ("You sit there,
fighting off jet lag and doing your best to look interested"), and brace themselves when the president asks King Abdullah of Saudi Arabia how he keeps
up with a dozen wives. (His Majesty's answer: "Very badly . . . It's more
complicated than Middle East politics.") And I'll never forget his first night
in the White House when, not knowing what else to do, he walked around
turning off lights before finally going to bed. Such a dad move.

But most illuminating is why Obama, after winning his US Senate seat
from Illinois, aspired to the presidency at all. "God, Barack ... when is it
going to be enough?" Michelle Obama reproaches early on. His own introspection is hardly more charitable. "Was it just vanity?" he wonders. "Or
perhaps something darker—a raw hunger, a blind ambition wrapped in the
gauzy language of service?" He eventually reached a series of justifications:

to stir a new kind of politics; to bridge the country's divides; and to expand the horizons of young people of color who would be inspired to see him take the oath.

Such self-aware symbolism, so powerful in the emotion of a historic campaign, can become a hindrance once poetry gives way to prose. "They had taken possession of my likeness and made it a vessel for a million different dreams," he writes. "I knew a time would come when I would disappoint them." Black activists and intellectuals—never sure he would win, anyway—wanted him to take "the most uncompromising positions" on issues such as affirmative action and reparations, Obama recalls. And he knows he disappointed many when he did not mete out "Old Testament justice," as one senior official described it, in response to bankers' misdeeds in the mortgage crisis. "I wonder whether I should have been bolder in those early months, willing to exact more economic pain in the short term in pursuit of a permanently altered and more just economic order," Obama writes.

But the wondering does not last long. If he had to do it all over again, "I can't say I would make different choices," he decides. Returning to a state of "pre-crisis normalcy" would be good enough.

This practicality recurs throughout *A Promised Land*. When an adviser suggests that the Rev. Jeremiah Wright should not deliver a public invocation at his 2008 campaign kickoff, Obama is frustrated by the need to soften blunt racial truths for white audiences, but he concludes that "as a matter of practical politics" the adviser was right. During the push for health-care reform, he wants to get tough on the pharmaceutical and insurance industries but decides that, "as a practical matter," a conciliatory approach is best. Same when he appeases some conservative Democrats by agreeing to strip the public option out of the health-care proposal. "It wasn't the first time I'd chosen practicality over pique," he confides.

Obama tends to see all sides of everything. On foreign policy, he admits that he was never quite the "starry-eyed idealist" he seemed during the presidential campaign and that he owed as much to the realist worldview, believing in restraint, wary of unforeseen consequences, cognizant of the limits of America's ability to remake the world. The splits among his foreign policy team—young idealists such as Ben Rhodes and Samantha Power, cautious veterans such as Bob Gates and Hillary Clinton—reflected Obama's own ambivalence. On the Arab Spring, for instance, "I shared both the hopes of younger advisors and the fears of my older ones," he writes.

In this book, you often see Obama talking himself into moderation, even though the very reason he'd left behind other roles—as a community organizer, lawyer, state senator, and US senator—was dissatisfaction with the limits they imposed on him. "My heart was now chained to strategic considerations and tactical analysis, my convictions subject to counterintuitive arguments ... in the most powerful office on earth, I had less freedom to say what I meant and act on what I felt than I'd had as a senator—or as an ordinary citizen."

But if you keep encountering the same discontent, the same restlessness, wherever you go, no matter the job, maybe it's you. In *A Promised Land*, Obama's on-the-other-handedness is his default setting. He worries about politicians redirecting white frustrations against racial minorities, yet he sympathizes with those frustrations. He understands the tea party anger, though he considers it misdirected. He affirms that the regulatory state conservatives so decry has made American lives "a hell of a lot better," then adds the obligatory caveat: "That's not to say that every criticism of federal regulation was bogus." It's a tic of temperament but also of design. As early as his college years, Obama cultivated the habit of questioning his assumptions, which he thinks "inoculated" him against the revolutionary zeal of the Reagan-era left. The vaccination has lasted.

Obama writes with the knowledge and weight of history, an occupational hazard of the presidency (though evidently not for all presidents). He constantly references his predecessors—by my count, at least twenty of them appear in *A Promised Land*—pondering how Abraham Lincoln consoled so many wounded soldiers or how Franklin Roosevelt explained his policies during the Depression.

He is a talented writer—and not just for a politician—but he overdoes the history lessons at times. Obama introduces virtually every decision or conflict with some dutiful background or policy overview, a habit that can make for tedious reading. "Though I hadn't majored in economics, I was familiar enough with John Maynard Keynes, one of the giants of modern economics," he explains in a discussion of the stimulus debates. "Since *Marbury v. Madison* . . . ," he intones when describing Supreme Court appointments. "Since the time of the czars, historians had noted . . . ," he lectures when musing on Russia's fatalism. I normally take notes while I read; here, I wanted to grab a red pen and slash out lines. For Obama, just about every moment is a teachable one.

He also gives detailed shout-outs to countless aides and staffers—an admirable quality in a manager, less so in the author of a 751-page book. He boasts that his first presidential campaign sought to "challenge the Washington playbook and tell hard truths," sentiments that are themselves straight out of the Washington playbook. (It's the audacity of trope.) And he can overapply the writerly gloss, as when he looks back on Election Day 2008: "Across the country millions of strangers step behind a black curtain to register their policy preferences and private instincts, as some mysterious collective alchemy determines the country's fate—and your own." (Alternatively: "People voted.")

Obama's erudition is most powerful not when he squeezes in more history but when he distills it. His recollection of a speech at West Point leads to a perfect, one-paragraph digression on the heroism and folly of America's wars, whether the Civil War, World War II, or Vietnam. "Glory and tragedy, courage and stupidity—one set of truths didn't negate the other," he writes. Just as he does not outright condemn American military action (he was, after all, a president who personally approved drone strikes against terrorist targets), neither does he decry America as a land of prejudice, beyond redemption. "The conviction that racism wasn't inevitable may also explain my willingness to defend the American idea: what the country was, and what it could become," he recalls.

And here we may get to the heart not just of the American idea but of Obama's idea, too. "Do we care to match the reality of America to its ideals?" he asks in his preface. It is the question that suffuses the book and the country it describes, just as closing the gap between ideal and reality—even simply acknowledging it can suffice sometimes—animates the man and his life.

Obama meant to write a single-volume memoir of his presidency, and I wish he had. *A Promised Land* ends in the aftermath of the 2011 raid that killed Osama bin Laden, with so much still left to revisit and reconsider. Syria and the red line. Trayvon Martin, Ferguson, and Black Lives Matter. Newtown and Charleston. The brutal 2016 campaign, Russian election interference, and the shock of the four years since Obama left office.

I don't want to wait to learn how Obama saw all this at the time or how he sees it now. He connects Trump's appeal to his own presidency—"for millions of Americans spooked by a black man in the White House, he promised an elixir for their racial anxiety"—but Trump is not the focus of this book, nor should he be. The forty-fifth president appears largely by implication and by contrast, as when Obama regards Sarah Palin's 2008 vice presidential nomination as a forerunner of the forces overtaking the Republican Party, and when he details the process for meetings and policy rollouts in his administration. "Every document issued was fact-checked, every person who showed up for a meeting was vetted, every event was planned to the minute, and every policy announcement was carefully scrubbed to make sure it was achievable," he writes. Today, that reads like a dispatch from a different world.

Obama also revisits his famous 2004 Democratic National Convention speech, another call to create an America aligned with what is best in us. That night, he saw a country that was not torn by politics or race, but united. Once again, though, he looks back with ambivalence. "I'd intended it more as a statement of aspiration than a description of reality," Obama now explains. "But it was an aspiration I believed in and a reality I strove for."

Those two impulses—hope tempered by caution and caution streaked with hope—capture the promise of *A Promised Land*.

November 2020

THE LAST THROES OF
DICK CHENEY

IT WAS A CLASSIC WASHINGTON split-screen moment.

On May 21, 2009, minutes apart and just a mile and a half away from each other, President Obama and former vice president Dick Cheney offered dueling visions of America's war on terrorism—of Guantánamo and torture, of surveillance and civil liberties. Speaking at the National Archives, Obama decried the previous administration's "hasty decisions" and said that essential American values had been discarded "as luxuries that we could no longer afford." Cheney, holding court at the hawkish American Enterprise Institute, defended "enhanced interrogations" as legal and valuable, and warned that "in the fight against terrorism, there is no middle ground, and half-measures keep you half-exposed."

I was in the second row at Cheney's speech, and I recall the energy in the room as he approached the lectern. Only recently out of office, Cheney still mattered. He embodied a worldview that held sway. In 2009, Obama versus Cheney was a heavyweight prizefight.

Six years later, Cheney is out with a new book on national security and is once again scheduled to deliver a speech at AEI, with Obama again as his foil. But it's hard to muster the same excitement. It is far from clear that Cheney's arguments, calcified in the intervening years, wield much influence anymore, even within his own party, or that they should. Rather than a slugfest, this feels like a swan song.

And it is a song he performs, in perfect Cheney pitch, with *Exceptional: Why the World Needs a Powerful America*. Cowritten with his daughter and former State Department official Liz Cheney, the book is part history of America's role in the world since World War II, part assault on Obama's record on foreign and defense policy, and part relentlessly militaristic to-do list for the next commander in chief. "Our next president must be committed to restoring America's power and strength," the Cheneys write. "Our security and the survival of freedom depend on it."

In the authors' telling, America's influence over world events has been almost entirely benevolent, as leaders from Roosevelt and Truman to Reagan and George W. Bush stared down tyrants and dispensed freedom and security. "We are, as a matter of empirical fact and undeniable history," the Cheneys explain, "the greatest force for good the world has ever known." From D-Day through the Cold War and into the age of terror, "security and freedom for millions of people around the globe have depended on America's military, economic, political, and diplomatic might."

Until 2009, that is. "President Obama has diminished American power and retreated from the field of battle, fueling rising threats against our nation," the authors write. "He has pursued a foreign policy built on appeasing our adversaries, abandoning our allies, and apologizing for America."

The Cheneys repeatedly accuse Obama and his administration of misleading the American public—particularly regarding the Iran nuclear deal and the Benghazi attack—subsuming foreign policy to domestic political considerations, underestimating the threat posed by the Islamic State and other terrorist groups, and ceding global initiative and influence to Moscow, Tehran, and Beijing. More fundamentally, they contend, Obama simply does not get America. "The touchstone of his ideology—that America is to blame and her power must be restrained—requires a willful blindness about what America has done in the world," the Cheneys write. "It is fundamentally counterfactual."

All histories are selective histories, and in this respect *Exceptional* does not disappoint. The Vietnam War receives perfunctory treatment, perhaps because it doesn't fit the storyline of unambiguous American goodness. "The objective of preventing a Communist takeover of South Vietnam was a worthy one," the Cheneys write. "There were many errors in the way America pursued this objective, about which much has been written elsewhere." The main error they raise is the one hawks always raise: that America did not fight to win.

On the Iraq war, *Exceptional* is entirely Cheneyesque—undoubting, unyielding and ultimately unconvincing. American forces "were, in fact, greeted as liberators," they write, a defense of Vice President Cheney's prediction on the eve of the invasion. While acknowledging that "we now know" Saddam Hussein did not possess stockpiles of weapons of mass destruction, the authors argue that the Iraqi leader was still a threat to US security, because Iraq was "the most likely nexus" between terrorists and the weapons they sought. And they emphasize all that America accomplished in Iraq, such as deposing a dictator and providing security for the people as they voted in their first free elections.

"Those who say the invasion of Iraq in 2003 was a mistake are essentially saying we would be better off if Saddam Hussein were still in power," they write. The Cheneys don't question whether Americans would have supported the invasion solely because Iraq was a "likely nexus" for terrorism and because US troops could bring freedom to a long-suffering people, rather than because of Iraq's supposed weapons of mass destruction, affirmed by the vice president and so many other Bush administration officials.

The closest *Exceptional* comes to contrition concerns the execution of the war, not its rationale, but even then it stops short. "The war to liberate Iraq was indisputably difficult," the authors write. "It included tragedy and challenges we did not foresee. Every war does, but these tragedies and challenges do not detract from the rightness of our cause."

History is written by the victors, and also by those who convince themselves that they won.

The Iraq experience adds an extra hurdle of credibility for the Cheneys' warnings about Iran and the nuclear accord the United States and other powers recently reached with that country. "The Obama agreement will lead to a nuclear-armed Iran, a nuclear arms race in the Middle East, and more than likely, the first use of a nuclear weapon since Hiroshima and Nagasaki," they write. Obama's successor must junk the deal, they argue—just one of many items a new president must get to right away.

Their list features a massive military buildup, including new missile-defense systems, more nuclear weapons, and a force prepared to wage war in multiple geographic locations simultaneously. The Cheneys also call for the restoration of the National Security Agency's surveillance authorities, the return of "enhanced" interrogation of terrorism suspects, the deployment of thousands of military "advisors" to battle the Islamic State, and a halt to the US withdrawal from Afghanistan. They also advocate aggressive actions against rival nations, such as sending troops to NATO countries that border Russia, in order to "signal American determination."

Otherwise, the authors write, militant Islam will spread across the globe; Iran and other countries will go nuclear; China will dominate Asia and target America; and Russia will overpower Europe, enslaving free nations and destroying NATO.

The Cheneys rarely grapple with counterarguments or inconvenient facts. They say that harsh interrogations "saved lives and prevented attacks" but ignore the Senate Intelligence Committee's 2014 report, which after a five-year investigation concluded that such techniques did not work. ("Feinstein, Dianne" does not appear in the book's index.) When they chastise Obama for setting a timetable for the withdrawal of US troops from Iraq, they forget that Bush did the same. They complain that President Dwight Eisenhower's farewell speech on the military-industrial complex has been "distorted" and selectively quoted by critics of the military, and then proceed to do the same with Obama's remarks on American exceptionalism.

At a time when the Republican presidential candidates offer get-tough rhetoric and obsess over the Mexican border, a thoughtful and reasoned critique of Obama's foreign policy is needed. But *Exceptional* does not provide it. It is heavy on self-justifications, light on self-awareness. "One might ask why the administration worked so hard to ignore evidence and peddle a false narrative about what happened," the Cheneys write regarding Benghazi. It is a question that might be asked of other administrations during other crises, too.

The former vice president has not endorsed anyone in the 2016 Republican field, and none of the candidates seems particularly eager to claim him as a foreign policy adviser. It's probably just as well. When American exceptionalism is conflated with militarism and jingoism, it leaves little room for the traditions of reinvention and self-assessment that make America's exceptional nature come alive.

America *is* exceptional. Dick Cheney is, too.

September 2015

HILLARY CLINTON'S ONLY MANIFESTO

HILLARY CLINTON FELT MISUNDERSTOOD.

It was late 1994, Republican revolutionaries had stormed the House, and the first lady worried that it was her fault. Had she pushed too hard on health-care reform? Did voters resent her influence in her husband's administration? During a meeting with confidantes in the White House residence, Clinton held back tears and contemplated stepping back from a visible role in politics and policy.

Instead, she decided to reintroduce herself to America. "I realized I needed to tell my own story and define my own values in a format that could be evaluated directly by people without being distorted or mischaracterized," she later explained. The result was *It Takes a Village*, a meditation on the needs of children in the United States—and the closest thing we've ever had to a political manifesto from Hillary Clinton. After the humiliating failure of Hillarycare and her party's midterm debacle, the book became a bestseller, her comeback.

In the decades since, it has also become her touchstone, the argument she still reaches for when explaining her vision. "I believe the idea of the village and its shared responsibility for our children is even more essential today than it was in 1996," Clinton wrote in the book's tenth anniversary edition. She drew on it again during her first run at the Democratic presidential nomination, in 2008. "After all these years, I still believe it takes a village to raise a child," she said in remarks before the Urban League, where she pledged, "as your president, to build that village." And Clinton returned to it in the speech launching her 2016 presidential campaign, calling for "an inclusive society"—or, she added, "what I once called 'a village' that has a place for everyone." As if we didn't remember.

Clinton has labeled herself "a progressive who likes to get things done," suggesting ideology leavened by pragmatism. Though some of her views have no doubt shifted since she wrote the book, *It Takes a Village* shows Clinton striving, sometimes struggling, to reconcile those two impulses. The Clinton in these pages is a self-described moderate, but one who wants an activist government to drive social policy transformations. She is an advocate for equal rights, with a surprising streak of social conservatism. And in a preview of one of her 2016 campaign's big challenges, she dismisses cross-generational nostalgia for a bygone America yet fears that young Americans don't recognize the sacrifices their elders once made for them.

Clinton today frequently hails the country's economic performance during her husband's presidency, but *It Takes a Village* begins with a bleak view of the 1990s. "Everywhere we look," she writes, "children are under assault: from violence and neglect, from the breakup of families, from the temptations of alcohol, tobacco, sex, and drug abuse, from greed, materialism, and spiritual emptiness."

Parents are the first defense for their kids—feeding, teaching, nurturing, encouraging—but children "exist in the world as well as in the family," Clinton explains. They depend on grandparents, neighbors, teachers, ministers, doctors, employers, and, yes, politicians. "It takes a village to raise a child," she writes. "I chose that old African proverb to title this book because it offers a timeless reminder that children will thrive only if their families thrive and if the whole of society cares enough to provide for them."

The whole of society—that's where Clinton's vision quickly expands. Although she highlights the importance of nonprofits, faith communities, businesses, and international nongovernmental groups, "it takes a village" often becomes code for "it takes Washington." Clinton writes passionately about the Family and Medical Leave Act, the Violent Crime Control and Law Enforcement Act, the Brady Bill, immunization campaigns, and other federal initiatives, deeming them essential to village life. "Let us stop stereotyping government or individuals as absolute villains or absolute saviors, and recognize that each must be part of the solution," she writes. "Let us use government, as we have in the past, to further the common good."

So, what is the proper role for that government? Clinton identifies competing strands in American history—a collective "gratitude" for a government that promotes the common good, alongside a deep skepticism of authority evident in constitutional checks and balances and the Bill of Rights—and then claims the center. "Most of us would describe ourselves as 'middle of the road'—liberal in some areas, conservative in others, moderate in most, neither exclusively pro- nor anti-government," she writes. It may not be the vision of 2016 primary voters seduced by Sanders's calls for political revolution, but it's entirely consistent with Bill Clinton's presidency, which, two weeks after the book's publication, declared the era of big government over.

On the economy, Hillary Clinton reflects the ambivalence that still dogs her as today's Democratic voters consider her Wall Street ties. She emphasizes the importance of regulations for strong financial markets and job growth, yet she brags about how the Clinton administration eliminated sixteen thousand pages of them. She blasts companies that lay off workers in the name of efficiency but adds that, "to be fair, while corporate restructuring is eliminating many jobs, the economy is also creating millions of new jobs, with small businesses starting at a record pace." *the practical benefits rather than the hegemonic benefits*

Centrist rhetoric doesn't stop Clinton from reaffirming her case for universal health care. *of healthcare reform* "Many people believe that we cannot guarantee health care to all because of cost," she writes. "In fact, a sensible universal system would, as in other countries, end up costing us less." She laments the nation's unwillingness to "commit ourselves to make affordable care available to every American." Today Clinton looks back with pride on her battles with the insurance industry, telling audiences that she fought hard and has "the scars to prove it." In her book, she appears defensive at times, the wounds still fresh.

Though her push for reform, like Obamacare after it, was assailed as a paternalistic, Washington-knows-best approach to social policy, in *It Takes a Village* Clinton also stresses the role of personal agency in staying healthy. Take the stairs instead of the elevator, she says. Teach kids to feel responsible for their own weight. Shut the refrigerator door and open the front door instead. "There's probably no area of our lives that better illustrates the connection between the village and the individual and between mutual and personal responsibility than health care," Clinton writes.

This emphasis on personal responsibility is consistent with one of the more unexpected aspects of *It Takes a Village*—its socially conservative views of family, sex, and popular culture.

Though Clinton writes that children can thrive in multiple family structures, she argues that "the nuclear family, consisting of an adult mother and father and the children to whom they are biologically related, has proved to be the most durable and effective means of meeting children's needs over time." She endorses uniforms in schools, calls for stricter codes for violence in movies, and praises Tipper Gore's efforts on warning labels for explicit music. Clinton also encourages sexual abstinence and wishes that young people would postpone decisions about sex until age twenty-one—all views that may feel anachronistic in her party today but that placed Clinton near the center in the 1990s culture wars.

She laments abortion among young people and says it's a "national shame that many Americans are more thoughtful about planning their weekend entertainment than they are about planning their families." Clinton calls for more research into family planning and wider access to contraception, and she asserts that "women and men should have the right to make this most intimate of all decisions free of discrimination or coercion." But then, in odd phrasing for the pro–abortion rights politician, she contends that "once a pregnancy occurs ... we all have a stake in working to ensure that it turns out well."

Perhaps most dissonant in an America—and a Democratic Party—focused on racial disparities in policing and criminal justice, *It Takes a Village* praises the 1994 crime bill for stopping "the revolving door for career criminals," hails the presence of more cops on the streets, and points approvingly to the rise of neighborhood watch groups. "It is realistic, not racist, to be cautious when walking through a high-crime neighborhood, or to want to avoid a corner where a drive-by shooting has taken place," Clinton writes.

"Such judgments become biased only when they are motivated by negative stereotypes rather than common sense."

Finally, Clinton decries widespread divorce, characterizing it as a personal failing of couples who don't try hard enough. "For a high proportion of marriages," she writes, "'till death do us part' means 'until the going gets rough.'" Clinton mentions her own efforts to keep her marriage together: "My strong feelings about divorce and its effect on children have caused me to bite my tongue more than a few times during my own marriage and to think instead about what I could do to be a better wife and partner," she acknowledges.

In her speech at the 1996 Democratic National Convention in Chicago, Clinton drew heavily from *It Takes a Village*, linking its arguments to her family and, most important, to her husband's case for reelection:

> For Bill and me, there has been no experience more challenging, more rewarding, and more humbling than raising our daughter. And we have learned that to raise a happy, healthy, and hopeful child, it takes a family. It takes teachers. It takes clergy. It takes businesspeople. It takes community leaders. It takes those who protect our health and safety. It takes all of us.
>
> Yes, it takes a village.
>
> And it takes a president. . . . It takes Bill Clinton.

Today, she is making that case for a different Clinton, in a different time. It's a tough balance, embracing elements of that past presidency, discarding others, and casting herself forward as her own person.

Even in *It Takes a Village*, Clinton is conflicted about the past. She dismisses the "nostalgia merchants" who would like to take us back to a Norman Rockwell–style America, but she worries that young people don't appreciate the hard-earned gains of those who came before. "When I look back on my childhood," she writes, "I see how my mother and my girlfriends' mothers worked to push open doors of opportunity for us." By contrast, younger Americans "don't remember that many of the most important advances grew out of controversy and were achieved only after great effort."

But others do remember, and Clinton's recitation of those who have benefited from the village almost resembles a Democratic electoral coalition. "Our children may not remember, but older African Americans who could not eat in restaurants or sleep in hotels or vote in elections surely do. Women who were not admitted into certain professions remember. ... Asian Americans who were told not even to apply for some jobs and Jewish Americans who were prohibited from buying homes in certain neighborhoods remember. Hispanic Americans who had no legal recourse against exploitative employers remember. Native Americans who lacked access to medical services before the expansion of the Indian Health Service remember. Men who went off to fight in World War II and were welcomed home by a grateful nation and the GI Bill of Rights remember."

The dust jacket of *It Takes a Village* features a smiling Clinton, bathed in sunlight, surrounded by adorable children. They look six or seven years old, and they're all laughing. The message is clear: these are the children Clinton fights for; the village she is building is for them.

Two decades later, those kids are in their twenties. They're the millennial generation. And they're feeling the Bern.

February 2016

THE EVERGREEN
HILLARY CLINTON

WHILE DONALD TRUMP CLAIMS TO be our voice, Hillary Clinton struggles to find hers.

Her speech Thursday at the Democratic National Convention will afford her yet another chance to argue her case, to explain why she's the best person for the presidency. For Clinton, whom we've known so well and so long, that's a challenge. Familiarity affords obvious strengths, but so far in this campaign, it often has posed a hindrance, with the proportion of Americans viewing Clinton unfavorably creeping up as the race has worn on. The candidate who said she "found my own voice" in New Hampshire in 2008 now faces an electorate that has trouble trusting what she says. "I have work to do on this point," she admitted recently.

That has been the work of a lifetime for Clinton, not only as a first lady, senator, presidential candidate, and secretary of state but as an author as well. If *It Takes a Village* (1996) was a statement of Clinton's values, then her two memoirs, *Living History* (2003) and *Hard Choices* (2014), are her story of those values in action. The memoirs show how Clinton perceives her life and record, and how she wants us to see them, too.

All memoir is, to some extent, propaganda, and the memoirs of striving politicians may be the most agitprop of all. Even so, the Hillary Clinton who emerges from these thousand-plus pages of autobiography is revealing in ways that she never will be in political ads, party platforms, or four-day Philadelphia infomercials. In her writing, she is torn over her generational and gender symbolism, incapable of separating the personal from the political, and loath to concede anything beyond tactical errors. She is trapped in what she calls "derivative" subordinate roles under more politically powerful men, yet finds ways to thrive in them. She is ever aware of the daggers surrounding her, but still careless in exposing herself to the blades. She recognizes the risks inherent in the most potent relationship of her life yet is unwilling to relinquish it. And she is a talented writer and expansive thinker whose writing and thinking grow more cautious as the prize of the presidency draws nearer.

Living History spans Clinton's life from childhood through her election as the junior senator from New York in 2000. *Hard Choices* chronicles her experiences as President Obama's secretary of state. *Hard Choices* is about her ability, *Living History* is about her humanity.

Clinton may be tempted to stress the former, to premise her election on expertise and predictability, especially when her Republican rival sells fear and division. Yet in reading her memoirs, that is the less compelling version of the candidate. *Living History* is riskier, more vulnerable, more real, especially read now, in an era when most campaigns have grown less so. Competence and experience have always been Clinton's calling card, but they've not sufficed. For the remainder of this campaign, her task, her hardest choice, will be to reveal the humanity behind the capability, the person inside the politician.

"While Bill talked about social change, I embodied it."

That's how Clinton describes her impact on her husband's 1992 presidential campaign, when Bill's suggestion that Americans would get "two for one" and Hillary's response to questions about her legal career—"I suppose I could have stayed home and baked cookies and had teas"—became embedded in Clinton lore, eliciting admiration, skepticism, and sexism in equal measure. "I had been turned into a symbol for women of my generation," she concludes, reliving the controversies over her professional background and policy ambitions versus the traditional duties of a political spouse. "In this era of changing gender roles, I was America's Exhibit A."

Yet if the generational symbolism felt imposed during the race, it was a burden she was happy to shoulder on other occasions. Her 1969 commencement speech at Wellesley College, the one that made her a national figure long before anyone had heard of a certain William Jefferson Clinton, was, she explains, a reflection of the aspirations of Clinton and her classmates, "women and Americans whose lives would exemplify the changes and choices facing our generation." At the 1992 Democratic National Convention, she writes, the young Clinton and Gore families waving at Madison Square Garden represented "a new generation's turn to lead." And when working with Bill on a major health-care speech early in his presidency, she reminded him that reform was "our generation's chance to answer a call on behalf of future generations."

Clinton is predisposed to see herself in such history-making terms. In *Hard Choices*, she recalls considering the legacies of notable predecessors as secretary of state—Thomas Jefferson, George C. Marshall, Dean Acheson— and envisioning how she would remake the role. "I believe, with all of my heart, that this is a new era for America," she told her cheering new colleagues on her first day on the job.

Even when Clinton's memoirs revel in life, family, and friendship, she invariably returns to politics. After Chelsea was born and Hillary took four months off from her Little Rock law firm, she and Bill "emerged from our experience committed to ensuring that all parents have the option to stay home with their newborn children." When, early in Bill's presidency, her father is dying and Hillary huddles with her family in his hospital room, "succumbing to the hypnotic whir and click of the respirator," she makes time to talk with doctors, nurses, and administrators about health-care reform, and the conversations reinforced "the importance of improving our system." While Clinton was attending the 1994 Winter Olympics in Norway, she recalls, Prime Minister Gro Brundtland asked her about the proposed health-care bill, which instantly made her "a friend for life."

Yes, chronic eye-rolling is an occupational hazard of reading Clinton's memoirs. Still, the deeper you go, the more you realize that she isn't just another politician mining life experiences for cheap talking points. This is really what it's like to walk around inside her head. Life and politics and policy are never separate—and nowhere is this clearer than in her relationship with the forty-second president.

Living History shows Bill and Hillary scoping each other out at the Yale Law Library, details their work on the 1972 McGovern campaign, and chronicles Bill's numerous proposals before she agrees to marry him. "When we first met as students, I loved watching him turn the pages of a book," Clinton writes, capturing the almost sensual intellectualism with which she regards him. But her doubts about him were prescient. "I thought of him as a force of nature," she explains, "and wondered whether I'd be up to the task of living through his seasons."

Winter arrived in the second term, and *Living History* describes Hillary's reaction to the Monica Lewinsky revelations. "I could hardly breathe. Gulping for air, I started crying and yelling at him," she writes. She details the distance, anger, and loneliness as the scandal played out, but more instructive is her explanation for how and why they reconciled. "As his wife, I wanted to wring Bill's neck," Clinton explains. "But he was not only my husband, he was also my President, and I thought that, in spite of everything, Bill led America and the world in a way that I continued to support."

All those who speculate that the Clintons share a marriage of political convenience—that they've reached an "arrangement," as Steve Kroft suggested in a *60 Minutes* interview—miss the point. In her telling, there is no trade-off between the personal and the political; they are fused. Later, when Hillary considers a run for a US Senate seat out of New York, political strategizing brings the couple together. "One benefit of my decision-making process was that Bill and I were talking again about matters other than the future of our relationship. Over time, we both began to relax."

Clinton, of course, regarded the investigations of the administration as fundamentally unfair, part of the "vast right-wing conspiracy" that she complained about in 1998. "I viewed the independent counsel's assault on the Presidency as an ever escalating political war," she writes, and in that war, she fought alongside Bill, never against him. The chapter titles of *Living History* list the battles: Vince Foster. Whitewater. Independent Counsel. Impeachment.

Looking back on the era, when even minor controversies exploded into lengthy investigations and endless press leaks, it astonishes that Hillary Clinton, years later, would risk using a private email server to communicate official State Department business—and then would take so long to admit her mistake. Yet this reluctance to admit error looms over the Clinton memoirs. "There are always choices we regret, consequences we do not foresee, and alternate paths we wish we had taken," she writes in *Hard Choices*, but her regrets are often situational, or poorly disguised attacks on political enemies.

On the failure of the Clintons' health-care initiative, she suggests that they tried to move "too quickly"—so zealous in helping the American people!— and concludes that she and Bill failed to promote reform "with enough clarity and simplicity to rouse public support or to motivate Congress to act in the face of well-financed, well-organized opponents." Essentially, a PR screw-up. Clinton also regrets how she and Bill succumbed to pressure from opponents, as well as White House political operatives, to request the appointment of an independent counsel to investigate Whitewater. "With the wisdom of hindsight, I wish I had fought harder and not let myself be persuaded to take the path of least resistance," she writes. Similarly, not settling the Paula Jones sexual harassment lawsuit against President Clinton early on was "the second biggest tactical mistake made in handling the barrage of investigations and lawsuits."

In *Hard Choices* Clinton describes her 2002 Senate vote authorizing military action in Iraq as a "mistake" but then explains why she long resisted calling it so. "It wasn't because of political expediency," she insists. "After all, primary voters and the press were clamoring for me to say that word. When I voted to authorize force in 2002, I said that it was 'probably the hardest decision I have ever had to make.' I thought I had acted in good faith and made the best decision I could with the information I had. And I wasn't alone in getting it wrong."

Such mea culpas are a rarity in *Hard Choices*, which reads like five hundred pages' worth of résumé bullet points, an affirmation of expertise. Seemingly every trip, however inconsequential, is dutifully detailed, and Clinton offers generic, clichéd descriptions of her destinations. We learn that China is a country "full of contradictions," that the Obama administration came to office "during a perilous time in the Middle East" and that "coaxing the Israelis and the Palestinians back to the negotiating table was not going to be easy." Also, Benjamin Netanyahu is a "complicated figure," while Vladimir

Putin is "thin-skinned and autocratic." And Clinton quotes Haitian president René Préval begging a State Department aide for help after the country's massive 2010 earthquake: "I need Hillary. I need her. And no one else."

Clinton has a weakness for foreign policy buzzwords (she relies on "smart power"; Syria poses a "wicked problem") and local proverbs ("When it rains, collect water," they say in Burma, apparently). She stresses her foresight and foreign policy savvy, suggesting that she saw the Arab Spring coming and anticipated the disheartening consequences. In a visit with activists in Egypt shortly after the fall of dictator Hosni Mubarak, "I came away worried that they would end up handing the country to the Muslim Brotherhood or the military by default, which in the end is exactly what happened."

Journalistic accounts have emphasized how tightly the Obama White House controls foreign policy, leaving the State Department far from the action at times. Clinton is careful to avoid such complaints, going out of her way to emphasize how closely she and President Obama worked, invariably characterizing theirs as a partnership, not a rivalry, let alone a boss-subordinate relationship. This is Clinton's time on the world stage, after all, and it grates to be a supporting actor. "I was at the White House more than seven hundred times during my four years," she writes, protesting a bit too much. "After losing the election, I never expected to spend so much time there."

Now, once again, Clinton seeks to take up permanent residence there. Unlike in her 2008 campaign, when she largely resisted playing up the historic appeal of a female candidate for the presidency—that unforgettable "eighteen million cracks" line only appeared in her speech conceding the Democratic primary race to Obama—Clinton has returned to form, embracing the symbolism that has followed her since Wellesley. No matter how taxing her first White House sojourn, and even though she says the best part of her time as secretary of state was that "partisan politics was almost entirely absent from our work," Clinton is headed once more unto the breach.

Why? Unquenched ambition is the easy, obvious answer, a chance to deploy all that experience and ability on her own, at last. But some version of a line recurs in these two memoirs, a Methodist lesson from Clinton's midwestern, mid-century upbringing: "Do all the good you can, by all the means you can, in all the ways you can, in all the places you can, at all the times you can, to all the people you can, as long as ever you can."

I won't be surprised if she invokes these words again in her convention speech claiming the Democratic nomination.* If you support Clinton, the sentiment is inspiring; if not, the notion of Clinton doing all she can by all means possible may terrify. But the final clause—"as long as you ever can"—is telling. It embodies the Clinton of her memoirs: familiar, enduring, scarred, but eager and available, if we'd only choose her. Even her Secret Service code name, "Evergreen," is apt, the perfect label for a candidate whose principal qualification for the presidency is her eternal readiness for it.

July 2016

---

* She did. Speaking at the party convention in Philadelphia on July 28, 2016, Clinton recalled her mother's influence. "She made sure I learned the words of our Methodist faith: 'Do all the good you can, for all the people you can, in all the ways you can, as long as ever you can.' "

HOW TO HATE HILLARY CLINTON, ESPECIALLY IF YOU ALREADY DO

IN THE MATTER OF THE Right-Wing Publishing Machine versus Hillary Rodham Clinton, I find for the defendant.

During the final months of this singular presidential campaign, a batch of bestselling anti-Clinton books has emerged, offering the most nefarious interpretations of the Democratic nominee. They are the case for the prosecution, and their closing arguments leave nothing out—if it's damning, or outlandish, or even contradictory, it's here. In these pages, the former first lady, senator, and secretary of state is invariably lawless and duplicitous, her record as horrifying as her hidden blueprint for national destruction. For those who already despise Clinton, these books affirm and amplify that loathing.

Clinton's plan "is the enslavement of America," writes Dinesh D'Souza in *Hillary's America*. "We have become serfs not of a plantation owner, but serfs of the progressive state." Clinton is "volcanic, impulsive, enabled by sycophants, and disdainful of the rules set for everyone else ... a cheerless grifter always on her scheming way," writes former Secret Service officer Gary J. Byrne in *Crisis of Character*, a memoir of his time serving in the Clinton White House. And in *Guilty as Sin*, the Clinton antagonist Edward Klein warns that "if Obama's abuse of power shocks you, just wait: Hillary has promised to go even further."

With chants of "lock her up" and "crooked Hillary" and simply "bitch" reverberating at Donald Trump's rallies, these works have found a ready audience, already spending a collective twenty-nine weeks on the *New York Times* bestseller list. If these books and authors sum up your knowledge of the Democratic nominee, if they are all you believe of Clinton, supporting her would seem impossible, regardless of her opponent's overwhelming shortcomings.

But if your feelings about her are even slightly more complex, if mistrust and admiration mingle with every Clinton speech or shimmy, such attacks may backfire. These books have taken me beyond Clinton fatigue; they've given me Clinton fatigue fatigue. I'm tired of being tired of Hillary Clinton.

Clinton has earned some of this criticism—but there's no way she deserves all of it. The focus on her personality and appearance is crude and sexist. The obsession with her scandals, so well known for so long, leaves her accusers looking nearly as dirty as the accused, and more desperate. And her allegedly ruinous policy projects and worldview come across as more improbable than terrifying.

Trump's vile statements about women have become campaign controversies, but the insults are consistent with the descriptions of Clinton scattered throughout these volumes.

"She is old, and mean, and even her laugh is a witch's cackle," D'Souza writes of the first woman to become the presidential nominee of a major US party. He asserts that in her youth, Clinton already came off as "ugly, petulant, and bitchy" and had a "sly, owlish" look, "with her terrible clothes and her peering eyes." Byrne, the former Secret Service officer, stresses Clinton's "booming voice" and "maniacal laugh" (the laugh is a constant obsession) and seems to imply that she is more vampire than witch. "Her true power was of the night—not the daylight," he writes.

Clinton's temper is another preoccupation. "She threw massive tantrums," Byrne contends of her time as first lady, a habit he attributes to Clinton's spoiled nature and an enabling, weak-willed staff. Klein notes that Clinton swears "like a drunken sailor," and he offers examples of her supposed "vulgar mouth," although his dubious quotations—always sourced anonymously to Clinton's closest friends—make the candidate sound like a B-movie gangster. "The motherf—ers have tried to get Bill and me ever since we entered politics, and we've always come out smelling like roses," Clinton supposedly said of the investigation into her use of a private email server while secretary of state. "I'm going to beat this FBI rap, too." Not only does this fail to resemble how any real human would talk, but it sounds nothing like the voice we encounter in the tens of thousands of Clinton emails that have been made public. (Her movie-mobster lingo must all be in the deleted ones.)

Such fixation on physical appearance and foul language is less likely to pester a male candidate—for guys, behind-the-scenes expletives are a sign of rugged leadership!—whereas strong female politicians must endure these charges, just as they endure speculation about their sexuality. Both D'Souza and Klein, for instance, raise "rumors" that Clinton is a lesbian. "I have to confess that I cannot refute this theory," D'Souza offers, "but I believe it is unsubstantiated." Klein writes: "Despite persistent rumors, and the testimony of at least one of Bill Clinton's former girlfriends, no one has ever definitively proven that Hillary was or is a lesbian." He even suggests that Clinton aide Huma Abedin may be the candidate's girlfriend and chastises the news media for not exploring the "intimate nature" of their relationship.

Dismissing, refuting, or even entertaining these notions only fulfills the authors' purpose, which is not to prove anything but merely to plant the ideas deep in the minds of their readers.

The news media has had no dearth of real Clinton scandals to report on over the years, and these authors relive each of them, from cattle futures to email servers. Unlike the scandals portrayed in the endless collection of anti-Obama books, which often enter the realm of make-believe (birtherism, secret Muslim allegiance, and the like), many of the Clinton scandals are anchored in reality. With her unfailing secrecy and endless entanglements—it's not like she can wipe that all away, like with a cloth or something—Clinton always gives these authors something to work with. Then they run with it, always magnifying her malevolence and culpability.

If you're too tender in years to get all the references (Webb Hubbell?), don't worry; the authors are recommending a massive ICYMI effort. "The Republicans need to run a targeted campaign against Hillary among younger voters," write Dick Morris and Eileen McGann, in *Armageddon*. "To those under 35, all the Hillary scandals are new. These voters, after all, were under 15 years of age when the Lewinsky scandal unfolded and were way too young to have followed Hillary's misadventures over the years."

Somehow, I can't imagine that refreshers on Bill Clinton's impeachment proceedings will rally millennials to the GOP cause. But in these authors' telling, it may as well have been Hillary who was impeached by the House of Representatives. "Far from being a victim, Hillary is the enabler of her husband's depredations," writes D'Souza. "She covers up for Bill while at the same time going after the women he abuses." This didn't just happen, he contends—it was the plan since they first met. As early as law school, Hillary recognized that "Bill's degeneracy could work to her advantage," D'Souza posits. "She could become his cover-up artist and his blame-the-victim specialist. ... In this way Hillary would make herself indispensable to Bill, and Bill would become increasingly dependent on her."

D'Souza has the gallantry to admit that this scenario is "less a description than an interpretation." Translation: it's made up. Such speculation is rampant in these volumes. "Could they actually be behind so many of the suspicious—or merely coincidental—deaths surrounding their activities?" Byrne asks about the former first couple in *Crisis of Character*. "Had they really killed Vince Foster? Was it even possible? It weighed on me." The 1993 death of Foster, a White House attorney and childhood friend of Bill Clinton, was ruled a suicide by multiple investigations, no matter what dark corners of the internet still insist on foul play. Writing a passage like that should weigh on Byrne. Heavily.

In their prosecutorial zeal—Morris and McGann even try to fact-check Hillary Clinton's middle-school extracurriculars—the books end up contradicting one another. Clinton lied about Benghazi, D'Souza writes, because she was lining up Libya reconstruction contracts for cronies and didn't want people to think things were falling apart there. But she actually lied, Morris and McGann explain, because she didn't want Americans to figure out that al-Qaeda was still a threat, despite Osama bin Laden's death. So which is it? Why not both? Don't forget that "for Hillary, lying is routine," Morris and McGann assert. "It comes naturally—like breathing."

The books add little to the current controversies surrounding the Clinton campaign. On the emails, Klein purports to show that the Democratic nominee is "guilty as sin," but adding words like "obvious" or "clearly" to that phrase doesn't quite nail the case, and his assertions that Bill Clinton, the Obama White House, and Attorney General Loretta Lynch pressured the FBI into exonerating Hillary are based largely on anonymous, secondhand descriptions of secret gatherings. Klein also relies on his own past anti-Clinton books, as well as the opinions of conservative commentators, as support for various assertions—convenient, if not quite journalistically sound.

Most scandalous of all, the authors write, is Clinton's policy agenda for America. While an objective reading of the Clinton-Kaine platform reveals a repetitive jumble of economic optimism and identity politics, in these books Clinton's intentions are always wicked, totalitarian, immoral.

So don't be fooled by Clinton's faux concern for the little guy. "Hillary's progressivism uses the bogus chants of 'inequality' and 'social justice' to implement wealth-confiscation and power-grabbing schemes much more expansive than anything previously attempted," D'Souza writes.

Morris and McGann offer similarly harsh visions of Clinton's policy plans, linking them to her odious personality. "Combine her unmistakable character flaws with her zealous commitment to four more years of Obama's unconstitutional, overreaching, anti-American, pro-international, socialist policies that will annihilate the core of America, and you get a feel for exactly what a Hillary administration would be like," they conclude. "It would be one we might never recover from." They also claim that Clinton is too much of a warmongering hawk to be commander in chief, but also far too weak on terrorism; she is an inveterate flip-flopper, but also far too rigid and pigheaded in her views. And they barely pause to note the inconsistencies.

Klein's concerns can be less wonky than prudish. He frets that Clinton's malign influence would further America's slide into what he calls a "decadent society," with current signs of decadence including generalized female weight gain, the proliferation of tattoos ("once limited to sailors and members of biker gangs"), and deteriorating dress codes, with now, even at work, people attired "as if in imitation of Shaggy from *Scooby-Doo*."

And she might get away with it, if not for these meddling authors.

———

There is little consternation in these works for the potential decadence of a Trump presidency. When the authors regard the Republican nominee at all, they are generous with praise and unstinting with the benefit of the doubt.

"Trump escapes distracting details and focuses on objectives—the big picture—using talented people around him to map out the path to achieving them," rave Morris and McGann. "He will get things done." They note his "laser-like" mind, his "uncanny" knowledge of policy issues and his "no-nonsense message." It's almost like they are hoping for consulting gigs from the Trump White House.

D'Souza acknowledges the frequent criticism of Trump's fascistic tendencies, but he mainly repeats it to pivot to his charge that the Democrats—and by extension, Clinton—are the true fascists. And Klein embraces Trump for the simple reason that he could free America of Clinton: "Her wooden inauthenticity and unlikeability would make her the perfect foil for tell-it-like-it-is Trump."

Together, these titles seek to expose, recall, or fabricate the worst possible version of Hillary Clinton, while disregarding, even embracing, the vices of her rival. So are they just part of that vast right-wing conspiracy Clinton has long feared? After all, when former consultants and Secret Service officers are writing books eviscerating you, you've earned the right to a little paranoia.

But if it is a plot, it is a messy, contradictory, and possibly self-defeating one, more of Twitter trolls than of cunning conspirators. The case they make against Hillary comes down to the fact that she's Hillary, with all the instant revulsion that name is supposed to conjure. But that works only if for you, as for them, hating Hillary Clinton comes naturally. Like breathing.

October 2016

THE COLLECTED WORKS OF DONALD TRUMP

Sitting down with the collected works of Donald J. Trump is unlike any literary experience I've ever had. I spent this past week reading eight of his books—three memoirs, three business-advice titles, and two political books, all published between 1987 and 2011—hoping to develop a unified theory of the man, or at least find a method in the Trumpness.

Instead, I found ... well, is there a single word that combines revulsion, amusement, respect, and confusion? That is how it feels, sometimes by turns, often all at once, to binge on Trump's writings. Over the course of 2,212 pages, I encountered a world where bragging is breathing and insulting is talking, where repetition and contradiction come standard, where vengefulness and insecurity erupt at random.

Elsewhere, such qualities might get in the way of the story. With Trump, they *are* the story. There is little else. He writes about his real estate dealings, his television show, his country, but after a while that all feels like an excuse. The one deal Trump has been pitching his entire career—the one that culminates in his play for that most coveted piece of property, at 1600 Pennsylvania Avenue—is himself.

"We need a leader that wrote *The Art of the Deal*," Trump declared during his presidential campaign announcement in June, and he has repeatedly cited that 1987 book in other appearances. In it, Trump, then forty-one, explains the power of psychology and deception—he calls it "bravado" or "truthful hyperbole"—in his early real estate acquisitions. Before he was a brand name, he had to convince people that he was worth their time.

It was small things here and there. Like asking his architect to gussy up the sketches for a hotel so it seemed like they spent huge sums on the plans, boosting interest in his proposal. Or having a construction crew drive machinery back and forth on a site in Atlantic City so that the visiting board of directors would be duped into thinking the work was far along. "If necessary," he instructed a supervisor, "have the bulldozers dig up dirt on one side of the site and dump it on the other."

Achieving an "aura" (a constant word in his writings) around his projects, his ideas, and himself is essential. "I play to people's fantasies," Trump explains. "... It's an innocent form of exaggeration—and a very effective form of promotion."

Trump has been mocked for emblazoning his name on every building, plane, boat, or company he touches. "Mostly it's a marketing strategy," he writes. "Trump buildings get higher rents." But this is more than branding. Trump writes of his buildings as if they were living beings, like friends or even lovers. "My relationship with 40 Wall Street began as a young man," he writes in *The Art of the Comeback*, published in 1997. "From the moment I laid eyes on it, I was mesmerized by its beauty and its splendor." Or, referring to his 110,000-square-foot private club in Palm Beach, Florida, Trump writes: "My love affair with Mar-a-Lago began in 1985." Or, of one of his longest-standing properties: "Trump Tower, like a good friend, was there when I needed it."

These relationships seem no less meaningful, and are certainly far more lasting, than those with, say, his two former wives. For all the gushing over his properties, Trump is hardheaded when it comes to married life, one of the few arenas he cannot fully control, where it is by definition not all about him. "My marriage, it seemed, was the only area of my life in which I was willing to accept something less than perfection," he writes in *Surviving at the Top*, released in 1990. He reflects at length in several books on the necessity of prenuptial agreements, which he says served him well with Ivana Trump, his first wife, and Marla Maples, his second. (*The Art of the Comeback* even includes a chapter titled "The Art of the Prenup.") And he tells a friend with a "nagging" wife that he's better off leaving and cutting his losses. "If he doesn't lose the ballbreaker, his career will go nowhere."

Trump has some experience at cutting those personal losses. Though he assures readers that he'll "never say a bad thing" about Ivana, he proceeds to paint his ex-wife as cold and duplicitous, even mocking her accent when he describes a phone call she made to him during their legal wranglings: "I vant my money now. I have decided to honor the contract, and I vant a check for ten million dollars and all the other things immediately." It's hard to know how intentional this is, because Trump disparages even when offering praise. "There's nothing I love more than women, but they're really a lot different than portrayed," he confides. "They are far worse than men, far more aggressive, and boy, can they be smart!" Boy.

To be fair, it is not just his wives, not just women; it's everyone. Trump's books are sprayed with insults, like he's trying to make sure we're still paying attention. He trashes a former Miss Universe for gaining weight. When he meets a one-star general, he asks, "How come you're only a one-star?" The Rolling Stones are "a bunch of major jerks." He dismisses Paul McCartney, "the poor bastard." (That was for not getting a prenup. Obviously.) Trump also slams complete unknowns—random bank executives or real estate types, lawyers or community activists, anyone who dared cross or disappoint him. "If someone screws you," he writes, "screw them back."

Trump's world is binary, divided into class acts and total losers. He even details how physically unattractive he finds particular reporters, for no reason that I can fathom other than that it crossed his mind. The discipline of book writing does not dilute Trump; it renders him in concentrated form. Restraint is for losers.

Streaks of insecurity run through the books. Trump constantly reminds readers that he studied at the University of Pennsylvania's Wharton School. ("I went to the great Wharton School of Finance and did well" … "I learned at the Wharton School of Finance that the economy runs in cycles" … "I have had friends, many friends, who went to the Wharton School with me who were very smart.") Everything he owns is the best, biggest, hottest. His apartment: "There may be no other apartment in the world like it." His yacht: "Probably the most beautiful yacht ever built." His living room: "While I can't honestly say I need an eighty-foot living room, I get a kick out of having one." And his third wife, Melania: "Considered by many, including me, to be one of the most beautiful women in the world."

Trump claims to dislike parties and socializing, but he can't help but boast about his celebrity-studded galas, exclusive dinners, and high-profile friendships. His books double as a wall of fame, stuffed with pictures of the Donald with notables from Liberace to Tiger Woods to Hillary Clinton. ("The First Lady is a wonderful woman who has handled pressure incredibly well," reads the caption.) He's not above betraying their confidences, either. Trump reports that at a dinner with Frank Sinatra, the Chairman of the Board went on a rant about "f—ing broads" being "the scum of the earth." And recalling the time Michael Jackson and his then-girlfriend Lisa Marie Presley stayed at his Palm Beach club, Trump puts all doubts about their liaison to rest. "People often ask me whether or not the relationship was a sham. ... I can tell you, at least for a period of time, those two folks were really getting it on."

Trump's books tend to blur together, with anecdotes and achievements enhanced with each retelling. Did you know, for example, that Trump renovated the Wollman ice skating rink in Central Park in the mid-1980s? (If not, pick up any of his books and you'll find the story there.) By the new millennium, Trump had moved on from autobiographies to business-advice books, adapting elements of his life into bite-size financial wisdom. "Don't let the brevity of these passages prevent you from savoring the profundity of the advice you are about to receive," he writes at the beginning of *How to Get Rich* (2004).

I'm no billionaire, but much of the advice usually falls between obvious and useless. Stay focused, he says. Hire a great assistant. Think big. Where he gets specific, it's stuff like: "The best way to ask for a raise is to wait for the right time." Or this gem from *Think Like a Billionaire* (2004): "People should always be encouraged to follow their dreams (my children have) but realize that a lot of time and money can be wasted chasing dreams that just weren't meant to be true."

Even if your dreams aren't meant to be, Trump's dreams are, because his dream is the American dream. Throughout the books, he conflates himself with New York City ("When I'm attacked, in a strange way, so is New York"), and because the Manhattan skyline embodies the country's aspirations, he becomes, by the transitive property of Trumpness, America. "When you mess with the American Dream, you're on the fighting side of Trump," he warns. He accuses regulators—or "burons," a cross between "bureaucrats" and "morons"—of "Dreamicide."

Trump's American dream, however, is born of a narrow view of America. They say presidents struggle to break out of their bubbles, but Trump has designed his quite deliberately. "The reason my hair looks so neat all the time is because I don't have to deal with the elements," he explains. "I live in the building where I work. I take an elevator from my bedroom to my office. The rest of the time, I'm either in my stretch limousine, my private jet, my helicopter, or my private club in Palm Beach Florida. ... If I happen to be outside, I'm probably on one of my golf courses, where I protect my hair from overexposure by wearing a golf hat." Even when Trump tries to relate, he can't pull it off. In one instance, he complains about awful traffic on the way to the airport. A common gripe. "Luckily," he adds, "it was my plane we were heading to, my plane, so it's not as if I could have missed the flight."

Beyond his bubble, Trump has other aspects of the commander in chief role down. He is reluctant to admit mistakes, for instance. When he does, he usually says he miscalculated how awful other people would be. Or it's the Trumpiest remorse possible: "I have only one regret in the women department—that I never had the opportunity to court Lady Diana Spencer ... a dream lady." His confrontations with the news media ("a business of distortions and lies") would make Ari Fleischer's and Jay Carney's press shops look cuddly. After questioning whether Ronald Reagan had "anything beneath that smile" in his first book, Trump eventually shifts to the standard GOP Gipper worship. Finally, he struggles to delegate. As president, he would appoint himself US trade representative, for example, and "take personal charge of negotiations with the Japanese, the French, the Germans, and the Saudis," he writes in *The America We Deserve* (2000). "Our trading partners would have to sit across the table from Donald Trump and I guarantee you the rip-off of the United States would end."

Yes, Trump has a serious savior complex, a common affliction for presidential hopefuls. "Look, I do deals—big deals—all the time," he writes in

Time to Get Tough (2011). "We need a dealmaker in the White House." The first Republican presidential debate this coming week should help clarify whether Trump is a real candidate or merely a sign of the GOP's disenchantment with its options. Either way, his rivals should brace themselves. "I'll do nearly anything within legal bounds to win," Trump writes. "Sometimes, part of making a deal is denigrating your competition."

But, judging from these books, I'm not sure how badly he really wants the presidency. To win it—yes, I think he'd love to close that deal and, of course, publish another book about it. But to actually be president, day to day? Trump has always been about the next big thing, whether the next deal, spouse, or fight. "The same assets that excite me in the chase, often, once they are acquired, leave me bored," he writes. "For me, you see, the important thing is the getting, not the having."

July 2015

DONALD TRUMP AND THE
FICTIONAL AMERICAN DICTATOR

AMERICANS HAVE SEEN THIS LEADER before. Boastful, deceptive, crudely charismatic. Dabbling in xenophobia and sexism, contemptuous of the rule of law, he spouts outlandish proposals that cater to the lowest instincts of those angry or frightened enough to back him. He wins the nation's top office, triggering fears of an authoritarian, even fascist US government.

Normally, though, this leader resides safely in the pages of American fiction.

Donald Trump's ascent to become the presumptive Republican presidential nominee has released a spasm of mea culpas from reporters and pollsters who failed to anticipate the biggest story in national politics—and a spate of literary and film references among those fearing a turn toward dictatorial government. It is Plato's *Republic* that anticipated the rise of Trump. Or maybe the 2006 political comedy *Idiocracy*. Or the 1981 young-adult novel *The Wave*. Or is it Howard Beale's mad-as-hell rants in 1976's *Network* that truly portended the anger erupting four decades later?

In particular, two novels depicting homegrown strongmen have become ways to interpret Trump's campaign and to imagine his presidency. Sinclair Lewis's *It Can't Happen Here* (1935) features a populist Democratic senator named Berzelius "Buzz" Windrip who wins the White House in the late 1930s on a redistributionist platform—with a generous side order of racism—and quickly fashions a totalitarian regime purporting to speak for the nation's Forgotten Men. *Salon* has dubbed it "the novel that foreshadowed Donald Trump's authoritarian appeal," while *Slate*'s Jacob Weisberg writes that you can't read the book today "without flashes of Trumpian recognition."

Philip Roth's *The Plot Against America* (2004) offers a similarly bleak vision of that era, imagining the slow implosion of a working-class Jewish family when the Republican Party nominates aviator Charles Lindbergh for the presidency in 1940. The victorious Lindy strikes a pact with Hitler, launches federal programs that break apart and resettle Jewish communities, and promotes anti-Semitic thuggery. "Roth's novel could use another reading in light of the very real possibility that Trump might be the Republican nominee," David Denby wrote in *The New Yorker*. "The counter-factual may be merging into fact just as virulently as Roth imagined."

Reading these works in this moment, it is impossible to miss the similarities between Trump and totalitarian figures in American literature—in rhetoric, personal style, and even substance. Yet the American-bred dictators are not the true protagonists. Ordinary citizens, those who must decide how to live under a leader who repudiates democratic values and institutions, are the real story. They must choose: Resist or join? Speak up or keep your head down? Fight or flee?

If Trump is elected and the fears of those crying "fascism" materialize, it is those characters and their choices that become especially relevant. In Donald Trump's anti-America, what would you do, and who would you be?

The trappings of fictional strongmen will be familiar to anyone observing US politics in the unimaginable year since a reality-television star took a Trump Tower down-escalator to launch a presidential bid. There's the obligatory *Art of the Deal*–style manifesto. In *It Can't Happen Here*, Windrip has a bestselling book, *Zero Hour*—"part biography, part economic program, and part plain exhibitionistic boasting"—that is required reading among the faithful. The leader also delivers awful yet captivating speeches. Doremus Jessup, the aging, small-town newspaper editor and hero of Lewis's novel, marvels at Windrip's "bewitching" power over large audiences. "The Senator was vulgar, almost illiterate, a public liar easily detected, and in his 'ideas' almost idiotic." But he captivates supporters, addressing them as if "he was telling them the truths, the imperious and dangerous facts, that had been hidden from them."

Much as Trump claims that only he is tough enough to restore national glory, in *The Plot Against America* Lindbergh is hailed as a "man's man who gets the impossible done by relying solely on himself." Republican leaders despair over Lindy's refusal to take any of their advice on how to run his campaign. Defenders believe that Lindbergh's strength of personality will enable him to strike deals—great ones, the best ones—with the world's bad guys. "Lindbergh can deal with Hitler, they said, Hitler respects him because he's Lindbergh."

Oh, and people swoon over Lindy's cool plane, too.

Like Trump, Windrip seeks to discredit the journalists covering him. "I know the Press only too well," he declares. "Almost all editors hide away ... plotting how they can put over their lies, and advance their own positions and fill their greedy pocketbooks by calumniating Statesmen who have given their all for the common good." As the novel progresses, Windrip detains them and takes over their publications, producing puff stories exalting the governing "Corpos," members of the newly created American Corporate State and Patriotic Party.

Trump, of course, has repeatedly called the press "dishonest" and has threatened to "open up" libel laws to attack unfriendly journalists. He, too, believes the media's job is to praise him, not to ask troublesome questions. "Instead of being like, 'Thank you very much, Mr. Trump' or 'Trump did a good job,' everyone's saying, 'Who got it, who got it, who got it,' and you make me look very bad," the candidate complained during a May 31 news conference about his promised donations to veterans groups. In life as in art, the expectation of adulatory coverage is a stamp of the strongman.

The dictators whom Roth and Lewis conjure share the intolerance underlying Trump's most controversial proposals—banning Muslims from entering the United States, building a wall straddling the US-Mexico border, deporting millions of undocumented immigrants—but the fictional characters often go further. Lindbergh moves Jews from urban centers into the rural heartland through an ominous Office of American Absorption, leaving them vulnerable to anti-Semitic violence. Windrip creates concentration camps for dissidents; establishes a sham judiciary; and bars black Americans from voting, holding public office, practicing law or medicine, or teaching beyond grammar school. "Nothing so elevates a dispossessed farmer or a

Sinclair lewis, "It can't Happen Here"

factory worker on relief," Jessup realizes, "as to have some race, any race, on which he can look down."

That's as true when the demeaned group is Jewish Americans or African Americans, Muslims seeking passage into the United States, or undocumented immigrants—or even an Indiana-born judge who is derided as anti-American, a hater, because of his Mexican heritage.

How ordinary people respond to oppressive authority has been the subject of disturbing studies, from the historical writings of Hannah Arendt to the obedience experiments of Stanley Milgram. In the novels of Lewis and Roth, denial, opportunism, compliance, fear, and violence are all at play, driven by high principle, base incentives, and self-deception.

Throughout the 2016 race, conservative skeptics and GOP leaders have fantasized that Trump has simply been saying what he must to win, latching on to the fading hope that he would eventually become more "presidential." This seemed savvy at first; now, desperate.

That hope recurs in the literature of totalitarianism. In *It Can't Happen Here*, Jessup hears all the time that he needn't worry. "You don't understand Senator Windrip," Jessup's son Philip, a lawyer, lectures him. "Oh, he's something of a demagogue—he shoots off his mouth a lot about how he'll jack up the income tax and grab the banks, but he won't—that's just molasses for the cockroaches." And the father believes it for a while, in denial even after Windrip imposes martial law. "The hysteria can't last; be patient, and wait and see, he counseled his readers. It was not that he was afraid of the authorities. He simply did not believe that this comic tyranny could endure."

In *The Plot Against America*, a leading Jewish figure assures the nation that Lindbergh is not really anti-Semitic, even though the president hosts a high-ranking Nazi official at the White House. "Before his becoming president he at times made public statements grounded in anti-Semitic clichés," Rabbi Bengelsdorf acknowledges. "But he spoke from ignorance then, and admits as much today. I am pleased to tell you that it took no more than two or three sessions alone with the president to get him to relinquish his misconceptions."

Herman Roth, the Jewish salesman and diminished hero of *The Plot Against America*, responds to Lindbergh's rhetoric in a manner reminiscent of many Trump opponents. "Others?" Herman demands. "He dares to call us others? He's the other. The one who looks most American—and he's the one who is least American. The man is unfit. ... He shouldn't be there, and it's as simple as that!"

The editor's son in *It Can't Happen Here* and the genial rabbi in *The Plot Against America* choose self-interested accommodation with their new leaders. As Jessup grows radicalized in his opposition to Windrip, his son feigns concern, warning Jessup that he's going to get into trouble if he keeps opposing local Corpos. But soon Philip's motive emerges: the government is offering him an assistant military judgeship, he admits, and the appointment could suffer over his father's intransigence. Rabbi Bengelsdorf, meanwhile, reaches the highest ranks of the Lindbergh administration, the token Jewish adviser, counseling the first lady and running the Office of American Absorption.

Consider how Trump's success has produced agony among longtime Republican foreign policy experts, to name one group, who wonder if they could live with themselves working in a Trump administration that threatens to target the families of terrorists and destroy trade deals. And top GOP elected officials, such as House Speaker Paul Ryan and New Jersey governor Chris Christie, have made their bed, if not their peace. Principle versus opportunity is their unending dilemma.

For others who embrace Trump, resentment is a more powerful motivator than careerism. Much has been made over the bond Trump has forged with white working-class voters, especially those with relatively less schooling— "I love the poorly educated!" the candidate gushed after the Nevada primary—and who feel abandoned in the rush toward globalization and multiculturalism. Darker is his tie with the alt-right; his tardy, unconvincing disavowals of white supremacists have done little to deter the growing insults, threats, and online targeting against Jewish journalists by Trump supporters.

This bond is also found in fictional accounts of American dictatorship. A fascinating character in *It Can't Happen Here* is Shad Ledue, handyman for the Jessups, an uneducated white laborer whom the family looks down upon but who exacts revenge when he acquires power—not much but just enough—under the Corpos. "I suppose you think I had a swell time when I was your hired man!" Shad says to Jessup, after overseeing the execution of the editor's son-in-law following a sham legal proceeding. "Watching you and your old woman and the girls go off on a picnic while I—oh, I was just your hired man, with dirt in my ears, your dirt!"

Jessup, a "small-town bourgeois Intellectual," espoused all the appropriate theoretical sympathies for the working class but long regarded Shad as a fool he must civilize. He saw him every day, but never knew him or understood what he could become. "With all the justified discontent there is against the smart politicians and the Plush Horses of Plutocracy—oh, if it hadn't been one Windrip, it'd been another . . . ," Jessup muses later. "We had it coming, we Respectables."

The options for opponents of the strongman are clear: fight or flight. Jessup hopes his traditional journalism can make a difference; he continues writing editorials that "would excite 3 per cent of his readers from breakfast time till noon and by 6 P.M. be eternally forgotten." But as the ruthlessness of the Corpos becomes clear, he joins an underground resistance group, producing leaflets in clandestine publishing shops, and even fantasizes about murdering Shad. He doesn't go through with it; others do.

In the 2016 race, anti-Trump protesters have crossed into violence; at a California event, some protesters assaulted supporters of the candidate. The allure of force, invariably justified as resistance, is prevalent in the novels, proving destructive to all sides. In *The Plot Against America*, a New Jersey Jewish community begins an armed self-defense patrol—the Provisional Jewish Police—which ends up clashing, fatally, not with anti-Semitic Lindbergh supporters but with local police. Herman, hiding with his family in a neighbor's home as fighting stalks their block, declines to wield a gun. "I believe in this country," he says simply.

In *It Can't Happen Here*, Jessup's daughter avenges her dead husband by killing the judge who sentenced him, herself dying in the process. "Now I know why men like John Brown became crazy killers!" Jessup rages, comparing the nation's plight to the abolitionist cause. He does not engage in violence, but his sedition gets him arrested and thrown into a concentration camp for his troubles.

When dissenting voices are silenced, exit is a last resort. In these novels, that usually means Canada, the land of American exile fantasies. Anyone vowing to move there if Trump wins will find fellow travelers in *It Can't Happen Here* and *The Plot Against America*, in which the Great White North offers the promise of freedom and the anguish of surrender. The Corpos guard even the smallest trails approaching the border—a big, beautiful wall of sorts, keeping people in—and interrogate families seeking to flee. Even when Jessup escapes his detention and makes it across the border, he regards his temporary home as a "prison of exile from the America to which, already, he was looking back with the pain of nostalgia."

For Herman, Canada implies defeat. When the government conspires with his employer to relocate Jewish salespeople to the American heartland, the family wonders whether they should join their many friends who have already gone north. Normally in control of his emotions, Herman explodes when his wife, Bess, brings it up. " 'No,' he replied, 'not Canada again!' as though Canada were the name of the disease insidiously debilitating us all. 'I don't want to hear it. Canada,' he told her firmly, 'is not a solution.' 'It's the only solution,' she pleaded. 'I am not running away!' he shouted, startling everyone. 'This is our country!' 'No,' my mother said sadly, 'not anymore.' "

The 2008 election told us something about America. The 2016 election is telling us something else. Both may be true, but only one can be right.

Like Doremus Jessup and Herman Roth, it is easy to grow despondent. "Why, there's no country in the world that can get more hysterical—yes, or more obsequious!—than America," Jessup moans. Or, as Herman wonders, "How can this be happening in America? ... If I didn't see it with my own eyes, I'd think I was having a hallucination."

Trump feels like an American hallucination: wealth, sex, reality television, social media—he is every national fixation in excess. Yet, more than electoral college math or the Democratic nominee, what stands against his brand of politics is America itself, its self-perception and self-knowledge. That is what the fictional Roth family concludes in a visit to Washington, where they encounter anti-Semitic Lindbergh supporters but soak in the historic buildings and recite hallowed inscriptions on national monuments. "It was American history, delineated in its most inspirational form, that we were counting on to protect us against Lindbergh," Herman's youngest son decides.

Perhaps American principles do provide that bulwark. When *It Can't Happen Here* was published, reviewers noted the rhetorical parallels between Windrip and Louisiana's Huey Long, for instance, but such leaders have not reached the presidency, at least not outside the realm of fiction. Even there, they can be airbrushed out. In *The Plot Against America*, Lindbergh mysteriously disappears—perhaps a plane crash, maybe a defection to Germany—and Franklin Roosevelt returns to the White House. Pearl Harbor happens, the United States joins World War II, and history resumes much as we've known it.

I don't imagine that is possible beyond a writer's imagination. Even now, whether or not Trump wins this election, whether or not he builds his walls and subverts our laws, he has set loose passions and compelled choices that will long mark us. If the politics he represents take root, as in so many other nations and times, tweeting #NeverTrump or slapping a "Don't Blame Me, I Voted for Hillary" sticker on the car will offer little solace. And the man promising to make America great again will have succeeded in rendering America, finally and conclusively, unexceptional.

June 2016

AMERICAN PRESIDENTS GET THE SCANDALS THEY DESERVE

RICHARD NIXON'S PARANOIA PRODUCED WATERGATE. Ronald Reagan's indifference contributed to Iran-Contra. Bill Clinton's appetites led to his impeachment. And Donald Trump's delusions—about his singular abilities and the impunity of his office—propel the crisis of legitimacy that threatens his presidency.

No matter how distinct presidential scandals appear in their origins, however, there is also a weary sameness to how presidents react to them, how Washington mobilizes for them, how history looms over them. Each crisis feels unprecedented at the time, yet some detailed journalistic accounts of presidential disgrace—*The Final Days*, Bob Woodward and Carl Bernstein's narrative of Nixon's end; *A Very Thin Line*, Theodore Draper's comprehensive look at Iran-Contra; and *The Breach*, Peter Baker's dissection of Clinton's impeachment trial—reveal how uniformly White House crises can unfold, explicitly drawing from one another, reliving dramas and pivots, and affecting how future scandals are judged.

Investigations and revelations. Fury and denial. Indictments and firings. Today, the White House is in crisis mode once again, and all in Washington are playing their parts. What distinguishes the Trump scandal is how its central character appears to combine the worst qualities of his troubled predecessors. How, rather than evolving into scandal, this presidency was born into it. And above all, how perceptions of the president's integrity and honor—which proved critical in the outcomes of past political and constitutional crises—are barely an issue for a man without moral high ground left to lose.

In the evenings, sitting alone in the White House residence, the president "surrendered to his distress, watching hours of television news or talk shows and phoning allies at home to vent." And at a dinner with a small group of White House staffers and dwindling Capitol Hill allies, the president complained about how "the liberals and the press hated him, and so the rules were being changed and he was going to be made to pay."

This is not President Trump in 2017 but rather descriptions of Clinton and Nixon, respectively, at the height of the Lewinsky and Watergate sagas. Indeed, one of the most persistent images of a White House in turmoil is the isolated and vengeful commander in chief, stewing at 1600 Pennsylvania Avenue. Trump may spend lonely nights and mornings with the remote in one hand and the phone in another, but historically speaking, he has plenty of company.

During presidential scandals, the White House offers the illusion that the president and top aides are undistracted, that the nation's business remains foremost in their minds, when in fact the political challenges threaten to overpower all else. Nixon was "increasingly moody, exuberant at one moment, depressed the next, alternately optimistic and pessimistic," Woodward and Bernstein write. He spent hours on end poring over his Oval Office tapes and pondering his survival. Though the president hoped that overseas trips and foreign policy moves might enhance his public standing, White House chief of staff Alexander Haig confided to a former Pentagon colleague that Nixon was "distracted, spending so much time on Watergate, it's destroying his ability to lead." Haig even repeatedly urged a top telecommunications policy official to not bring anything substantive to Nixon's attention. "The President isn't in any shape to deal with this," he explained.

Clinton's famous ability to compartmentalize, to carry on amid the ever-expanding inquiry by independent counsel Kenneth Starr, was largely for show, Baker reports. "In private, Clinton was consumed with the Starr investigation and its collateral damage, sometimes so preoccupied that he appeared lost during meetings." Clinton told cabinet members that he had woken up "profoundly angry" every day for four and a half years. Imagine what his morning tweetstorms would have been like.

Such presidential anger requires a focal point: for Nixon, it included special counsel Archibald Cox and former White House counsel John Dean;

for Clinton, it was Starr and his Republican defenders. Trump's wrath is less discriminating, targeting special counsel Robert Mueller as well as the FBI, the Justice Department, and virtually all journalists save his loyalists at Fox News. In the same way Trump says digging into his personal finances would be a red line Mueller should not cross, Nixon regarded Cox's attempts to secure his tapes as "the ultimate defiance" meriting dismissal.

The effort by Trump and his supporters in the right-wing media to depict Mueller's probe as a partisan "witch hunt"—another common phrase across these scandals—is a time-honored tactic for any White House under siege. Haig and Nixon press secretary Ron Ziegler agreed on the need to "place the impeachment issue in as partisan a light as possible," and the Clinton team reached the same conclusion more than twenty years later. Baker describes the latter group's strategy during the impeachment fight: "Attack the accusers, demonize the investigators, complain about partisanship while doing everything to foment it."

Cracks invariably emerge among the true believers, the deeply conflicted, and the suddenly departed members of each administration. Once a loyalist, Dean provided a catalogue of accusations against the Nixon White House before the Senate Watergate committee: wiretapping, secret funds, money laundering, cover-ups, and more. The Reagan team split among senior officials who had opposed arms sales to Iran, such as Secretary of State George Shultz, and those dedicated to advancing the initiative, such as John Poindexter, the national security adviser. Poindexter, who saw himself as "the head of an American version of a Roman praetorian guard around the president, loyal and responsible to him alone," Draper writes, was eventually convicted of lying to Congress and obstructing investigations of Iran-Contra, though the convictions were reversed on appeal.

Disillusioned staffers try to make their peace with flawed presidents. Clinton aide Paul Begala "sank into a deep depression" during the Monica Lewinsky scandal, Baker writes, and vowed never again to appear on television defending the president. (It was a vow he did not honor.) White House chief of staff Erskine Bowles sought to keep his distance from the details of the whole affair: when former United Nations ambassador Bill Richardson wanted to describe how he'd offered Lewinsky a job, Bowles interrupted: "I don't want to know a f—ing thing about it!" And during Watergate, Haig and Nixon lawyer James St. Clair refused to read transcripts or listen to certain portions of the president's tapes until late in the game. They didn't want to know, either.

For Trump staffers and enablers, the dilemma is different. There are few illusions about their leader left to be shattered. Their true challenge is less about surviving Trump's eruptions than simply living with the choice they've made, convincing themselves that service to the nation—passing a tax cut, forestalling a war, reducing immigration—is worth it.

For the presidents involved, enduring a scandal means convincing yourself of a good many things as well. Trump's refusal to accept the US intelligence finding that the Kremlin sought to tilt the 2016 election in his favor mirrors the stubbornness of his predecessors. Reagan went along with the sale of arms to Iran in an effort to free American hostages, though "always telling himself that it was not an arms-for-hostages deal," Draper writes. Nixon lawyer J. Fred Buzhardt concluded that the thirty-seventh president lied not just to others but to himself. It was an easy tell, Woodward and Bernstein explain: "Almost invariably when [Nixon] lied, he would repeat himself, sometimes as often as three times—as if he were trying to convince himself." And the Clinton White House held political strategy sessions during the impeachment saga, meetings that had an "unreal feel," Baker writes, because the president and his aides would cover everything except their most overriding political challenge: saving Clinton's presidency.

It makes Trump's fawning cabinet meetings—in which department heads recite prayers and offer thanks for their leader—seem almost normal.

Attaching a "-gate" suffix to every minor White House scandal is an occupational hazard of political journalism. Some overzealous commentators compared Trump's dismissal in January of acting attorney general Sally Yates to the "Saturday Night Massacre" of 1973, when Nixon's order to fire the special prosecutor prompted both the attorney general and the deputy attorney general to resign. It was a premature comparison but not an unusual one.

During Iran-Contra and the Clinton impeachment trial, the memories of Watergate were ever present—a constant reference, yardstick, and warning.

Edwin Meese, attorney general during Reagan's second term, was "haunted" by Nixon's attempted cover-up, Draper writes, and was "determined at all costs to avoid a repetition" with Iran-Contra. Mike McCurry, Clinton's press secretary, decided to leave the White House before the impeachment proceedings got underway, in part to avoid "becoming the Ron Ziegler of his era," Baker explains.

At times, Watergate became a call for restraint over hyperbole. House minority leader Richard Gephardt, a Democrat, told House Republicans that Watergate should be the model for cooperation between both sides in the Clinton proceedings, Baker reports. Some took that model quite literally: the House Judiciary Committee lawyer charged with producing the first draft of the articles of impeachment was so taken by the Nixon precedent that he borrowed liberally from the Watergate-era draft, using the same three-paragraph introduction, the same wording at the start of each article, and the same two concluding paragraphs. (*The Breach* notes that even a password to access committee computer files was an homage of sorts: "RODINO," for Rep. Peter Rodino, the New Jersey Democrat who chaired the Judiciary Committee during Watergate.)

But by replicating the Watergate format, Baker argues, House Republicans were "implicitly raising the bar for the substance of the charges as well—lying under oath and covering up an affair might pale in comparison to paying hush money and using the CIA to thwart an FBI investigation of political espionage." That was the case Democrats made. Baker summarizes in three words the argument by the White House lawyers defending Clinton before the House committee: it ain't Watergate.

The Trump investigation is not Watergate, either—at least not yet. We are just two indictments and two guilty pleas into this thing, and the *Washington Post* reports that the Mueller investigation could last deep into 2018, no matter how soon the Trump White House expects it to conclude. It is precisely that longevity, however, that could exhaust the forbearance of a notoriously impatient president. Thus far, Trump and his supporters seem intent on discrediting Mueller's inquiry rather than shutting it down. A latter-day Saturday Night Massacre or a wholesale pardoning of top aides would propel the crisis of the Trump presidency to far more precarious heights.

"Watergate was a series of discrete, unrelated transactions," members of Nixon's legal team concluded, according to Woodward and Bernstein. "There had been no grand strategy, just consistently bad judgment." History's judgment may have proved otherwise—certainly Woodward and Bernstein have come to see Watergate in far more expansive and insidious terms—but it's not a bad description of Trump's presidency to date, one driven not by ideology but by impulse, incompetence, and the quest for loyalty and personal benefit. Henry Kissinger lamented that Nixon was "a man who let his enemies dictate to him, whose actions were often reactions." Or as White House press secretary Sarah Huckabee Sanders has said of Trump, "When he gets hit, he's going to hit back."

Trump appears Nixonian in his disregard for democratic norms, Clintonian in his personal recklessness, and beyond Reaganesque in his distance from the details of policy. But where the parallels and parables of past scandals fall apart is with Trump's well-documented disregard for truth. In Watergate, Iran-Contra, and the Clinton impeachment, views of the president's honesty played a significant role for the public, for administration officials, and for lawmakers torn over how to proceed.

Normally, revelations of presidential deceit are consequential. When Nixon speechwriter Patrick Buchanan, among the most devoted of the president's men, explained to Nixon family members why a damning Oval Office recording meant that the president's resignation was inevitable, he emphasized not law but dishonesty. "The problem is not Watergate or the cover-up," he argued. "It's that he hasn't been telling the truth to the American people. The tape makes it evident that he hasn't leveled with the country for probably eighteen months. And the President can't lead a country he has deliberately misled." When Sen. Susan Collins of Maine (one of a handful of Senate Republicans who ultimately voted against both articles of impeachment for Clinton) was agonizing over the decision, her misgivings centered on the president's forthrightness. "She could not get over Clinton's recklessness—it was as if he could not stop doing wrong, could not tell the truth," Baker reports. And some of Reagan's worst Iran-Contra moments came in statements the president made in late 1986 and early 1987, when his questionable mastery of details and shifting rationales received tough scrutiny. In a March 1987 Oval Office speech, he finally (and mostly) fessed up. "A few months ago I told the American people I did not trade arms for hostages," Reagan said. "My heart and my best intentions still tell me that's true, but the facts and the evidence tell me it is not."

Trump does not even attempt to save face. Fact-checkers have documented so many of his false or misleading statements during the 2016 campaign and into the first year of his presidency that there is no presumption of honesty left to squander. Even when Trump dismisses the fact checks as fake news—in effect, being dishonest about his dishonesty—it doesn't seem to matter. Trump's relentless attacks against anyone seeking to hold him accountable help neutralize the impact on his supporters.

During Watergate, top Nixon aides worried that the material on the Oval Office tapes—not just the disclosures of wrongdoing but also the "amorality" of Nixon's words and thoughts—would hurt the president and the presidency. Ziegler was adamantly opposed to releasing transcripts, Woodward and Bernstein write, because "there was rough language on the tapes," candid discussions that would "offend Middle America, destroy his mandate." Once certain transcripts were made public, Nixon lawyer Leonard Garment worried that the president had "allowed America into the ugliness of his mind—as if he wanted the world to participate in the despoliation of the myth of presidential behavior. ... That was the truly impeachable offense: letting everyone see."

With Trump, we've already seen it, and we already know it. His tweets are his Nixon tapes; the *Access Hollywood* recording his Starr report; his heedlessness for checks, balances, and the rule of law his Iran-Contra affair. Offending does not destroy his mandate, it fulfills it. The expectation of integrity has given way to a cynical acceptance of deceit. As much as anything Mueller uncovers, this is the scandal of our time.

December 2017

MEET THE TRUMPS

WHEN THE EXTENDED TRUMP FAMILY gathered in the White House in April 2017 to celebrate the birthdays of the president's two sisters, President Trump pointed out a framed black-and-white photograph behind the Resolute Desk in the Oval Office—the image of a mustachioed man in a jacket and tie, with receding dark hair and a commanding air. "Isn't that a great picture of Dad?" Trump asked his sister Maryanne. She replied with a reprimand: "Maybe you should have a picture of Mom, too."

The president seemed never to have considered it. "That's a great idea," he said. "Somebody get me a picture of Mom."

Many presidents have had daddy issues: dreaming of their absent fathers, chafing at their judgments, or struggling under their legacies. When discussing his father in his memoir *Trump: The Art of the Deal*, Donald Trump stresses the business savvy he gleaned from the late Fred C. Trump. "I learned about toughness in a very tough business, I learned about motivating people, and I learned about competence and efficiency."

In *Too Much and Never Enough: How My Family Created the World's Most Dangerous Man*, Mary L. Trump, the president's niece, describes those lessons somewhat differently. In her telling, her wealthy grandfather was a suffocating and destructive influence: emotionally unavailable, cruel, controlling. Fred Trump both instilled and fortified his middle son's worst qualities—Donald's bullying, disrespect, lack of empathy, insecurity, and relentless self-aggrandizement—while lavishing on him every opportunity and financing every mistake, to the point that both men came to believe the myths they had created. In the wreckage of this relationship, Mary Trump writes, is a "malignantly dysfunctional family" that engages in "casual dehumanization" around the dinner table, a family in which privilege and anxiety go together, in which money is the only value, in which lies are just fine and apologies are just weak.

All happy families are alike; each unhappy family can at least give thanks that they're not the Trumps of Queens.

Too Much and Never Enough is an account of cross-generational trauma, and a book suffused by an almost desperate sadness. Mary Trump brings to this effort the insider perspective of a family member, the observational and analytical abilities of a clinical psychologist, and the writing talent of a former graduate student in comparative literature. But she also brings the grudges of estrangement. Mary Trump writes that her own father, Freddy, the oldest son of the Trump family, was robbed of his birthright and happiness for committing the unforgivable sin of failing to meet Fred's demands and expectations. Freddy was supposed to take over the family business, was supposed to be a "killer," which in the Trump family means being utterly invulnerable. But he preferred to become a commercial airline pilot, an ambition his father constantly mocked.

"Freddy simply wasn't who he wanted him to be," Mary Trump writes. "Fred dismantled his oldest son by devaluing and degrading every aspect of his personality and his natural abilities until all that was left was self-recrimination and a desperate need to please a man who had no use for him." Instead, Donald was elevated while Freddy, suffering from alcoholism and heart ailments, was cast aside, his entire family line "effectively erased," Mary explains, written out of wills, eulogies, and simple kindnesses.

The Trump family, perhaps fearing shame or worse, tried hard to quash this book, based on the terms of a settlement in a long-ago lawsuit. (The suit was over money—what else.) They failed, and Mary Trump does offer some embarrassing, even silly, stories about growing up Trump: that Donald paid a friend to take the SATs for him; that, for all their riches, Trump and his wives skimped on Christmas presents, regifting old food baskets and used designer handbags; that Maryanne, a former appeals court judge, described her younger brother Donald as "a clown" with "no principles." Mary Trump also recalls an instance when, while visiting Mar-a-Lago, she joined Donald and his then-wife, Marla, for an outdoor lunch following a swim, wearing her bathing suit and a pair of shorts. As she approached, Donald gawked. "Holy s—, Mary. You're stacked." (Trump passing judgment aloud on the size of his then-twenty-nine-year-old niece's breasts, in the presence of his wife, may rank as one of the least surprising reveals of 2020.)

More memorable than any such details are this book's insights and declarations. Mary describes her grandfather as a "high-functioning sociopath," a condition that can include abusiveness, ease with deceit, and indifference to right and wrong. Couple that with a mother who was often absent because of health problems, and young Donald began to develop "powerful but primitive" coping mechanisms, Mary Trump writes, including hostility, aggression, and indifference to the neglect he experienced. Unable to have his emotional needs met, "he became too adept at acting as though he didn't have any."

Books and essays have been written speculating on the mental health of the forty-fifth president, and to the frequent armchair diagnoses of "narcissistic personality disorder," Mary Trump might add "antisocial personality disorder" (chronic criminality, arrogance, disregard for others) and "dependent personality disorder" (inability to make decisions or take responsibility, discomfort with being alone). She even suggests that Trump suffers a "long undiagnosed learning disability" that hinders his processing of information. She provides little specific evidence or context for this assertion—a habit on display throughout the book, as the author makes definitive pronouncements about her uncle's state of mind.

"His ego is a fragile thing that must be bolstered every moment because he knows deep down that he is nothing of what he claims to be," she argues. "He knows he has never been loved." The president withdraws to comfort zones such as Twitter and Fox News because "he is and always will be a terrified little boy." And she contends that Trump has been "institutionalized" for most of his adult life, in the sense that he has been shielded from his shortcomings—whether by his father bailing him out of terrible investments or by a federal government deployed to protect his ego. "Donald's pathologies are so complex and his behaviors so often inexplicable that coming up with an accurate and comprehensive diagnosis would require a full battery of psychological and neuropsychological tests that he'll never sit for," Mary Trump concludes.

A lesson for the Trump family: keep your friends close, but your nieces with doctorates in psychology closer.

Mary Trump's most convincing moments are those when she draws out behavioral parallels between Fred and Donald. Just like his son in the Oval Office, Fred Trump "always made his supplicants come to him, either at his Brooklyn office or his house in Queens, and he remained seated while they stood." Fred Trump often engaged in hyperbole while speaking; "everything was 'great,' 'fantastic,' and 'perfect,'" just like Trump's "perfect" phone call with the leader of Ukraine. Their professional habits seem similar, too: "Working the refs, lying, cheating—as far as Fred was concerned, those were all legitimate business tactics."

Most personally for the author, Donald also emulated his father when it came to his treatment of Freddy—ridiculing him, ostracizing him, and, ultimately, ignoring him. Donald did not attend Freddy's wedding, and on the day Freddy was rushed to the hospital in the direst of conditions, his brother was too busy to stop by. "As my father lay dying alone," Mary Trump writes, "Donald went to the movies."

Too Much and Never Enough is a kind of revenge, perhaps. Mary Trump comes across as that oddity, a relatively normal Trump, but she is still a Trump, after all. When she becomes a secret source for the *New York Times*'s Pulitzer-winning investigation of the Trump family's taxes—delivering nineteen boxes of legal and financial documents to three overjoyed reporters—she privately ponders the need to "take Donald down," the sort of mob talk that does the family proud. It's her most killer moment.

But her ultimate sin against the family is not helping the *Times* or trashing her uncle in print. It's that her book is not really about Donald but about Fred—not the new patriarch but the old one. All the chaos playing out on the national and world stage is a form of family dysfunction writ largest, she explains, with the president's incessant bragging and bluster directed at his "audience of one," his late father. As Mary Trump puts it, "Every one of Donald's transgressions became an audition for his father's favor, as if he were saying, 'See, Dad, I'm the tough one. I'm the killer.'"

Normally when we keep photographs of loved ones near our desks, it is so we can remember them, look upon their faces and think back on good times. But after reading this book, I wonder if the photograph hovering behind the president's shoulder in the Oval Office serves the opposite purpose—not so Donald can gaze upon Fred but so Fred can look upon that frightened little boy, now at the height of his power, and finally, truly, approve.

July 2020

THREE WAYS TO WRITE ABOUT DONALD TRUMP

When journalists write books on the presidency of Donald Trump, they tend to choose one of three options. They write about personality, they write about paper, or they write about people.

This choice not only determines what kinds of work they produce but also affects how their audiences interpret Trump's continuing influence over American life. In personality-driven narratives, the former president's uniqueness and unpredictability render him mesmerizing but always verging on self-destruction; after all, when you suck all the air out of the room, you risk bursting. Writers who focus on paper—meaning the investigations, memos, and ritual documentation of Washington, which Trump challenged with equal measures of deliberation and carelessness—depict his presidency as a tug between discontinuity and procedure, as the political system and Trump resisted and adapted to each other. An emphasis on people tells the story of Trump's craven enablers, his true believers, his embattled opponents, and, looking ahead, his most opportunistic imitators.

The personality stories fascinate for their color and detail; they appeal to the versions of history that place a singular individual at their center. The paper stories resonate for their clash of cultures and institutional heft; the findings and accusations of the House's January 6 committee offer but the latest plot point in this dramatic arc. The people stories captivate for their steady supply of characters who, facing the unthinkable, decide to go ahead and think it, who, having experienced Trump's America, opt to live there full time. Just about every Trump book that aims to shape the historical record and not just cater to momentary passions is a variation on one of these themes, even if most contain elements of all three. Depending on the accounts you choose and trust, you may come to believe that America is experiencing the death throes of the Trump era, awaiting its miraculous resurrection, or feeling the birth pangs of Trumpism by another name.

In the epilogue of *Confidence Man: The Making of Donald Trump and the Breaking of America,* Maggie Haberman recalls an interview with Trump in which he muses that talking to her is like talking to his psychiatrist. Haberman, a *New York Times* reporter, dismisses the line as a "meaningless" attempt at flattery. "He treats everyone like they are his psychiatrist," she writes. Even so, *Confidence Man* constitutes a study of Trump's "personality and character traits," as Haberman affirms. She writes of his stunted emotional development, of the loneliness "that always seemed to be stalking him," of the "emotional balm" that campaign rallies provide for him, of how he displays "both the thickest and thinnest skin" of any public figure she has covered, of his tendency to live in the moment yet inhabit an "eternal past" full of unquenchable grievance, and of his "irrepressible self-destructive streak." Haberman concludes that her subject is "a narcissistic drama seeker who covered a fragile ego with a bullying impulse."

Haberman may not be Trump's shrink, but she puts him on the couch, takes detailed notes, and offers a diagnosis.

This focus surfaces some odd Trumpian obsessions and tendencies. On multiple occasions in the book, for instance, Trump wonders aloud about who is and isn't gay, and he even seeks heterosexual reassurance from former New Jersey governor Chris Christie. "Me and you, just chicks—right, buddy?" Trump asks Christie. Trump appears to enjoy mocking his son-in-law Jared Kushner: "Can you imagine Jared and his skinny ass camping? It'd be like something out of *Deliverance.*" And, in the pettiest way possible, to assert his authority, he makes sure to get one more scoop of ice cream for dessert than the Democratic House members attending a dinner he hosted in 2017. Haberman distinguishes between what some confidants call the "Good" Trump, capable of generosity and humor, and the "Bad" Trump, who is abusive and insecure, but Bad Trump is the lead actor of *Confidence Man*, with only rare cameos by his alter ego.

This emphasis on personality should not be confused with journalistic superficiality. Haberman makes clear how Trump's instincts and impulses shaped the substance of the presidency day to day, minute to minute. "His aversion to hearing bad news led to people tiptoeing around him or trying to avoid telling him certain things," she writes, a dangerous trait when your job involves managing all manner of emergencies.

Trump relished fights with Republicans more than with Democrats, Haberman explains, because he prefers battles about "interpersonal dynamics such as loyalty and respect" over discussions of ideology or policy, of which he cares little and knows less. She suggests that the move to clear anti–police violence protesters from Washington's Lafayette Square on June 1, 2020, and the subsequent photo op in front of St. John's Church, with the president brandishing a Bible and a get-off-my-lawn scowl, flowed in part from his humiliation at a *Times* report that he had taken refuge in a White House bunker. And Trump's transactional response when Christie urged him to disavow white-supremacist supporters during the 2016 campaign helps clarify why Trump socializes with anti-Semites, white nationalists, and QAnon adherents in 2022. "A lot of these people vote," he told Christie.

Trump "reoriented an entire country to react to his moods and emotions," Haberman asserts in her book's closing paragraph. From his Trump Tower campaign announcement in 2015 to the spasms of January 6, 2021, the story of Trump's personality became the story of America.

It was not, however, the story of Washington. That tale is told in *The Divider: Trump in the White House, 2017–2021*, by another *New York Times* reporter, Peter Baker, and Susan Glasser, a *New Yorker* staff writer. This volume captures how the political establishment dealt with Trump the only way it knew how—with lots and lots of paper.

Documents assume enormous importance in *The Divider*, a preoccupation that feels retro for a presidency so dominated by social media and cable news yet one that more than merits its place. In moments of high drama, resignation letters by key cabinet members and top advisers are started but not finished, drafted but not sent, delivered and rejected but not immediately returned. Washington's Trump-era dilemma—whether you can serve this president without being corrupted by him—is usually answered in an anguished affirmative, only to elicit profound regret soon thereafter.

Memos, letters, and reports tell the story of the administration. The May 2017 memo by Rod Rosenstein, the deputy attorney general, made the case for firing James Comey as FBI director, but it left Rosenstein as the White House's "fall guy" for the move, Baker and Glasser explain. Rosenstein in turn appointed Robert Mueller as special counsel to investigate the Trump campaign's links to Russia, but Mueller's 448-page report was neutered on arrival by another document: the four-page letter to Congress by Attorney General William P. Barr, which painted the report in "the best possible light," the authors write, allowing Trump to claim exoneration.

Read those three documents, and you have the story.

From Trump's perspective, the Mueller investigation constituted the "ultimate showdown" against his deep-state enemies, Baker and Glasser write, meaning "the Democrats, the FBI, the intelligence agencies, the news media, the State Department, the Pentagon, the career civil service, the establishment writ large, fellow Republicans who had never fully accepted him. In other words, Washington." Indeed, *The Divider* is the story of Trump versus Washington, so much so that I began to read the book's title as a reference not only to how Trump divided the country but also to how he set himself against the capital—and how Washington fought back.

When Gen. John Kelly became Trump's chief of staff in mid-2017, White House staff secretary Rob Porter drafted memos aimed at helping Kelly professionalize the place. "Decisions are not final—and therefore may not be implemented—until the staff secretary secures a cleared [decision memorandum] that has been signed by the president," one of them read. In other words, Trump could tweet whatever he wanted, but without a formal process, nothing was official. "The sentence was underlined to make the point clear," Baker and Glasser write, and you can almost see them rolling their eyes. Imagine trying to neutralize Trump's Twitter feed with a formal paper trail.

Special counsel reports don't deter him. Vote counts don't deter him. Not even the Constitution fazes Trump, whose call for the document's "termination" is the ultimate battle against paper. His initial response to the January 6 committee's conclusion that he committed multiple federal crimes reflected a standard Trump tactic. "These folks don't get it that when they come after me, people who love freedom rally around me," he declared. "It strengthens me." Trump always tries to turn paper fights into personality fights and then rallies people to defend him. For Trump, personality beats paper, and the support of his people beats everything.

Paper matters in *Confidence Man*, too, though mainly because it offers insight into Trump's personality. Haberman reports on how the president tore up documents and tossed them in the trash or the toilet, episodes that could reflect mere "behavioral tics" or signal the president's "inherent paranoia." Personality matters in *The Divider*, too, though mainly as an indication of how removed Trump's presidency felt from the traditions of the office. "The psychological state of the world's most powerful man was a source of never-ending speculation, commentary and concern in a way that simply had no parallel in American history," Baker and Glasser write.

In an odd coincidence, the two books rely on the same Hollywood metaphor to explain the former president. *The Divider* cites a Trump-era national security official who, describing how Trump learned to undermine his administration's so-called axis of adults, likens him to the velociraptor in *Jurassic Park* who learned new ways to hunt his prey. "It was a chilling thought," Baker and Glasser write. "Who can forget the scene where the audience discovers this, when one of the predators chases the film's child protagonists into an industrial kitchen by turning a handle to open a door?" Haberman cites the son of a Trump Organization executive who recalls the first time the future president fired off a tweet on his own, without staff help. "He later compared the moment to the scene in the movie *Jurassic Park*," Haberman writes, "when dinosaurs realize they can open doors themselves."

Apparently the secret to writing a Trump bestseller is to compare him to an angry, carnivorous beast that terrifies little kids. In the first instance, Trump is testing the constraints on his power and manipulating the obstacles in his way. In the second, Trump is not just learning new methods but affirming old instincts. "No longer having to rely on staff meant there was no one to mediate his worst impulses," Haberman writes. One is a Washington brawl, the other a personality unleashed.

In Robert Draper's *Weapons of Mass Delusion*, Trump is not the one battling

Washington or undergoing a psychological assessment. Draper, a staff writer with the *New York Times Magazine*, studies the Republican House members who emulate Trump's "performance art of cultural vendetta" and the MAGA supporters who, having absorbed the conservative media's vilification of the left for so long, forgive whatever their side might do to counter the enemy. Even an assault on the Capitol is acceptable if the opponents arrayed against them are not just wrong but wicked. "So long as there was evil, there was righteousness," Draper writes. "Identify evil, and the details did not matter."

This is the third category of Trump books, the kind that concentrates less on his calculations or psychology than on the actions of those who come next, those who, viewing Trump as a mere baseline, have "plunged deeper into a Trumpian cult of compulsive dissembling and conspiracy mongering," Draper writes.

Marjorie Taylor Greene, the QAnon-friendly Republican House member from Georgia who has minimized the Capitol riot as "Witch Hunt 2.0," is one of Draper's main characters. First Greene blamed the violence of January 6 on antifa infiltrators, and later she excused it because the Declaration of Independence encouraged the people to overthrow tyrants. She has taken her statements even further, telling a Republican gathering in New York that if she and Steve Bannon had organized the attack on the Capitol, it would have succeeded, and it would have been armed. She later dismissed the remark as a "sarcastic joke," but Draper emphasizes how even "her most outlandish rhetoric has become GOP talking points."

Conventional members of Congress often yearn for a "legacy project," Draper writes, that one piece of legislation or vital initiative that constituents, colleagues, and historians will long remember. For politicians like Greene, deep and abiding grievance is the project that matters and the most consequential legacy. "Millions of Americans believed as she did," Draper writes. "Their once-great country was under assault from within." Though he provides sketches of ordinary Americans caught up in conspiracy theories and political violence, he still struggles to grasp the "emotional kinetics" that would compel so many people to gather in Washington on a single day and commit violence upon the seat of American democracy. "Will be wild!" Trump told them. So they came, and they were wild.

The emotional kinetics may be easier to understand if we recognize that Stop the Steal was never just about the presidency or the 2020 vote or even Trump himself. For those gathered on January 6, what was stolen was not just the election; it was America itself, or at least the fantasy version of the country that the rioters and their supporters felt had been promised and never delivered yet somehow wrested away. The 2022 midterm election results may signal a weakening of such forces, and Trump's early poll numbers for 2024 are not exactly commanding, but how often have we heard that a fever was finally breaking?

"The question of Trump's influence was the wrong one," Draper concludes. "The more salient question of the 2022 political season was whether it would augur the return of sanity to the Republican Party." Too much of the GOP has morphed into standard-issue Trumpism, no matter whether Trump is its standard-bearer.

Personality, paper, and people are not just three ways to understand Trump. Even Haberman admits at the end of *Confidence Man* that, despite her best efforts, "almost no one really knows him." They are also three lenses through which to make sense of the politics we are living through and the history we are writing. In her book, Haberman suggests that what began as Trump's "personality-driven populism" has hardened into a longer-term political realignment. In *The Divider*, Baker and Glasser conclude that "there will be no return to the pre-Trump era of American politics." Draper wonders if both Trump and Greene have become victims of their success, if they risk being "drowned out amid the Greek chorus of MAGA supplicants."

One of the great questions of this time has always been whether Trump changed the country or revealed it more clearly. The answer is yes; it is both. He changed America by revealing it. On January 6, Trump was the man who could win the country back for those who yearned for him long before they imagined him. If he can't do it, someone like him will do. Or someone like him, perhaps, but more so.

December 2022

THE PREMATURE REDEMPTION
OF MIKE PENCE

MIKE PENCE HAD A GO-TO line during his tenure as vice president of the United States. When his boss would ask him to carry out some task or duty—say, take an overseas trip or run the response to a pandemic—Pence would look President Trump in the eye, nod, and say, "I'm here to serve."

The phrase recurs in Pence's *So Help Me God*, which covers his years as a congressman, governor of Indiana, and vice president, with a focus on his actions during the assault on the Capitol on January 6. It is the tale of the loyalist who finally had enough, of the prayerful stand-taker who insisted that he did not have the power to overturn an election, no matter the arguments concocted by Trump and his air-quote lawyers.

With rioters calling for his hanging and Trump tweeting that Pence lacked "the courage to do what should have been done," the vice president turned to the aides and family members with him in an underground loading dock at the Capitol. "It doesn't take courage to break the law," he told them. "It takes courage to uphold the law." It is an inspiring scene, marred only by Pence then asking his daughter to write down what he said.

Pence has been busy promoting *So Help Me God* on television, distancing himself from Trump (urging him to apologize for dining with a Holocaust-denying white supremacist at Mar-a-Lago), and even teasing a White House run of his own in 2024. The book debuted at No. 2 on the *New York Times* hardcover nonfiction bestseller list, and the Justice Department is now seeking to question Pence in its investigation of Trump's efforts to remain in power after the 2020 election. Clearly, the former veep is having his moment.

Feel free to buy the book, but don't buy the redemption tale just yet. Pence was indeed in the White House to serve, but he served the president's needs more than those of the nation. In *So Help Me God* he rarely contradicts the president, even in private, until the days immediately preceding January 6. He rarely attempts to talk Trump out of his worst decisions or positions. He rarely counters Trump's lies with the truth.

Most damning, Pence failed to tell the president or the public, without hedging or softening the point, that the Trump-Pence ticket had lost the 2020 election, even after Pence had reached that conclusion himself. Americans should be enormously grateful that the vice president did not overstep his authority and attempt to reverse the will of the voters on January 6. But you shouldn't get the glory for pulling democracy back from the brink if you helped carry it there in the first place. And, so help me God, Pence did just that.

Why wouldn't Trump—a man Pence invariably calls "my president" and "my friend"—assume that his vice president would help steal the election? Pence had agreed to so much else, had tolerated every other indignity with that faraway, worshipful gaze. The irony is that Pence's record of reliable servility was a key reason he was in position to be the hero at the end. And so the vice president became that rarest of Trump-era creatures: a dedicated enabler who nonetheless managed to exit the administration with a plausible claim to partial credit. If Pence got to do the right thing on January 6, it was because he had done the wrong one for so long.

The purpose of the vice president, of course, is to serve as second banana, preferably without getting too mottled by lousy assignments, presidential indifference, or embarrassing deference. (Pence fills his sycophancy quotas in the book, extolling the president's physical stamina, likening Trump to Jimmy Stewart's character in *Mr. Smith Goes to Washington*, and noting that he displayed a signed copy of *The Art of the Deal* in his West Wing office during his entire vice presidency.) Still, I searched through the 542 pages of this memoir for any instances in which Pence exercised enough character and independent judgment to tell Trump that he might have been on the wrong course about something, about anything. I found two such cases before the events surrounding January 6. Two.

No, it's not when the president fired FBI director James Comey in May

2017, an action Trump took not for self-serving reasons, he assured Pence, but because it was "the right thing to do for the country." (Apparently Pence is so persuaded by this argument that he quotes it twice.) It's not when Trump praised the "very fine people" on both sides of the Charlottesville tragedy in August 2017. (Any notion of a false equivalence between neo-Nazis and those opposing them, Pence explains, was an unfortunate "narrative" that "smeared" his good friend in the Oval Office.)

It's not when the administration separated children from their parents at the southern US border. (On immigration, Pence writes, Trump "led with law and order but was prepared to follow with compassion.") It's not when Trump pressed Ukraine's leader to investigate a potential Democratic rival in the 2020 election. ("It was a less-than-perfect call," Pence acknowledges, but its imperfections were stylistic, the product of Trump's "casual" and "spontaneous" approach to foreign relations.)

It's not when Trump confused a frightened populace with his nonsensical coronavirus briefings in the spring of 2020. Pence explains away those sessions by suggesting that Trump believed that "seeing him and the press argue was in some way reassuring to the American people that life was going on." And it's not when Trump shared a stage with Vladimir Putin in Helsinki in July 2018 and accepted the Russian president's denials about election interference. Pence says he encouraged Trump to "clarify" his views, but the vice president seemed far more troubled by media coverage of the event. "The press and political establishment went wild," he writes. "It sounded as though the president was taking Putin's side over that of his national security officials." If it sounded that way, it was because that was the sound the words made when they left the president's mouth.

That is a standard Pence feint: when Trump says or does something wildly objectionable, Pence remains noncommittal on the matter and just condemns the "ever-divisive press" that covered it. When Trump derided Haiti, El Salvador, and various African nations as "shithole countries" in an Oval Office conversation in early 2018, "the media predictably went into a frenzy," Pence laments. The former vice president even faults journalists for drawing attention to Covid infection numbers in May 2020, "at a time,"

Pence writes, "when cases in more than half of the states were dropping, and case rates were also in decline, numbering 20,000 a day, down from 30,000 in April." As if 20,000 new Americans infected with a dangerous virus each day was not newsworthy.

The two meaningful disagreements that Pence expressed to the president in real time were these: First, Pence demurred when Trump considered inviting Taliban representatives to Camp David; he suggested that the president "reflect on who they are and what they've done and if they have truly changed." Second, the president and vice president had a testy exchange when Corey Lewandowski, a former Trump campaign manager, left a pro-Trump super PAC and joined Pence's political action committee. Pence reminded Trump that he had encouraged the move, but Trump denied having done so. "By that point I was angry," Pence acknowledges; he even admits to raising his voice. Somehow, the Taliban and Corey Lewandowski rated equally as lines that shall not be crossed.

Between Election Day on November 3, 2020, and the tragedy of January 6, 2021, while Trump and his allies propagated the fiction of a stolen vote, Pence enabled and dissembled. Describing the outcome of the vote in his memoir, he offers a gloriously exculpatory euphemism, writing that "we came up short under circumstances that would cause millions of Americans to doubt the outcome of the election." (Circumstances could not be reached for comment.) When Trump declared victory in the early hours of November 4, Pence stood alongside him in the East Room of the White House, in front of dozens of US flags and behind a single microphone, and "promised that we would remain vigilant to protect the integrity of the vote," Pence recalls. In the days that followed, Pence addressed conservative audiences and pledged to continue the fight "until every legal vote is counted and every illegal vote is thrown out!"

Note those slippery, wiggle-room formulations. Pence does not directly state that he believed the election had been stolen, yet his rhetoric still appears fully in line with Trump's position. The ovations at his speeches were "deafening," Pence notes. So was his public silence about the truth. Less than a week after the election, Pence had already admitted to Jared Kushner that "although I was sure that some voter fraud had taken place, I wasn't convinced it had cost us the election." Why not share that conclusion with the public? Why stand by as the big lie grew bigger and January 6 grew inevitable?

The memoir revisits several conversations between Pence and Trump in the weeks immediately preceding January 6—all missed opportunities to convey the truth to the boss. Instead, Pence reassured Trump that "the campaign was right to defend the integrity of America's elections." (Pence often refers obliquely to the actions of "the campaign," as if he played no role in it, as if his name was not even on the ballot.) He dances around reality, coming closest to it when he advised the president that "if the legal challenges came up short and if he was unwilling to concede, he could simply accept the results of the elections, move forward with the transition, and start a political comeback."

On December 14, 2020, state electors officially voted and delivered an electoral college majority to Joe Biden and Kamala Harris, leading Pence to acknowledge that "for all intents and purposes, at that point the election was over." He says so now in his memoir; if only he had said it in public at the time. Yes, he told Trump repeatedly that the vice president lacks the authority to overturn the results of the election. But not once in his book does Pence say to the president that, *even if I had the authority, I would not exercise it—because we lost.*

Throughout *So Help Me God*, readers find Pence still running interference for Trump, still minimizing his transgressions. When he quotes the president's video from the afternoon of January 6, in which Trump finally called on the rioters to stand down, Pence makes a revealing omission. Here is how he quotes Trump: "I know your pain, I know your hurt . . . but you have to go home now, we have to have peace." What did Pence erase with that ellipsis? "We had an election that was stolen from us," Trump said in the middle of that passage. "It was a landslide election, and everyone knows it, especially the other side." So much of Pence's vice presidency is captured in those three little dots.

Sometimes the problem is not the relevant material Pence leaves out but

the dubious material he puts in. Pence writes, with an overconfidence border-
ing on overcompensation, that he was going to win reelection as Indiana governor in 2016, that his victory "was all but assured." In fact, Pence's approval
ratings in the final stretch of his governorship were low and polls indicated a
tight contest against his Democratic opponent.

Pence writes that Trump "never tried to obscure the offensiveness of what
he had said" on the infamous *Access Hollywood* tape, perhaps forgetting that
Trump dismissed his words as mere "locker room talk" and later suggested
that the voice on the recording might not have been his own.

Pence also writes that the White House, busy with its Covid response,
did not have "much time for celebrating" after the president's acquittal in his
first Senate impeachment trial in February 2020, even though the next day
Trump spoke about the outcome in the White House for more than an hour
before a crowd of lawmakers, aides, family members, and lawyers. Trump
explicitly called the speech a "celebration" and referred to that day, February
6, 2020, as "a day of celebration," as Pence, sitting in the front row, no doubt
heard. The day would indeed prove a high point in the administration's final
year, as a pandemic, electoral defeat, and insurrection soon followed.

"I prayed for wisdom to know the right thing to do and the courage to
do it," Pence writes of the days before January 6. Unsurprising for a book
with this title, Pence's Christian faith is a constant reference point. Raised
Catholic, Pence describes being born again during his college years and joining an evangelical church with his wife. Throughout the memoir, he is often
praying, and often reminding readers of how often he prays.

Each chapter begins with a Bible passage, and Pence highlights individuals he deems particularly "strong" or "devout" Christians, with Rep. Julia
Carson of Indiana, who died in 2007, Sen. Josh Hawley, Rep. Jim Jordan,
and Secretary of State Mike Pompeo making the cut. I kept wondering if he
would consider the role that his outspoken faith may have played in getting
him on the ticket in the first place. If Trump picked him to reassure Christian conservatives, how does Pence feel about that bargain?

In the epilogue, Pence provides a clue. Of all the Trump administration's
accomplishments, he writes, the "most important of all" was making possi-

ble the Supreme Court's decision in *Dobbs v. Jackson Women's Health*, which overturned *Roe v. Wade* and ended the constitutional right to abortion. "The fact that three of the five justices who joined that opinion were appointed during the Trump-Pence administration makes all the hardship we endured from 2016 forward more than worth it." Pence, in other words, is the ultimate "But Gorsuch!" voter. That is what he got out of the bargain, plus a new national profile that he may leverage into a bid for the only higher office left to seek.

In the book's appendix, Pence reprints several documents that emphasize different aspects of his public service. There is his 2016 Republican convention speech, in which he hailed Trump as both an "uncalculating truth-teller" and "his own man, distinctly American"; his 2016 State of the State of Indiana address; his letter to Congress on January 6, 2021, in which he stated that the vice president's role in certifying an election is "largely ceremonial"; and his letter to then-Speaker Nancy Pelosi, six days after the attack on the Capitol, refusing to invoke the Constitution's Twenty-Fifth Amendment to remove Trump from office. Pence also adds two texts in which he takes special pride, and which I imagine him citing in any future presidential run.

First is an essay titled "Confessions of a Negative Campaigner," which Pence published in 1991 after his second failed run for Congress. "It is wrong, quite simply, to squander a candidate's priceless moment in history, a moment in which he or she could have brought critical issues before the citizenry, on partisan bickering," Pence wrote. He was describing himself, with regret. The second is a speech that Pence, then representing Indiana's Sixth Congressional District, delivered at Hillsdale College in 2010. "You must always be wary of a president who seems to float upon his own greatness," Pence declared. He was describing the Obama presidency, with disdain. The president, he wrote, "does not command us; we command him. We serve neither him nor his vision." Pence warned that "if a president joins the power of his office to his own willful interpretation, he steps away from a government of laws and toward a government of men."

These documents provide an apt coda to Pence's vice presidency. One day, he may use them to distinguish himself from his president and his friend, to try to show that he, too, can be his own man. For now, he does not make the obvious connection between the sentiments in his essay and speech and his experience campaigning and governing alongside Donald Trump. Or if he does, he is calculating enough to keep it to himself.

After all, Mike Pence was there to serve.

November 2022

THE LUCK OF JOE BIDEN

SOMETIMES A BOOK IS SO eager to take readers behind the scenes that it neglects the scenes themselves. This is often so with journalistic works chronicling presidential elections, obsessed as they are with the machinations of high-priced operatives, the strategizing of rival campaigns, or the "optics" of who stands where on a debate stage. Read enough of them and it gets hard to discern whether that is all the authors choose to emphasize or if that is all there really is to see.

Lucky: How Joe Biden Barely Won the Presidency, a detailed account of the 2020 election by Jonathan Allen of NBC News and Amie Parnes of *The Hill*, is the first volume to tell the story of this unusual electoral contest, with several competing works scheduled later in 2021 and into 2022. In 2017, Allen and Parnes coauthored the bestselling *Shattered*, an examination of Hillary Clinton's failed 2016 campaign, in which they placed the blame largely on the ineptitude of the losing side. In this sequel, they are only slightly more generous with the Democratic nominee. Joe Biden won, yes, but mainly because he "caught every imaginable break." He was the "process-of-elimination candidate," emerging from a crowded set of more exciting Democratic contenders. He was "lousy in debates and lackluster on the trail," prevailing despite "a bland message and a blank agenda." Biden, they argue, got lucky.

The fiasco of the Iowa caucuses, where the app designed to report the results failed miserably, temporarily obscured Biden's fourth-place showing. "This was a gift," a campaign aide later explained. Luck returned when rival Democrats such as Pete Buttigieg (who ended up winning Iowa) and Mike Bloomberg (who won American Samoa) suffered debate-night takedowns by Amy Klobuchar and Elizabeth Warren—and when Biden survived his own hit from Kamala Harris over his past positions on school busing and desegregation. (That almost cost Harris the subsequent veep nod, Allen and

Parnes report.) Fortune showed up again when the Democratic establishment rushed to Biden's side after his victory in the South Carolina primary, even if it was less about devotion to him than panic that Bernie Sanders might secure the nomination. "On Super Tuesday, you got very lucky," President Donald Trump told Biden at their first debate. The Democrat did not disagree.

But Trump offered his rival some luck, too, when the president failed to deal effectively with the coronavirus pandemic. Allen and Parnes quote then–senior campaign official Anita Dunn, who later became a White House adviser, discussing how the outbreak affected Biden's prospects. "COVID is the best thing that ever happened to him," she told an associate early in the crisis, according to the authors. It's a cynical way to regard a disaster that would take the lives of hundreds of thousands of Americans, even if it was, they write, what Biden campaign aides "believed but would never say in public." Well, it's public now.

Such blunt talk is the lifeblood of *Lucky*. Biden campaign pollster John Anzalone, for instance, worries about the vagueness of his candidate's speeches. "No one knows what this 'soul of America' bulls— means," he complains. At a New York event with black corporate leaders in the fall of 2019, Barack Obama praised Warren's candidacy and listed several reasons Buttigieg couldn't win. "He's thirty-eight, but he looks thirty," the former president said, eliciting laughs in the room. "He's the mayor of a small town. He's gay, and he's short." And top Sanders campaign adviser Jeff Weaver chewed out fellow adviser Chuck Rocha as the early Nevada primary results came in. "Where are the Latinos? You spent three million dollars. Where are the Latinos?"

A simplistic focus on identity is evident throughout the Democratic field, with new aides often hired to make staffs look young and more diverse— only to complicate things by, you know, having ideas of their own that diverged from those of entrenched advisers. Allen and Parnes portray a Biden campaign split along "deep fault lines mostly based on generation, race, ideology, and time in Bidenworld." Biden was in the middle of it, in every sense, hewing to centrist positions on health care, racial justice, and law enforcement, no matter the pressures from his campaign team and his party. He may not have been "Sleepy Joe," but he remained "Unwoke Joe," Allen and Parnes quip. "That was the ugly truth many Democrats had to face in the aftermath of the 2020 election: To beat Trump, they had to swallow their progressive values and push forward an old white man who simply promised to restore calm."

That "simply" is a little deceptive. The 2020 race took place against the backdrop of a deadly pandemic, widespread racial-justice protests, and threats to American democracy emanating from the presidency itself. In *Lucky*, such critical context matters largely to the extent that it affects the candidates' rhetoric and fundraising. (George Floyd's death, for instance, required some "nimble positioning" by Biden, Allen and Parnes write, trying to keep both moderate white voters and party activists happy.)

As a result, the moments of high drama in *Lucky* can feel small-bore. Should Biden leave New Hampshire and head to South Carolina before the Granite State's full primary results are announced, thus potentially alienating supporters there for the general election? (Spoiler: He did leave early. It was fine.) And how do longtime Biden campaign staffers react when the interloping new campaign boss, Jennifer O'Malley Dillon, receives a glowing write-up in the *Washington Post*'s opinion section, complete with a portrait-type photo? "The profile landed like the mother of all bombs in the civil war between the Obama veterans and Biden's primary crew," Allen and Parnes overwrite.

There are memorable moments in *Lucky* revealing vital negotiations or highlighting truths that parties and campaigns would rather avoid. For example, planners of the Democratic Party's virtual convention thought about featuring a national map that would highlight the locations of various speakers, thus countering the notion that the party was a club for coastal elites—only to kill the idea when they realized multiple speakers would be broadcasting from Martha's Vineyard. And the all-important endorsement of Rep. James E. Clyburn of South Carolina was in play when Clyburn cornered Biden during a commercial break at a Charleston debate and urged him to promise to appoint a black woman to the Supreme Court.

"This wasn't offered as a condition of Clyburn's endorsement, but it was an expectation," the authors write, parsing a bit too finely. Biden awkwardly complied.

Unfortunately, Allen and Parnes clutter their story with italicized descriptions of what various players are really thinking at particular moments, a tic that carries over from *Shattered* but that in *Lucky* grows more noticeable. "Obviously, we are not able to read minds," they acknowledge in an author's note, explaining that they divine such thoughts from first- or secondhand sources, or from "documents that suggest what a person was thinking." Even so, these asides are distracting and often unnecessary. *"How the hell can they do that?"* Trump thought when Fox News called Arizona for Biden on election night. (Yes, we all heard he was upset.) And Warren's supposed inner monologue before eviscerating Bloomberg on a Las Vegas debate stage closely resembled—no shock—what she said to Bloomberg's face on national television.

Note to political reporters and nonfiction authors: italics are not a get-out-of-quote-free card.

The most persuasive case that Biden "barely won" the presidency, as the book's subtitle states, is found not in the details of Allen and Parnes's reporting but in their description of the election's final tallies. Yes, Biden received 81 million votes, the most in US presidential history, but "many voters didn't realize how close the president had come to winning a second term." Allen and Parnes note that Trump's collective margin of defeat in three states that would have given him an electoral college victory—Wisconsin, Georgia, and Arizona—was 42,918 votes, less than the 77,000-plus votes that cost Clinton Wisconsin, Michigan, and Pennsylvania four years earlier. That is certainly close.

Lucky provides useful detail to understand Biden's victory, even if the framing is not particularly novel. What candidate has not experienced some luck or misfortune during a long presidential bid? One time it might be a major public-health crisis, another time, a self-righteous FBI director. Stuff happens, and the best candidates figure out how to react. "Knowing who he was, and where he wanted to be politically, allowed Biden's campaign to capitalize when luck ran his way," Allen and Parnes conclude in their final pages.

In other words, Biden was more than lucky. And for political reporters as for political candidates, spending too much time on optics is just not a good look.

February 2021

THE FALSE CHOICES OF
KAMALA HARRIS

SEN. KAMALA HARRIS MENTIONS JOE Biden only once in her memoir, *The Truths We Hold: An American Journey*, and she does so in passing. "I was sworn in on January 3, 2017, by Vice President Joe Biden during his final month in office." That's it.

But if Harris had been gaming out her own veep prospects under a potential Biden nomination when her book was published in 2019, she could have done no better. In her book, Harris praises Biden's eldest son, the late Beau Biden—who served as Delaware's attorney general while Harris held that post in California—as "an incredible friend ... a man of principle and courage." They worked together during the Great Recession, she recalls, investigating banks involved in the foreclosure crisis and seeking more money for struggling homeowners. "Beau and I talked every day," she writes. "We had each other's backs." When Harris and Joe Biden made their first public appearance as running mates in mid-August 2020, they both invoked the memory of Beau in bringing them together.

The Truths We Hold, published in advance of Harris's failed run at the 2020 Democratic presidential nomination, is a conventional political memoir—a mix of biography, reflections, and policy prescriptions. Even its title and subtitle are a generic combo of American civics and political-speak. Its most memorable moments are those personal touches: Harris's recollections of family and friendship and, above all, her late mother, an Indian immigrant and cancer researcher.

But the book also illuminates Harris's philosophy and aspirations, and the qualities she brings to a national presidential campaign. In these pages, Harris emerges as something between a feel-your-pain Democrat and a policy wonk, though not fully either. She takes pride in her record as a district attorney and attorney general, yet she acknowledges the pitfalls of the criminal justice system in which she labored and thrived. Harris constantly dismisses as "false choices" the dilemmas that politicians encounter in policy debates. She wants to be a "joyful warrior in the battle to come," and whether joy or war prevails may be the story of her campaign.

Harris's record as a prosecutor—long considered an asset for Democrats hoping to project a tough, no-nonsense image as they pursued higher office— is a potential liability now that the excesses of law enforcement and mass incarceration have prompted movements for social, cultural, and legal change. Harris acknowledges the nation's "deep and dark history" of prosecutorial power wielded as an instrument of injustice, and she admits that critics have questioned "how I, as a black woman, could countenance being part of 'the machine' putting more young men of color behind bars."

Yet even as she decries mass incarceration as "a living monument to lost potential" and criticizes sentencing guidelines that are "harsh to the point of being inhumane," Harris believes that serious crimes deserve serious consequences. "We cannot overlook or ignore that mother's pain, that child's death, that murderer who still walks the streets," she writes.

Harris attempts to square these positions with the idea of a "progressive prosecutor," one who holds serious offenders accountable but understands that preventing crime, not just punishing it, helps create safe communities. "The job of a progressive prosecutor is to look out for the overlooked, to speak up for those whose voices aren't being heard, to see and address the causes of crime, not just their consequences, and to shine a light on the inequality and unfairness that lead to injustice," she writes. "It is to recognize that not everyone needs punishment, that what many need, quite plainly, is help."

Harris's "Back on Track" initiative, a reentry program for former prisoners that she developed as San Francisco district attorney, featuring GED courses, job training, community service, and drug testing, became a national model. But when she brought another policy she developed in that position, to reduce truancy among schoolchildren, to the state level as attorney general, some California parents faced jail time as a result. In her book, Harris laments that critics did not appreciate her good intentions. "They assume that my motivation was to lock up parents," she writes, "when of course that was never the goal." Except policies aren't judged solely by intentions but also by outcomes, intended or otherwise.

Harris doesn't like being forced into absolutes. She offers solidarity with those protesting systemic racism and police brutality but also believes that "most police officers deserve to be proud of their public service and commended for the way they do their jobs." (In her 2009 book, *Smart on Crime*, Harris branded as "myth" the notion that low-income residents don't want police in their communities.) "It is a false choice to suggest that you must either be for the police or for police accountability," she writes in her latest book. "I am for both."

During the campaign, Harris will no doubt be pushed to clarify and detail her positions, some of which may have shifted—or "evolved," in politicians' preferred nomenclature—since her memoir's publication. (In the book, she expresses unequivocal support for Medicare for All. Remember all that?) Yet *The Truths We Hold* suggests that Harris hews to positions that seem fairly centrist for today's Democratic Party. Her selection as Biden's running mate has been hailed as historic and groundbreaking, in part given her personal background as the daughter of Jamaican and Indian immigrants and the first woman of color on a major presidential ticket, but Harris is notable in part for her decidedly nonrevolutionary politics.

Growing up between Oakland and Berkeley in California in the 1960s and 1970s, Harris was "surrounded by adults shouting and marching and demanding justice from the outside," she writes. "But I also knew there was an important role on the inside, sitting at the table where the decisions were being made." At each step, Harris pursues that insider role. At Howard University and then the University of California's Hastings College of the Law, Harris was more careerist than activist, winning competitive internships and joining academic societies. And as district attorney, state attorney general, US senator, and now vice presidential candidate, Harris has continued scaling the heights of institutionalism.

"When activists came marching and banging on doors, I wanted to be on the other side to let them in," she writes. The vice presidency would afford her a wider door to swing open.

Like every proud legislator, Harris cites the many bills she has introduced during her time in the Senate—proposals to reform bail systems, place body cameras on immigration agents, provide relief to renters, protect critical election infrastructure, invest in quantum computing—as if legislative proposals were accomplishments in themselves, regardless of whether they become law. The bar is higher in the White House.

Other experiences, such as winning a close vote for attorney general in 2010 even after her opponent was prematurely declared the victor, may come in handy if election night 2020 proves contentious and uncertain. Harris's understanding of the immigrant experience, one she witnessed in her home state and in her own family, watching her mother's struggles and indignities, also provides an essential vantage point. There, too, she resists dichotomies. When a constituent at a Sacramento town hall complained that Harris cared more about undocumented immigrants than American citizens, the distinction was just another "false choice," she writes. "I cared deeply about them both."

Harris mixes in chapters on various policy debates—health care, marriage equality, housing, national security—in ways that feel a bit dutiful, even boilerplate. ("If not for ourselves, shouldn't we at least do this work for our children and grandchildren?" is a sentence that appears in this book.) She concludes with some principles for leadership and management, which are instructive for anyone trying to imagine a Vice President Harris.

"Test the hypothesis" is one, meaning that lasting innovations come from trial and error, not from imposing big plans right away. "Go to the scene" is another, with Harris urging politicians to look closely at the conditions they want to fix and the communities they mean to help. In her final principle, Harris recalls her mother reminding her to bring others along with her as she moves ahead: "You may be the first. Don't be the last."

Harris understands the scrutiny that comes with attempting to be a new first. "When you break through a glass ceiling, you're going to get cut," she writes. But this "joyful warrior" seems prepared to wage necessary battles and endure the verdict issued by future generations. "I don't want us to just tell them how we felt," she writes in her final sentences. "I want us to tell them what we did."

August 2020

RON DeSANTIS AND HIS ENEMIES

Ron DeSantis has an enemies list, and you can probably guess who's on it.

There's the "woke dumpster fire" of the Democratic Party and the "swamp Republicans" who neglect their own voters. There's the news media, with modifiers like "legacy" or "corporate" adding a nefarious touch. There's Big Tech, that "censorship arm of the political left," and the powerful corporations that cave to the "leftist-rage mob." There are universities like Harvard and Yale, which DeSantis attended but did not inhale. There's the administrative state and its pandemic-era spin-off, the "biomedical security state." These are the villains of DeSantis's *The Courage to Be Free: Florida's Blueprint for America's Revival*, and its author feels free to assail them with a fusillade of generically irate prose.

There is one more antagonist—not an enemy, perhaps, but certainly a rival—whom DeSantis does not attack directly in his book, even as he looms over much of it. The far-too-early national polls for the 2024 Republican presidential nomination show a two-person contest with Donald Trump and DeSantis (who has yet to announce his potential candidacy) in the lead, and the Haleys, Pences, and Pompeos of the world fighting for scraps. During his 2018 governor's race, DeSantis aired an obsequious ad in which he built a cardboard border wall and read Trump's *Art of the Deal* with his children, one of whom wore a MAGA onesie. Now DeSantis no longer bows before Trump. Instead, he dances around the former president; he is respectful but no longer deferential, critical but mainly by implication.

Yes, there is a DeSantis case against Trump scattered throughout these pages. You just need to squint through a magnifying glass to find it.

In the book's 250-plus pages, there is not a single mention of the events of January 6. DeSantis cites Madison, Hamilton, and the nation's founding principles, but he does not pause to consider a frontal assault on America's democratic institutions encouraged by a sitting president. The governor does not go so far as to defend Trump's lies about the 2020 election; he just ignores them.

However, DeSantis does write that an energetic executive should lead "within the confines of a constitutional system," and he criticizes unnamed elected officials for whom "perpetuating themselves in office supersedes fulfilling any policy mission." Might DeSantis ever direct such criticisms at a certain former president so willing to subvert the Constitution to remain in power? Perhaps. For the moment, though, such indignation exists at a safe distance from any discussion of Trump himself.

When DeSantis explains how he chose top officials for his administration in Florida, he offers an unstated yet unsubtle contrast to Trump's leadership. "I placed loyalty to the cause over loyalty to me," DeSantis writes. "I had no desire to be flattered—I just wanted people who worked hard and believed in what we were trying to accomplish." Demands for personal fealty have assumed canonical status in Trump presidential lore (who can forget his "I need loyalty" dinner with the soon-to-be-fired FBI director James Comey?), and it is hard to recall another recent leader whose susceptibility to flattery so easily overpowered any political or ideological coherence.

Where he describes his personal dealings with the former president, DeSantis jabs at Trump even as he praises him. In a meeting with Trump after Hurricane Michael struck Florida in late 2018, DeSantis asked for increased federal aid, particularly for northwestern Florida, telling the president that the region was "Trump country." In the governor's account, Trump responded with Pavlovian enthusiasm: "I must have won 90 percent of the vote out there. Huge crowds. What do they need?" DeSantis recalls how, after the president agreed to reimburse a large portion of the state's cleanup expenses, Mick Mulvaney, then the acting White House chief of staff, pulled the governor aside and urged him to wait before announcing the help, explaining that Trump "doesn't even know what he agreed to in terms of a price tag."

Even as DeSantis appears to thank Trump for assistance to Florida, he is showcasing an easily manipulated president who does not grasp the basics of governing.

DeSantis boasts of how Florida stood apart from other states' lockdown policies and how Tallahassee dissented from the federal response. Though he criticizes Trump-era federal guidelines, particularly early in the crisis, he rarely blames the president directly. "By the time President Trump had to decide whether the shutdown guidance should be extended beyond the original fifteen days, there were reasons to question the main model used by the task force to justify a shutdown," DeSantis writes, in his most pointed—yet still quite polite—disapproval.

Rather than question the former president's actions on Covid, DeSantis goes after Anthony Fauci, "one of the most destructive bureaucrats in American history," an official whose "intellectual bankruptcy and brazen partisanship" turned major US cities into hollowed-out "Faucivilles." Fauci is the supervillain of DeSantis's book, the destroyer of jobs and freedoms, the architect of a "Faucian dystopia." Trump, it seems, was not in charge during the early months of Covid, but Fauci wielded unstoppable and unaccountable power—until a courageous governor had finally had enough. "As the iron curtain of Faucism descended upon our continent," DeSantis writes, "the State of Florida stood resolutely in the way."

In *The Courage to Be Free*, DeSantis displays only enough courage to reprimand Trump by proxy.

In fact, DeSantis's broadest attack against Trump is also his most oblique. In the governor's various references to Trump, the former president emerges less as a political force in his own right than a symptom of preexisting trends that Trump was lucky enough to harness. Trump's nomination in 2016 flowed mainly from the failure of Republican elites to "effectively represent the values" of Republican voters, the governor writes. DeSantis even takes some credit for Trump's ascent: the House Freedom Caucus, of which DeSantis was a member, "identified the shortcomings of the modern Republican establishment in a way that paved the way for an outsider presidential candidate who threatened the survival of the stale D.C. Republican Party orthodoxy."

Trump has argued, not without reason, that he enabled DeSantis's election as governor with his endorsement in late 2017—and now DeSantis suggests he helped clear the path for Trumpism. The governor even notes the "star power" that Trump brought to American politics, the kind of thing critics used to say when dismissing Barack Obama as a celebrity candidate.

If Trump's success was not unique to him but flowed from larger cultural or economic forces that rendered him viable, presumably someone else could channel the same forces, perhaps more efficiently, if only Republican voters had the courage to be free of Trump. And who might that alternative be?

DeSantis pitches himself as not only a culture warrior but a competent culture warrior. The culture warrior who stood up for parents and stood against Disney (yes, the Magic Kingdom rates its own chapter here). The culture warrior with the real heartland vibe (DeSantis's family's roots in Ohio and Pennsylvania come up a lot). The culture warrior who is "God-fearing, hard-working and America-loving" in the face of enemies who are oppressive, unbelieving, unpatriotic. The culture warrior who takes "bold stands," displays "courage under fire," and is willing to "lead with conviction," "speak the truth," and "stand for what is right."

The Free State of Florida, as DeSantis likes to call it, is not just the national blueprint of his book's subtitle. It is "a beachhead of sanity," a "citadel of freedom in a world gone mad," even "America's West Berlin." (The rest of us must still live behind the iron curtain of Faucism.) No wonder Trump, who says he regrets endorsing DeSantis for governor, has begun denigrating his rival's achievements in the state where they both live.

The governor's prose can be flat and clichéd: Throughout the book, cautions are thrown to winds, less-traveled roads are taken, hammers are dropped, new sheriffs show up in town, dust eventually settles, and chips fall wherever they may. When members of Congress attempt to "climb the ladder" of seniority, he writes, they "get neutered" by the time they reach the top. (That is one painful metaphor—and ladder.) And DeSantis's red meat tastes a bit overcooked. "Clearly, our administration was substantively consequential," he affirms in his epilogue. Still, his broad-based 2022 reelection victory suggests that the competent culture warrior may have an appeal that extends beyond the hard-core MAGA base, even if Make America Substantively Consequential Again doesn't quite fit on a hat.

At times, DeSantis's culture-war armor slips, as with his awkward ambivalence about his Ivy League education. He experienced such "massive culture shock" when arriving at the "hyper-leftist" Yale, he writes, that after graduating he decided to go on to . . . Harvard Law School? "From a political perspective, Harvard was just as left-wing as Yale," DeSantis complains. Yes, we know. DeSantis informs his readers that he graduated from law school with honors, even if "my heart was not into what I was being taught in class," and he mentions (twice) that he could have made big bucks in the private sector with a Harvard Law degree but instead chose to serve in the navy. "I am one of the very few people who went through both Yale and Harvard Law School and came out more conservative than when I went in," he assured voters during his 2012 congressional campaign.

DeSantis wants both the elite validation of his Ivy League credentials and the populist cred for trash-talking the schools. Pick one, Governor. Even Trump just straight-up brags about Wharton.

Of course, whether DeSantis's culture-war instincts are authentic or shtick matters less than the fact that he is waging that war; the institutions, individuals, and ideologies he targets are real regardless of his motives. But the blueprint of his subtitle implies a more systematic worldview than is present in this book. DeSantis's professed reliance on "common sense" and "core" national values is another way of saying he draws on his own impulses and interpretations. It's a very Trumpian approach.

When DeSantis highlights his state's renewed emphasis on civics education and a high-school civics exam modeled on the US naturalization test—an idea that this naturalized citizen finds intriguing—it is a particularistic vision informed by the governor's own political preferences. When DeSantis goes after Disney's governance or tax status over its opposition to a Florida law concerning what can and cannot be taught in elementary schools, he is not making a statement of principle about business and politics; he just opposes the stance Disney has taken. When he brings up Russia more than two dozen times in his book, it never concerns Vladimir Putin's challenges to America or war against Ukraine; it is always about DeSantis's disdain for the "Trump-Russia collusion conspiracy theory." (DeSantis's subsequent dismissal of the war as a mere "territorial dispute" is therefore little surprise.) When he accuses the news media of pushing "partisan narratives," he is not striking a blow for objective, independent coverage; he just prefers narratives that fit his own.

DeSantis asserts that he has a "positive vision," beyond just defeating his enemies on the left. But in *The Courage to Be Free*, defeating his enemies is the only thing the governor seems positive about. That may be enough to compete for the Republican nomination, but it's not a blueprint for America. It's not a substantive vision, even if it proves a consequential one.

March 2023

BIDEN'S "STILL" VERSUS TRUMP'S "AGAIN"

PRESIDENTS ARE FOREVER LINKED TO their most memorable lines or slogans, phrases that become inseparable from their passage through history. Ronald Reagan proclaimed morning in America. Barack Obama promised America hope and change. Donald Trump pledged to make America great again. Our leaders also utter words they might rather take back—say, about lip-reading or the meaning of "is"—but their go-to lines can capture a message, signal an attitude, and even betray a worldview.

Joe Biden has long settled on his preferred pitch. "We are living through a battle for the soul of this nation," he wrote in 2017, after the darkness of Charlottesville. Biden highlighted the battle for that soul again in his 2020 and 2024 campaign announcements and has revisited it in multiple speeches. It is ominous and a bit vague—John Anzalone, Biden's 2020 pollster, complained during that race that no one knows what "soul of America" means and that the line fails to "move the needle." But it does provide the rationale for Biden's candidacy and presidency. Under Trump, Biden contends, America was becoming something other than itself.

Yet there is another Biden line—a single word, really—that also stands out, and it comes up whenever this president reflects on that American soul, on what the country is and what it might become. It is *still*.

"We have to show the world America is still a beacon of light," Biden wrote in that same post-Charlottesville essay.

"We have to prove democracy still works—that our government still works and we can deliver for our people," he said in a speech to a joint session of Congress in April 2021.

"We are still an America that believes in honesty and decency and respect for others, patriotism, liberty, justice for all, hope, possibilities," the president said in a speech in September at Independence Hall in Philadelphia, where he asserted that the foundations of the Republic were under assault by MAGA forces. "We are still, at our core, a democracy."

There is an insistent quality, almost a stubbornness, to Biden's "still." Its implicit assumption is that many Americans may no longer believe in the nation's professed virtues or trust that they will last much longer, that we must be persuaded of either their value or their endurance. To say that America is a democracy is to issue a statement of belief. To say that we are *still* a democracy is to engage in an argument, to acknowledge—and push back against—mounting concerns to the contrary.

The contrast between Biden saying America is still a democracy and Trump vowing to make it great again is more than a quirk of speechwriting. What presidents say—especially what they grow comfortable repeating—can reveal their underlying beliefs and impulses, shaping their administrations in ways that are concrete, not just rhetorical. Biden's "still" stresses durability; Trump's "again" revels in discontinuity. "Still" is about holding on to something good that may be slipping away; "again" is about bringing back something better that was wrested away. Both candidates, now in a dead heat in the 2024 presidential race, look to the nation's past but through divergent lenses. It's the difference between America as an ideal worth preserving and an illusion worth summoning.

Biden's use of "still" is both soothing and alarming. It connotes permanence but warns of fragility. The message of "still" is that we remain who we are, but that this condition is not immutable, that America as Biden envisions it exists somewhere between reality and possibility. "If we do our duty in 2022 and beyond," Biden said ahead of that year's midterm elections, "then ages still to come will say we—all of us here—we kept the faith. We preserved democracy. We heeded not our worst instincts but our better angels. And we proved that for all its imperfections, America is still the beacon to the world."

Remember, it's only when life is wretched that presidents reach for Lincoln. In good times, no one gives a damn about our better angels.

Americans do recognize the threat to our system of government, but they just don't seem that energized by the dangers. A *New York Times*/Siena College poll in fall 2022 found that more than 70 percent regarded American democracy as being at risk, but only 7 percent thought that was the nation's most important problem. Biden's message demands that we care. "Democracy is hard work," the president said at a Summit for Democracy meeting in March 2023.

In that speech, Biden also indulged in a bit of a victory lap. "Here in the United States, we've demonstrated that our democracy can still do big things and deliver important progress for working Americans," he said, citing lower prescription-drug costs, new infrastructure investments, electoral reform, and his administration's efforts against climate change. It was an answer to his speech before Congress in 2021, when he said we had to prove that democracy still functions. "It's working," he told the summit. "It's working."

But three months later, after the Supreme Court declared affirmative action in college admissions unconstitutional, the president reiterated his concern that the basic American promise of equal opportunity remains unfulfilled. "The truth is—we all know it," he stated. "Discrimination still exists in America. Discrimination still exists in America. Discrimination still exists in America." That third and final *still* was especially adamant.

Even as Biden affirms what he believes we still are, he also reminds us of all he believes we still must do—his "still" entails duty along with reassurance. The president can declare, as he did in 2021, that "it's never, ever, ever, been a good bet to bet against America, and it still isn't," but the need to state it so emphatically acknowledges that the stakes are rising, and that the odds are not improving.

Over the years, Biden has offered varying visions about what America still means to him. In his 2007 memoir, *Promises to Keep*, he reflected on the nation's ability to inspire the globe after a visit to a refugee camp in Chad. "We sometimes forget that America is the one country in the world that still shimmers, like that 'shining city on the hill,' as a promise of a brighter tomorrow," he wrote. But in Evan Osnos's *Joe Biden: The Life, the Run, and What Matters Now* (2020), Biden considered a different vision of what America still is. "Watching [George] Floyd's face pinned against that curb and his nose being crushed, I mean, the vividness of it was, like, 'Holy God. That still happens today?'"

Biden's "still" was once a contrast to the plight of other countries; then it came to be more about competing visions of our own.

In Jon Meacham's *The Soul of America* (2018), that presidential biographer and Biden wordsmith points to the "universal American inconsistency" of upholding rights and freedoms for some but not others. "The only way to make sense of this eternal struggle," Meacham concludes, "is to understand that it is just that: an eternal struggle."

At times, Biden seems torn over whether the struggle is eternal or temporary. In his 2017 essay on the battle for the soul of the nation, he noted that charlatans and political con artists "have long dotted our history," invariably blaming immigrants for our troubles and capitalizing on the despair of struggling communities. But in the video launching his 2020 campaign, he expressed confidence that history will deem Trump an "aberrant moment" in the national timeline, and only if Trump was granted eight years in the White House would he "forever and fundamentally" transform the national character. In other words, vote for Biden and America would still be America.

Of course, Biden didn't say Trump would need eight consecutive years to remake the nation; two nonconsecutive terms could prove even more definitive. That would mean that we tried Trump, attempted an alternative, and then decided we wanted him back after all. It would mean we chose Trump, again.

August 2023

II. FIGHTING

9/11 WAS A TEST, AND WE FAILED

DEEP WITHIN THE CATALOGUE OF regrets that is the 9/11 Commission report—long after readers learn of the origins and objectives of al-Qaeda, past the warnings ignored by consecutive administrations, through the litany of institutional failures that allowed terrorists to hijack four commercial airliners—the authors pause to make a rousing case for the power of the nation's character.

"The U.S. government must define what the message is, what it stands for," the report asserts. "We should offer an example of moral leadership in the world, committed to treat people humanely, abide by the rule of law, and be generous and caring to our neighbors. … We need to defend our ideals abroad vigorously. America does stand up for its values."

This affirmation of American idealism is one of the document's more opinionated moments. Looking back, it's also among the most ignored.

Rather than exemplify the nation's highest values, the official response to 9/11 unleashed some of its worst qualities: deception, brutality, arrogance, ignorance, delusion, overreach, and carelessness. This conclusion is laid bare in the sprawling literature to emerge from 9/11 over the past two decades— the works of investigation, memoir, and narrative by journalists and former officials that have charted the path to that day, revealed the heroism and confusion of the early response, chronicled the battles in and about Afghanistan and Iraq, and uncovered the excesses of the war on terror. Reading or rereading a collection of such books today is like watching an old movie that feels more anguishing and frustrating than you remember. The anguish comes from knowing how the tale will unfold; the frustration from realizing that this was hardly the only possible outcome.

Whatever individual stories the 9/11 books tell, too many describe the repudiation of US values, not by extremist outsiders but by our own hand. The betrayal of America's professed principles was the friendly fire of the war on terror. In these books, indifference to the growing terrorist threat gives way to bloodlust and vengeance after the attacks. Official dissembling justifies wars, then prolongs them. In the name of counterterrorism, security is politicized, savagery legalized, and patriotism weaponized.

It was an emergency, yes, that's understood. But that state of exception became our new American exceptionalism.

It happened fast. By 2004, when the 9/11 Commission urged America to "engage the struggle of ideas," it was already too late; the Justice Department's initial torture memos were already signed, the Abu Ghraib images had already eviscerated US claims to moral authority. And it has lasted long. The latest works on the legacy of 9/11 show how war-on-terror tactics were turned on religious groups, immigrants, and protesters in the United States. The war on terror came home, and it walked in like it owned the place.

"It is for now far easier for a researcher to explain how and why September 11 happened than it is to explain the aftermath," Steve Coll writes in *Ghost Wars*, his 2004 account of the CIA's pre-9/11 involvement in Afghanistan. Throughout that aftermath, Washington fantasized about remaking the world in its image, only to reveal an ugly image of itself to the world.

The literature of 9/11 also considers Osama bin Laden's varied aspirations for the attacks and his shifting visions of that aftermath. He originally imagined America as weak and easily panicked, retreating from the world—in particular from the Middle East—as soon as its troops began dying. But bin Laden also came to grasp, perhaps self-servingly, the benefits of luring Washington into imperial overreach, of "bleeding America to the point of bankruptcy," as he put it in 2004, through endless military expansionism, thus beating back its global sway and undermining its internal unity. "We anticipate a black future for America," bin Laden told ABC News more than three years before the 9/11 attacks. "Instead of remaining United States, it shall end up separated states and shall have to carry the bodies of its sons back to America."

Bin Laden did not win the war of ideas. But neither did we. To an unnerving degree, the United States moved toward the enemy's fantasies of what it might become—a nation divided in its sense of itself, exposed in its moral and political compromises, conflicted over wars it did not want but would not end. When President George W. Bush addressed the nation from the Oval Office on the evening of September 11, 2001, he asserted that America was attacked because it is "the brightest beacon for freedom and opportunity in the world, and no one will keep that light from shining."

Bush was correct. Al-Qaeda could not dim the promise of America. Only we could do that to ourselves.

"The most frightening aspect of this new threat ... was the fact that almost no one took it seriously. It was too bizarre, too primitive and exotic." That is how Lawrence Wright depicts the early impressions of bin Laden and his terrorist network among US officials in *The Looming Tower: Al-Qaeda and the Road to 9/11*. For a country still basking in its post–Cold War glow, it all seemed so far away, even as al-Qaeda's strikes—on the World Trade Center in 1993, on US embassies in 1998, on the USS *Cole* in 2000—grew bolder. This was American complacency, mixed with denial.

The books traveling that road to 9/11 have an inexorable, almost suffo-cating feel to them, as though every turn invariably leads to the first crush of steel and glass. Their journeys begin at different places. Wright dwells on the influence of Egyptian thinker Sayyid Qutb, whose mid-twentieth-century sojourn in the United States animated his vision of a clash between Islam and modernity, and whose work would inspire future jihadists. In *Ghost Wars*, Coll laments America's abandonment of Afghanistan once it ceased serving as a Cold War proxy battlefield against Moscow. In *The Rise and Fall of Osama bin Laden*, Peter Bergen stresses the moment bin Laden arrived in Afghanistan from Sudan in 1996, when Khalid Sheikh Mohammed first pitched him on the planes plot. And the 9/11 Commission cites bin Laden's declarations of war against the United States, particularly his 1998 fatwa calling it "the individual duty for every Muslim" to murder Americans "in any country in which it is possible."

Yet these early works also make clear that the road to 9/11 featured plenty of billboards warning of the likely destination. A Presidential Daily Brief item on August 6, 2001, titled "Bin Ladin Determined to Strike in US," became infamous in 9/11 lore, yet the commission report notes that it was the thirty-sixth PDB relating to bin Laden or al-Qaeda that year alone. ("All right. You've covered your ass now," Bush reportedly sneered at the briefer.) Both the FBI and the CIA produced classified warnings on terrorist threats in the mid-1990s, Coll writes, including a particularly precise National Intelligence Estimate. "Several targets are especially at risk: national symbols such as the White House and the Capitol, and symbols of U.S. capitalism such as Wall Street," it stated. "We assess that civil aviation will figure prominently among possible terrorist targets in the United States." Some of the admonitions scattered throughout the 9/11 literature are too over-the-top even for a movie script: there's the exasperated State Department official complaining about Defense Department inaction ("Does al Qaeda have to attack the Pentagon to get their attention?"), and the earnest FBI supervisor in Minneapolis warning a skeptical agent in Washington about suspected terrorism activity, insisting that he was "trying to keep someone from taking a plane and crashing it into the World Trade Center."

In these books, everyone is warning everyone else. Bergen emphasizes that a young intelligence analyst in the State Department, Gina Bennett, wrote the first classified memo warning about bin Laden in 1993. Pockets within the FBI and the CIA obsess over bin Laden while regarding one another as rivals. On his way out, President Bill Clinton warns Bush. Outgoing national security adviser Sandy Berger warns his successor, Condoleezza Rice. And White House counterterrorism coordinator Richard Clarke, as he incessantly reminds readers in his 2004 memoir, *Against All Enemies*, warns anyone who will listen and many who will not.

With the system "blinking red," as CIA director George Tenet later told the 9/11 Commission, why were all these warnings not enough? Wright lingers on bureaucratic failings, emphasizing that intelligence collection on al-Qaeda was hampered by the "institutional warfare" between the CIA and the FBI, two agencies that were not on speaking terms. Coll writes that Clinton regarded bin Laden as "an isolated fanatic, flailing dangerously but quixotically against the forces of global progress," whereas the Bush team was fixated on great-power politics, missile defense, and China.

Clarke's conclusion is simple, and it highlights America's we-know-better swagger, a national trait that often masquerades as courage or wisdom. "America, alas, seems only to respond well to disasters, to be undistracted by warnings," he writes. "Our country seems unable to do all that must be done until there has been some awful calamity." *like health care*

The problem with responding only to calamity is that underestimation is usually replaced by overreaction. And we tell ourselves it is the right thing, maybe the only thing, to do. *the catastrophe response*

A last-minute change of flight. A new job at the Pentagon. A retirement from the fire station. The final tilt of a plane's wings before impact. If the books about the lead-up to 9/11 are packed with unbearable inevitability, the volumes on the day itself highlight how randomness separated survival from death. "The ferocity of the attacks meant that innocent people lived or died because they stepped back from a doorway, or hopped onto a closing elevator, or simply shifted their weight from one foot to another," Jim Dwyer and Kevin Flynn write in *102 Minutes*, their narrative of events inside the World Trade Center from the moment the first plane hit through the collapse of both towers. Their detailed reporting on the human saga—such as a police officer asking a fire chaplain to hear his confession as they both flee a collapsing building—is excruciating and riveting at once.

Yet, as much as the people inside, the structures and history of the World Trade Center are key actors, too. They are not just symbols and targets but fully formed and deeply flawed characters in the day's drama.

Had the World Trade Center, built in the late 1960s and early 1970s, been erected according to the city building code in effect since 1938, Dwyer and Flynn explain, "it is likely that a very different world trade center would have been built." Instead, it was constructed according to a new code that the real estate industry had avidly promoted, a code that made it cheaper and more lucrative to build and own skyscrapers. "It increased the floor space available for rent ... by cutting back on the areas that had been devoted, under the earlier law, to evacuation and exit," the authors write. The result: getting everybody out on 9/11 was virtually impossible.

Under the new rules, the Port Authority of New York and New Jersey was able to rent three-quarters of each floor of the World Trade Center, Dwyer and Flynn report, a 21 percent increase over the yield of older skyscrapers. The cost was dear. Some one thousand people inside the North Tower who initially survived the impact of American Airlines Flight 11 could not reach an open staircase. "Their fate was sealed nearly four decades earlier, when the stairways were clustered in the core of the building, and fire stairs were eliminated as a wasteful use of valuable space." (The authors write that "building code reform hardly makes for gripping drama," an aside as modest as it is inaccurate.) The towers embodied the power of American capitalism, but their design embodied the folly of American greed. On that day, both conditions proved fatal.

The assault on the Pentagon, long treated as an undercard to New York's main event, could have yielded even greater devastation, and again the details of the building played a role. In his oral history of 9/11, *The Only Plane in the Sky*, Garrett Graff quotes Defense Department officials marveling at how American Airlines Flight 77 struck a part of the Pentagon that, because of new anti-terrorism standards, had recently been reinforced and renovated. This meant it was not only stronger but, on that morning, also relatively unoccupied. "It was truly a miracle," army branch chief Philip Smith said. "In any other wedge of the Pentagon, there would have been 5,000 people, and the plane would have flown right through the middle of the building." Instead, fewer than two hundred people were killed in the attack on the Pentagon, including the passengers on the hijacked jet. Chance and preparedness came together.

The bravery of police and firefighters is the subject of countless 9/11 retrospectives, but these books also emphasize the selflessness of civilians who morphed into first responders. Port Authority workers Frank De Martini, Pablo Ortiz, Carlos da Costa, and Peter Negron saved at least seventy people in the World Trade Center's North Tower by pulling apart elevator doors, busting walls, and shining flashlights to find survivors, only to not make it out themselves. "With crowbar, flashlight, hardhat, and big mouths, De Martini and Ortiz and their colleagues had pushed back the boundary line between life and death," Dwyer and Flynn write. The authors also note how the double lines of people descending a World Trade Center staircase would automatically blend into single file when word came down that an injured person was behind them. And Graff cites a local assistant fire chief who recalls the "truly heroic" work of civilians and uniformed personnel at the Pentagon that day. "They were the ones who really got their comrades, got their workmates out," he says.

The civilians aboard United Airlines Flight 93, whose resistance forced the plane to crash into a Pennsylvania field rather than the US Capitol, were later lionized as emblems of swashbuckling Americana. But one off-hand detail in the 9/11 Commission report underscores just how American their defiance was. The passengers had made phone calls when the hijacking began and had learned the fate of other aircraft that day. "According to one call, they voted on whether to rush the terrorists in an attempt to retake the plane," the commission report states. "They decided, and acted."

They voted on it. *They voted.* Even in that moment of unfathomable fear and distress, the passengers paused to engage in the great American tradition of popular consultation before deciding to become this new war's earliest soldiers. Was there ever any doubt as to the outcome of that ballot?

Such episodes, led by ordinary civilians, embodied values that the 9/11 Commission called on the nation to display. Except those values would soon be dismantled, in the name of security, by those entrusted to uphold them.

Lawyering to death.

The phrase appears in multiple 9/11 volumes, usually uttered by top officials adamant that they were going to *get things done*, laws and rules be damned. Anti-terrorism efforts were always "lawyered to death" during the Clinton administration, Tenet complains in *Bush at War*, Bob Woodward's 2002 book on the debates among the president and his national security team. In an interview with Woodward, Bush drops the phrase amid the macho-speak—"dead or alive," "bring 'em on," and the like—that became typical of his anti-terrorism rhetoric. "I had to show the American people the resolve of a commander in chief that was going to do whatever it took to

win," Bush explains. "No yielding. No equivocation. No, you know, lawyering this thing to death." In *Against All Enemies*, Clarke recalls the evening
of September 11, when Bush snapped at an official who suggested that international law looked askance at military force as a tool of revenge. "I don't
care what the international lawyers say, we are going to kick some ass," the
president retorted.

The message was unmistakable: the law is an obstacle to effective counterterrorism. Worrying about procedural niceties is passé in a 9/11 world, an
annoying impediment to the essential work of ass-kicking.

Except they did lawyer this thing to death. Instead of disregarding the
law, the Bush administration enlisted it. "Beginning almost immediately
after September 11, 2001, [Vice President Dick] Cheney saw to it that some
of the sharpest and best-trained lawyers in the country, working in secret in
the White House and the United States Department of Justice, came up with
legal justifications for a vast expansion of the government's power in waging
war on terror," Jane Mayer writes in *The Dark Side*, her relentless 2008 com-
pilation of the arguments and machinations of government lawyers after the
attacks. Through public declarations and secret memos, the administration
sought to remove limits on the president's conduct of warfare and to deny
terrorism suspects the protections of the Geneva Conventions by redefining
them as unlawful enemy combatants. Nothing, Mayer argues of the latter
effort, "more directly cleared the way for torture than this."

To comprehend what our government can justify in the name of national
security, consider the torture memos themselves, authored by the Justice Department's Office of Legal Counsel between 2002 and 2005 to green-light
CIA interrogation methods for terrorism suspects. Tactics such as cramped
confinement, sleep deprivation, and waterboarding were rebranded as "enhanced interrogation techniques," legally and linguistically contorted to
avoid the label of torture. Though the techniques could be cruel and inhu-
man, the OLC acknowledged in an August 2002 memo, they would constitute torture only if they produced pain equivalent to organ failure or death,
and if the individual inflicting such pain really *really* meant to do so: "Even
if the defendant knows that severe pain will result from his actions, if causing

such harm is not his objective, he lacks the requisite specific intent." It's quite the sleight of hand, with torture moving from the body of the interrogated to the conscience of the interrogator.

After devoting dozens of pages to the metaphysics of specific intent, the true meaning of "prolonged" mental harm or "imminent" death, and the elasticity of the Convention Against Torture, the memo concludes that none of it actually matters. Even if a particular interrogation method would cross some legal line, the relevant statute would be considered unconstitutional because it "impermissibly encroached" on the commander in chief's authority to conduct warfare. Almost nowhere in these memos does the Justice Department curtail the power of the CIA to do as it pleases.

In fact, the OLC lawyers rely on assurances from the CIA itself to endorse such powers. In a second memo from August 2002, the lawyers ruminate on the use of cramped confinement boxes. "We have no information from the medical experts you have consulted that the limited duration for which the individual is kept in the boxes causes any substantial physical pain," the memo states. Waterboarding likewise gets a pass. "You have informed us that this procedure does not inflict actual physical harm," the memo states. "Based on your research ... you do not anticipate that any prolonged mental harm would result from the use of the waterboard."

You have informed us. Experts you have consulted. Based on your research. You do not anticipate. Such hand-washing words appear throughout the memos. The Justice Department relies on information provided by the CIA to reach its conclusions; the CIA then has the cover of the Justice Department to proceed with its interrogations. It's a perfect circle of trust.

Yet the logic is itself tortured. In a May 2005 memo, the lawyers conclude that because no single technique inflicts "severe" pain amounting to torture, their combined use "would not be expected" to reach that level, either. As though embarrassed at such illogic, the memo attaches a triple-negative footnote: "We are not suggesting that combinations or repetitions of acts that do not individually cause severe physical pain could not result in severe physical pain." Well, then, what exactly are you suggesting? Even when the OLC in 2004 officially withdrew its August 2002 memo following a public outcry and declared torture "abhorrent," the lawyers added a footnote to the new memo assuring that they had reviewed the prior opinions on the treatment of detainees and "do not believe that any of their conclusions would be different under the standards set forth in this memorandum."

In these documents, lawyers enable lawlessness. Another May 2005 memo concludes that, because the Convention Against Torture applies only to actions occurring under US jurisdiction, the CIA's creation of detention sites in other countries renders the convention "inapplicable." Similarly, because the Eighth Amendment's prohibition on cruel and unusual punishment is meant to protect people convicted of crimes, it should not apply to terrorism detainees—because they have not been officially convicted of anything. The lack of due process conveniently eliminates constitutional protections. In his introduction to *The Torture Memos: Rationalizing the Unthinkable*, David Cole describes the documents as "bad-faith lawyering," which might be generous. It is another kind of lawyering to death, one in which the rule of law that the 9/11 Commission urged us to uphold becomes the victim.

Years later, the Senate Intelligence Committee would investigate the CIA's post-9/11 interrogation program. Its massive report—the executive summary of which appeared as a 549-page book in 2014—found that torture did not produce useful intelligence, that the interrogations were more brutal than the CIA let on, that the Justice Department did not independently verify the CIA's information, and that the spy agency impeded oversight by Congress and the CIA inspector general. It explains that the CIA purported to oversee itself and, no surprise, that it deemed its interrogations effective and necessary, no matter the results. (If a detainee provided information, it meant the program worked; if he did not, it meant stricter applications of the techniques were needed; if still no information was forthcoming, the program had succeeded in proving he had none to give.)

"The CIA's effectiveness representations were almost entirely inaccurate," the Senate report concluded. It is one of the few lies of the war on terror unmasked by an official government investigation and public report, but just one of the many documented in the 9/11 literature.

Officials in the war on terror didn't deceive or dissemble just with lawmakers or the public. In the recurring tragedy of war, they lied just as often to themselves.

In *To Start a War: How the Bush Administration Took America into Iraq*, Robert Draper considers the influence of the president's top aides. Deputy Defense Secretary Paul Wolfowitz (long obsessed with ousting Saddam Hussein), Pentagon chief Donald Rumsfeld (eager to test his theories of military transformation) and Cheney (fixated on apocalyptic visions of America's vulnerability) all had their reasons. But Draper identifies a single responsible party: "The decision to invade Iraq was one made, finally and exclusively, by the president of the United States, George W. Bush," he writes.

A president initially concerned about defending and preserving the nation's moral goodness against terrorism found himself driven by darker impulses. "I'm having difficulty controlling my bloodlust," Bush confessed to religious leaders in the Oval Office on September 20, 2001, Draper reports. It was not a one-off comment; in Woodward's *Bush at War*, the president admitted that before 9/11, "I didn't feel that sense of urgency [about al-Qaeda], and my blood was not nearly as boiling."

Bloodlust, moral certainty, and sudden vulnerability make a dangerous combination. The belief that you are defending good against evil can lead to the belief that whatever you do to that end is good, too. Draper distills Bush's worldview: "The terrorists' primary objective was to destroy America's freedom. Saddam hated America. Therefore, he hated freedom. Therefore, Saddam was himself a terrorist, bent on destroying America and its freedom."

Note the asymmetry. The president assumed the worst about what Hussein had done or might do, yet embraced best-case scenarios of how an American invasion would proceed. "Iraqis would rejoice at the sight of their Western liberators," Draper recaps. "Their newly shared sense of national purpose would overcome any sectarian allegiances. Their native cleverness would make up for their inexperience with self-government. They would welcome the stewardship of Iraqi expatriates who had not set foot in Baghdad in decades. And their oil would pay for everything."

There are lies, and then there is self-delusion. The Americans did not have to anticipate the specifics of the civil war that would engulf the country after the invasion; they just had to realize that managing postwar Iraq would never be as simple as they imagined. It did not seem to occur to Bush and his advisers that Iraqis could simultaneously hate Hussein and resent the Americans—feelings that could have been discovered by speaking to Iraqis and hearing their concerns.

Anthony Shadid's *Night Draws Near: Iraq's People in the Shadow of America's War*, published in 2005, is among the few books on the war that gets deep inside Iraqis' aversion to the Americans in their midst. "What gives them the right to change something that's not theirs in the first place?" a woman in a middle-class Baghdad neighborhood asks Shadid. "I don't like your house, so I'm going to bomb it and you can rebuild it again the way I want it, with your money?" In Fallujah, where Shadid hears early talk of the Americans as "kuffar" (heathens), a fifty-one-year-old former teacher complains that "we've exchanged a tyrant for an occupier." The occupation did not dissuade such impressions when it turned the former dictator's seat of government into its own luxurious Green Zone, or when it retrofitted the Abu Ghraib prison ("the worst of Saddam's hellholes," Shadid calls it) into its own chamber of horrors.

Shadid understood that governmental legitimacy—who gets to rule, and by what right—was a matter of overriding importance for Iraqis. "The Americans never understood the question," he writes; "Iraqis never agreed on the answer." It's hard to find a better summation of the trials of Iraq in the aftermath of America's invasion. When the United States so quickly shifted from liberation to occupation, it lost whatever legitimacy it enjoyed. "Bush handed that enemy precisely what it wanted and needed, proof that America was at war with Islam, that we were the new Crusaders come to occupy Muslim land," Clarke writes. "It was as if Usama bin Laden, hidden in some high mountain redoubt, were engaging in long-range mind control of George Bush, chanting 'invade Iraq, you must invade Iraq.'"

The foolishness and arrogance of the American occupation didn't help. In *Imperial Life in the Emerald City: Inside Iraq's Green Zone*, Rajiv Chandrasekaran explains how, even as daily security was Iraqis' overwhelming concern, viceroy L. Paul Bremer, Bush's man in Baghdad, was determined to turn the country into a model free-market economy, complete with new investment laws, bankruptcy courts, and a state-of-the-art stock exchange. In charge of the new exchange was a twenty-four-year-old American with no academic background in economics or finance. The man tasked with remaking Iraq's sprawling university system had no experience in the Middle East—but did have connections to the Rumsfeld and Cheney families. A new traffic law for Iraq was partially cut and pasted from Maryland's motor vehicle code. An antismoking campaign was led by a US official who was a closet smoker. And a US Army general, when asked by local journalists why American helicopters must fly so low at night, thus scaring Iraqi children, replied that the kids were simply hearing "the sound of freedom."

It seems freedom sounds terrifying.

For some Americans, inflicting that terror became part of the job, one more tool in the arsenal. In *The Forever War*, by Dexter Filkins, a US Army lieutenant colonel in Iraq assures the author that "with a heavy dose of fear and violence, and a lot of money for projects, I think we can convince these people that we are here to help them." (Filkins asked him if he really meant it about fear and violence; the officer insisted that he did.) Of course, not all officials were so deluded and so forthright; some knew better but lied to the public. Chandrasekaran recalls the response of a top communications official under Bremer, when reporters asked about waves of violence hitting Baghdad in the spring of 2004. "Off the record: Paris is burning," the official told the journalists. "On the record: Security and stability are returning to Iraq."

In *The Rise and Fall of Osama bin Laden*, Bergen sums up how the Iraq war, conjured in part on the false connections between Iraq and al-Qaeda, ended up helping the terrorist network: it pulled resources from the war in Afghanistan, gave space for bin Laden's men to regroup, and spurred a new generation of terrorists in the Middle East. "A bigger gift to bin Laden was hard to imagine," Bergen writes.

If Iraq was the war born of lies, Afghanistan was the one nurtured by them. Afghanistan was where al-Qaeda, supported by the Taliban, had made its base—it was supposed to be the good war, the right war, the war of necessity and not choice, the war endorsed at home and abroad. "U.S. officials had no need to lie or spin to justify the war," *Washington Post* reporter Craig Whitlock writes in *The Afghanistan Papers*, a book that provides a damning contrast of the war's reality versus its rhetoric. "Yet leaders at the White House, the Pentagon and the State Department soon began to make false assurances and to paper over setbacks on the battlefield." As the years passed, the deceit became entrenched, what Whitlock calls "an unspoken conspiracy" to hide the truth.

Drawing from a "Lessons Learned" project that interviewed hundreds of military and civilian officials involved with Afghanistan, as well as from oral histories, government cables, and reports, Whitlock finds commanding generals privately admitting that they long fought the war "without a functional strategy." That, two years into the conflict, Rumsfeld complained that he had "no visibility into who the bad guys are." That Lt. Gen. Douglas Lute, a former coordinator of Iraq and Afghanistan policy, acknowledged that "we didn't have the foggiest idea of what we were undertaking." That US officials long wanted to withdraw American forces but feared—correctly so, it turns out—that the Afghan government might collapse. "Bin Laden had hoped for this exact scenario," Whitlock observes. "To lure the U.S. superpower into an unwinnable guerrilla conflict that would deplete its national treasury and diminish its global influence."

All along, top officials publicly contradicted these internal views, issuing favorable accounts of steady progress. Bad news was twisted into good: Rising suicide attacks in Kabul meant the Taliban was too weak for direct combat, for instance, while increased US casualties meant America was taking the fight to the enemy. The skills and size of the Afghan security forces were frequently exaggerated; by the end of President Barack Obama's second term, US officials concluded that some thirty thousand Afghan soldiers on the payroll didn't actually exist; they were paper creations of local commanders who pocketed the fake soldiers' salaries at US taxpayer expense. American officials publicly lamented large-scale corruption in Afghanistan but enabled that corruption in practice, pouring massive contracts and projects into a country ill-equipped to absorb them. Such deceptions transpired across US presidents, but the Obama administration, eager to show that its first-term troop surge was working, "took it to a new level, hyping figures that were misleading, spurious or downright false," Whitlock writes. And then under President Donald Trump, he adds, the generals felt pressure to "speak more forcefully and boast that his war strategy was destined to succeed."

Long before President Biden declared the end of the war in Afghanistan in the summer of 2021, the United States twice made similar pronouncements, proclaiming the conclusion of combat operations in 2003 and again in 2014—yet still the war endured. It did so in part because "in public, almost no senior government officials had the courage to admit that the United States was slowly losing," Whitlock writes. "With their complicit silence, military and political leaders avoided accountability and dodged reappraisals that could have changed the outcome or shortened the conflict."

It's not like nobody warned them. In *Bush at War*, Woodward reports that CIA Counterterrorism Center director Cofer Black and Deputy Secretary of State Richard Armitage traveled to Moscow shortly after 9/11 to give officials a heads-up about the coming hostilities in Afghanistan. The Russians, recent mourners at the graveyard of empires, cautioned that Afghanistan was an "ambush heaven" and that, in the words of one of them, "you're really going to get the hell kicked out of you." Cofer responded confidently: "We're going to kill them. . . . We're going to rock their world."

Now, with US forces gone and the Taliban having reclaimed power in Afghanistan, Washington is wrestling with the legacy of the nation's longest war. Why and how did America lose? Should we have stayed longer? Was it worth its price in blood and billions? How does the United States repay the courage of Afghans who worked alongside US military and civilian authorities? What if Afghanistan again becomes a haven for terrorists attacking US interests and allies, as the airport suicide bombing in Kabul that killed thirteen US service members last month may signal? Biden asserted that "the war in Afghanistan is now over" but has pledged to continue the fight against terrorists there—so what are the limits and the means of future US military and intelligence action in the country?

These are essential debates, but a war should not be measured only by the timing and the competence of its end. We still face an equally consequential appraisal: How good was this good war if it could be sustained only by lies?

In the two decades since the 9/11 attacks, the United States has often attempted to reconsider its response. Take two documents from late 2006: the report from the Iraq Study Group, co-chaired by James A. Baker III and Lee H. Hamilton, which argued that Washington needed to radically rethink its diplomatic and political strategy for Iraq; and *The U.S. Army/Marine Corps Counterinsurgency Field Manual*, written by a team led by Lt. Gen. David H. Petraeus, which argued that US officials needed to radically rethink military tactics for insurgency wars of the kind it faced in Iraq and Afghanistan.

They are written as though intending to solve problems. But they can be read as proof that the problems have no realistic solution, or that the only solution is to never have created them.

"There is no magic formula to solve the problems of Iraq," the ISG report begins, yet its proposed fixes would have required plenty of fairy dust. The report calls for a "diplomatic offensive" to gain international support for Iraq, to persuade Iran and Syria to respect Iraq's territory and sovereignty, and to commit to "a comprehensive Arab-Israeli peace on all fronts." Simple! Iraq, meanwhile, needed to make progress on national reconciliation (in a country already awash in sectarian bloodletting), boost domestic security (even though the report deems the Iraqi army a mess and the Iraqi police worse), and deliver social services (even as the report concludes that the government was failing to adequately provide electricity, drinking water, sewage services, and education).

The recommendations seem written in the knowledge that they will never happen. "Miracles cannot be expected," the report states—twice. Absent divine intervention, the next step is obvious. If the Iraqi government can't demonstrate "substantial progress" toward its goals, the report asserts, "the United States should reduce its political, military, or economic support" for Iraq. Indeed, the report sets the bar for staying so high that leaving appears to be its primary purpose.

The counterinsurgency manual is an extraordinary document. Implicitly repudiating notions such as "shock and awe" and "overwhelming force," it argues that the key to battling insurgencies in countries such as Iraq and Afghanistan is to provide security for the local population and to win its support through effective governance. It also attempts to grasp the nature of America's foes. "Most enemies either do not try to defeat the United States with conventional operations or do not limit themselves to purely military means," the manual states. "They know that they cannot compete with U.S. forces on those terms. Instead, they try to exhaust U.S. national will." Exhausting America's will is an objective that al-Qaeda understood well.

"Soldiers and Marines are expected to be nation builders as well as warriors," the manual proclaims, but the arduous tasks involved—reestablishing government institutions, rebuilding infrastructure, strengthening local security forces, enforcing the rule of law—reveal the tension at the heart of the new doctrine. "Counterinsurgents should prepare for a long-term commitment," the manual states. Yet, just a few pages later, it admits that "eventually all foreign armies are seen as interlopers or occupiers." How to accomplish the former without descending into the latter? No wonder so many of the historical examples of counterinsurgency that the manual highlights, including accounts from the Vietnam War, are stories of failure.

The manual seems aware of its importance. The 2007 edition contains a foreword, followed by an introduction, then another foreword, a preface, then some brief acknowledgments and finally one more introduction. But the throat-clearing is clarifying. In his foreword, US Army Lt. Col. John Nagl writes that the document's most lasting impact may be as a catalyst not for remaking Iraq or Afghanistan, but for transforming the army and Marine Corps into "more effective learning organizations," better able to adapt to changing warfare. And in her introduction, Sarah Sewall, then director of Harvard's Carr Center for Human Rights Policy, concludes that its "ultimate value" may be in warning civilian officials to think hard before engaging in a counterinsurgency campaign.

At best, then, the manual helps us rethink future conflicts—how we fight and whether we should. It's no coincidence that Biden, in recent remarks defending the decision to withdraw American troops from Afghanistan, specifically repudiated counterinsurgency as an objective of US policy. "I've argued for many years that our mission should be narrowly focused on counterterrorism, not counterinsurgency or nation-building," the president affirmed. Even the longest war was not long enough for a counterinsurgency effort to succeed.

In *The Good Soldiers* (2009), David Finkel chronicles the experiences of an army battalion deployed in Iraq during the US troop surge in 2007 and 2008, a period of the war ostensibly informed by the new counterinsurgency doctrine. In his 2013 sequel, *Thank You for Your Service*, the author witnesses these men when they come home and try to make sense of their military experience and adapt to their new lives. "The thing that got to everyone," Finkel explains in the latter book, "was not having a defined front line. It was a war in 360 degrees, no front to advance toward, no enemy in uniform, no predictable patterns, no relief." It's a powerful summation of battling an insurgency.

Adam Schumann returns from war because of post-traumatic stress disorder and traumatic brain injury, "the result of a mortar round that dropped without warning out of a blue sky," Finkel explains. Schumann suffers from nightmares, headaches, and guilt; he wishes he needed bandages or crutches, anything to visibly justify his absence from the front. His wife endures his treatments, his anger, his ambivalence toward life. "He's still a good guy," she decides. "He's just a broken good guy." Another returning soldier, Nic DeNinno, struggles to tell his wife about the time he and his fellow soldiers burst into an Iraqi home in search of a high-value target. He threw a man down the stairs and held another by the throat. After they left, the lieutenant told him it was the wrong house. "The wrong f—ing house," Nic says to his wife. "One of the things I want to remember is how many times we hit the wrong house."

Hitting the wrong house is what counterinsurgency doctrine is supposed to avoid. Even successfully capturing or killing a high-value target can be counterproductive if in the process you terrorize a community and create more enemies. All of Iraq was the wrong house. America's leaders knew it was the wrong house. They hit it anyway.

In the eleventh chapter of the 9/11 Commission report, just before all the recommendations for reforms in domestic and foreign policy, the authors get philosophical, pondering how hindsight had affected their views of September 11. "As time passes, more documents become available, and the bare facts of what happened become still clearer," the report states. "Yet the picture of *how* those things happened becomes harder to reimagine, as that past world, with its preoccupations and uncertainty, recedes." Before making definitive judgments, then, they ask themselves "whether the insights that seem apparent now would really have been meaningful at the time."

It's a commendable attitude, one that helps readers understand what the attacks felt like in real time and why authorities responded as they did. But that approach also keeps the day trapped in the past, safely distant. Two of the latest additions to the canon, *Reign of Terror* by Spencer Ackerman and *Subtle Tools* by Karen Greenberg, draw straight, stark lines between the earliest days of the war on terror and its mutations in our current time, between conflicts abroad and divisions at home. These works show how 9/11 remains with us, and how we are still living in the ruins.

When Trump declared that "we don't have victories anymore" in his 2015 speech announcing his presidential candidacy, he was both belittling the legacy of 9/11 and harnessing it to his ends. "His great insight was that the jingoistic politics of the War on Terror did not have to be tied to the War on Terror itself," Ackerman writes. "That enabled him to tell a tale of lost greatness." And if greatness is lost, someone must have taken it. The backlash against Muslims, against immigrants crossing the southern border, and against protesters rallying for racial justice was strengthened by the open-ended nature of the global war on terror. In Ackerman's vivid telling—his prose can be hyperbolic, even if his arguments are not—the war is not just far away in Iraq or Afghanistan, in Yemen or Syria, but it's happening here, with mass surveillance, militarized law enforcement, and the rebranding of immigration as a threat to the nation's security rather than a cornerstone of its identity. "Trump had learned the foremost lesson of 9/11," Ackerman writes, "that the terrorists were whomever you said they were."

Both Ackerman and Greenberg point to the Authorization for Use of Military Force, drafted by administration lawyers and approved by Congress just days after the attacks, as the moment when America's response began to go awry. The brief joint resolution allowed the president to use "all necessary and appropriate force" against any nation, organization, or person who committed the attacks, and to prevent any future ones. It was the "Ur document in the war on terror and its legacy," Greenberg writes. "Riddled with imprecision, its terminology was geared to codify expansive powers." Where the battlefield, the enemy, and the definition of victory all remain vague, war becomes endlessly expansive, too, "with neither temporal nor geographical boundaries."

This was the moment the war on terror was "conceptually doomed," Ackerman concludes. This is how you get a forever war.

There were moments when an off-ramp seemed visible. The killing of bin Laden in 2011 was one such instance, Ackerman argues, but "Obama squandered the best chance anyone could ever have to end the 9/11 era." The author assails Obama for making the war on terror more "sustainable" through a veneer of legality—banning torture yet failing to close the detention camp at Guantánamo Bay and relying on drone strikes that "perversely incentivized the military and the CIA to kill instead of capture." There would always be more targets, more battlefields, regardless of president or party. Failures became the reason to double down, never wind down.

The longer the war went on, the more that what Ackerman calls its "grotesque subtext" of nativism and racism would move to the foreground of American politics. Absent the war on terror, it is harder to imagine a presidential candidate decrying a sitting commander in chief as foreign, Muslim, illegitimate—and using that lie as a successful political platform. Absent the war on terror, it is harder to imagine a travel ban against people from Muslim-majority countries.

Absent the war on terror, it is harder to imagine American protesters labeled terrorists, or a secretary of defense describing the nation's urban streets as a "battle space" to be dominated. Trump was a disruptive force in American life, but there was much continuity there, too. "A vastly different America has taken root" in the two decades since 9/11, Greenberg writes. "In the name of retaliation, 'justice,' and prevention, fundamental values have been cast aside."

In his latest book on bin Laden, Bergen argues that 9/11 was a major tactical success but a long-term strategic failure for the terrorist leader. Yes, he struck a vicious blow against "the head of the snake," as he called the United States, but "rather than ending American influence in the Muslim world, the 9/11 attacks greatly amplified it," with two lengthy, large-scale invasions and new bases established throughout the region.

Yet the legacy of the 9/11 era is found not just in Afghanistan or Iraq but also in an America that drew out and heightened some of its ugliest impulses—a nation that is deeply divided (like those "separated states" bin Laden imagined); that bypasses inconvenient facts and embraces conspiracy theories; that demonizes outsiders; and that, after failing to spread freedom and democracy around the world, seems less inclined to uphold them here. More Americans today are concerned about domestic extremism than foreign terrorism, and on January 6, 2021, our own citizens assaulted the same Capitol building that al-Qaeda had hoped to strike on September 11, 2001. Seventeen years after the 9/11 Commission called on the United States to offer moral leadership to the world and to be generous and caring to our neighbors, our moral leadership is in question, and we can barely be generous and caring to ourselves.

In *The Forever War*, Dexter Filkins describes a nation in which "something had broken fundamentally after so many years of war ... there had been some kind of primal dislocation between cause and effect, a numbness wholly understandable, necessary even, given the pain." He was writing of Afghanistan, but his words could double as an interpretation of the United States over the past two decades. Still reeling from an attack that dropped out of a blue sky, America is suffering from a sort of post-traumatic stress democracy. It remains in recovery, still a good country, even if a broken good country.

September 2021

THE CAUTIONARY TALE OF
H. R. MCMASTER

IT'S A BRUTAL VERDICT ON the failings so evident in the president and his top advisers: "arrogance, weakness, lying in the pursuit of self-interest, and, above all, the abdication of responsibility to the American people."

That is the judgment of Lt. Gen. H. R. McMaster, national security adviser to President Trump. But McMaster is not describing Trump; he is portraying President Lyndon B. Johnson, Defense Secretary Robert McNamara, and the members of the Joint Chiefs of Staff in the mid-1960s. In *Dereliction of Duty*, published in 1997, McMaster explains how a culture of deceit and deference, of divided and misguided loyalties, of policy overrun by politics, resulted in an ever-deeper US involvement in Vietnam—a war, McMaster writes, that "led Americans to question the integrity of their government as never before."

Twenty years ago, McMaster authored a cautionary tale. Today, he risks becoming one.

McMaster is one of the few credible voices remaining in a White House that is once again making Americans question the integrity of their government. Even before the Justice Department appointed a special counsel to investigate possible ties between Russian officials and the 2016 Trump campaign, McMaster was defending the increasingly indefensible behavior of the president, such as Trump's off-the-cuff disclosure of classified intelligence to senior Russian officials in an Oval Office meeting. The general publicly described the president's actions as "wholly appropriate" (resorting to the phrase nine times in a single appearance), attacked the reporting on Trump by rebutting allegations that had not been made, and reminded reporters that he was "in the room" when Trump met with Russia's ambassador and foreign minister. Message: if you don't trust the president, you can still trust me.

In *Dereliction of Duty*, which grew out of the author's doctoral dissertation in history, McMaster accuses the Joint Chiefs of Staff who served Johnson of failing to provide the president and Congress with honest advice on national security and insufficiently challenging the administration's flawed strategy in Vietnam. Profiles and news stories about McMaster invariably cite the book as proof that he grasps the importance of telling the president things he may not want to hear. But even more than his views on the Joint Chiefs—whom he depicts as torn by interservice rivalries and deliberately marginalized from key policy debates by Johnson and McNamara—it is McMaster's views on Johnson that feel most relevant when reading the book today.

McMaster displays nothing but disdain for LBJ, for reasons that echo. He was a president with a "real propensity for lying," McMaster writes, obsessed with loyalty, focused on his political fortunes at the expense of the nation's needs, paranoid about dissent and leaks, and willing to consume the credibility of decorated military officers to cover for his duplicity. Those around him, however well intentioned, became complicit or compromised, manipulators or manipulated. The Johnson White House found itself sinking in "a quicksand of lies" about the war's strategy, troop levels, and costs, McMaster writes, posing a dilemma for Johnson's military advisers. "The president was lying, and he expected the Chiefs to lie as well or, at least, to withhold the whole truth," McMaster explains. "Although the president should not have placed the Chiefs in that position, the flag officers should not have tolerated it when he had."

But how exactly do you not tolerate a president who lies and expects you to back him up? By challenging him and jeopardizing your job? By going public with your disagreements? Or are you the good soldier, staying and hoping to quietly exert some positive influence over a commander in chief and administration that need your help as much as your reputation?

This is a matter of individual conscience, both for Johnson's advisers four decades ago and Trump's today. What is clear, however, is that in his book McMaster displays contempt and disappointment toward those who do not speak clearly and honestly, whether in public or in direct conversations with the president and lawmakers. He derides the Joint Chiefs of Staff as "five silent men" for not revealing to Congress what they truly thought about McNamara's Vietnam strategy and Johnson's tendency to guide national security policies according to electoral and domestic priorities. (The Marine Corps commandant, Gen. Wallace Greene, is one of the few leaders McMaster praises, because he finally told Johnson that he believed it would take five hundred thousand troops and five years to win in Vietnam—even if he was largely ignored.) And McMaster is particularly damning regarding Gen. Earle Wheeler, chairman of the Joint Chiefs from 1964 to 1970, whom the president "used" on several occasions to "lend uniformed credibility to his decisions."

McMaster highlights congressional hearings in August 1964, shortly after the Gulf of Tonkin incident, in which Wheeler appeared alongside McNamara as a sort of administration prop, while the defense secretary was less than forthcoming in his description of Johnson's Vietnam policies. "Although Wheeler did not make any false statements to the senators or congressmen, by not revealing the truth he showed the president that he would go along with his and McNamara's attempts to mislead Congress and the American people," McMaster writes. "Sitting silently next to McNamara, Wheeler, dressed in his uniform, the light from the Capitol's crystal chandeliers reflecting off his brass insignia, lent indispensable credibility to his defense secretary's remarks."

Trump, we know, likes to surround himself with generals, perhaps for the macho vibe or because he hopes some additional respect will rub off on him. He appointed Marine Gen. Jim Mattis to run the Pentagon and Marine Gen. John F. Kelly to lead the Department of Homeland Security, while McMaster replaced yet another general, the oft-investigated Michael Flynn, as national security adviser. In his book, McMaster recounts how often the Johnson administration would stage presidential photo ops with generals to create a veneer of consultation and would trot out the brass to defend positions they had neither formulated nor supported.

"Above all President Johnson needed reassurance," McMaster writes. "He wanted advisers who would tell him what he wanted to hear, who would find solutions even if there were none to be found. Bearers of bad news or those who expressed views that ran counter to his priorities would hold little sway." When Vice President Hubert Humphrey expressed concern about the escalation of US forces in Vietnam, "Johnson responded by excluding Humphrey from future deliberations" over the war, McMaster explains, and Johnson's other advisers reached "the paradoxical conclusion that to protect their influence with the president, they had to spare him their most deeply held doubts." It became influence without purpose.

Gen. Harold Johnson, the army chief of staff at the time, "did not resign, resist, or object" to the president's policies, despite his personal misgivings, McMaster writes with clear disapproval. Gen. Johnson later explained his rationale: "What should my role have been? I'm a dumb soldier under civilian control. ... I could resign, and what am I? I'm a disgruntled general for 48 hours and then I'm out of sight. Right?" Better to stay in office, he concluded, and "try and fight and get the best posture that we can."

He came to regret the choice, McMaster writes. "Harold Johnson's inaction haunted him for the rest of his life."

When Trump announced McMaster as his new national security adviser at a brief Mar-a-Lago event on February 20, the general, in full uniform, chose his words carefully. "I'd just like to say what a privilege it is to be able to continue serving our nation," he said. "I'm grateful to you for that opportunity, and I look forward to joining the national security team and doing everything I can to advance and protect the interests of the American people."

Note his phrasing. Serving the nation, joining the team, protecting the interests of the people. McMaster was keeping his distance from Trump, even as he entered the most inner of circles. And he established his independence on some matters, such as nudging White House strategist Stephen K. Bannon out of the National Security Council and encouraging Trump, though not quite successfully, to cut back his references to "radical Islamic terrorism."

But with his strident and unconvincing defense of Trump's inadvertent intelligence disclosures to the Russians, McMaster put his own reputation and credibility at risk. Some observers are now referring to McMaster as

Trump's "shield." It is the same word McMaster used to describe Wheeler's relationship to President Johnson, and he did not mean it as a compliment. "Although his influence as a military adviser was low," McMaster writes, "Wheeler had become a valuable 'shield' to protect the administration from attacks on its decisions regarding Vietnam."

This book makes clear that McMaster has the analytical skills, and not just the war-fighting experience, to serve as national security adviser in times of military and foreign policy crises. It is a shame that he is doing so for a White House in which so many of the threats are internal and the wounds self-inflicted, and in which the main weapon McMaster must wield is his credibility. I can imagine a future officer-scholar writing a dissertation about the dilemmas faced by McMaster and the other generals, both active-duty and retired, serving in the Trump administration. Will they be deemed heroes or warnings?

They could be both. Working for this president might mean not the dereliction of duty, but the duty of dereliction.

May 2017

HOW TO READ VLADIMIR PUTIN

THE MOMENT IS ETCHED IN the lore of Vladimir Putin: the Berlin Wall had just succumbed to hammers, chisels, and history, and a KGB officer still shy of forty and stationed in Dresden, East Germany, was in a panic, burning documents and requesting military support as a crowd approached. "We cannot do anything without orders from Moscow," Putin was told on the phone. "And Moscow is silent." In an interview that appears in his 2000 book, *First Person*, Putin recalls that dreadful silence. "I got the feeling then that the country no longer existed," he said. "That it had disappeared." Two years after the wall came down, the Union of Soviet Socialist Republics did, too. A decade after, Putin would ascend to power in Russia, talking about a revival.

The death of the Soviet Union, and Putin's autopsy of the corpse, helps explain why he has risked a European conflict—and a confrontation with Washington—by launching a brutal assault on Ukraine. The USSR, he continued in that interview more than two decades ago, collapsed because it was suffering "a paralysis of power." If the phrase sounds familiar, that's because Putin repeated it in a defiant speech justifying his new war. The demise of the USSR, Putin stated on February 24, "has shown us that the paralysis of power . . . is the first step toward complete degradation and oblivion." The end of the Cold War, in his view, was not a matter of ideology or economics but of attitude and will. The Soviets blinked, and the Americans seized the opportunity. "We lost confidence for only one moment, but it was enough to disrupt the balance of forces in the world," Putin declared. So much of what has followed—the unipolar era of US supremacy that Putin reviles, the expansion of NATO he decries, the diminishment of Russia he rejects and the restoration he seeks—only affirms his fixation on that moment.

"What Putin Really Wants" is a perennial topic for cable news debates and big-think magazine covers; the invasion of Ukraine has prompted questions about the Russian leader's mental health and pandemic-era isolation.

But his motives can also be gleaned in part from his book and his frequent essays and major speeches, all seething with resentment, propaganda, and self-justification. In light of these writings, Russia's attack on Ukraine seems less about reuniting two countries that Putin considers "a single whole," as he put it in a lengthy essay last year, than about challenging the United States and its NATO minions, those cocky, illegitimate winners of the Cold War. "Where did this insolent manner of talking down from the height of their exceptionalism, infallibility, and all-permissiveness come from?" Putin demanded during his declaration of war. A world with one dominant superpower is "unacceptable," he has stated, and he constantly warns that this imbalance—exemplified in NATO's expansion—threatens Russia's existence. "For our country, it is a matter of life and death," he contends.

In *First Person*, a collection of interviews with Putin and various relatives and associates, he brags that he received top grades in high school, except for one subject. "I had gotten a B in composition," he admits. If so, the teacher got it about right. His writing elsewhere veers from straightforward to over-wrought, from reflective to overwhelmingly self-serving. Even so, these compositions serve as memos dictated for the archives of history: Putin's attempts to strike a posture of perpetual defiance, to articulate a Russian exceptionalism immune from rules and norms. They portray a leader intent on redressing a perceived historical wrong inflicted on his country and himself, and a man convinced that Moscow must never fall silent again.

In late 1999, Putin, then prime minister, issued a long essay, "Russia at the Turn of the Millennium," lamenting his country's deteriorating international standing. He blames Russia's economic decline of the 1990s on the "historic futility" of Soviet-era communism and on "schemes taken from foreign text-books," a dig at the Western consultants who had parachuted in carrying market models and bullet-point reforms. With weak infrastructure, low foreign investment, and lousy health indicators, Putin writes, Russia faced the real possibility of "sliding to the second, and possibly even third, echelon of world states."

Nonetheless, Putin is adamant that the nation could be glorious once again, that "it is too early to bury Russia as a great power." The answer is not a return to Communist Party values—they were "a road to a blind alley"—but a long-term strategy for economic development and moral, even spiritual, renewal. The details are hazy, but for one: "Russia needs a strong state power and must have it," he declares. Putin couches that requirement in almost mystical terms. "From the very beginning, Russia was created as a supercentralized state," he later explains in his book. "That's practically laid down in its genetic code, its traditions, and the mentality of its people."

The 1999 manifesto, published shortly before Boris Yeltsin resigned the presidency and handed power to Putin, is more grandiose than grand; Putin even considers Russia's restoration among the "signal events" of the new millennium and the anniversary of Christendom. But when he argues that "responsible socio-political forces" should build the strategy for Russian renewal, it is pretty obvious whom Putin has in mind. In *First Person*, he ponders his "historical mission," praises the stability of monarchies, and considers the possibility of amending the constitution to lengthen presidential terms. "Maybe four years is enough time to get things done," he says. "But four years is a short term." A colleague quoted in *First Person* who worked with Putin in the St. Petersburg mayor's office in the early 1990s recalls how, rather than hang the standard portrait of Yeltsin in his office, Putin chose an image of Peter the Great. Russia's glory is his goal, but Putin's own power is always the convenient means.

Standing in the way of that greatness and power, Putin has long concluded, is the United States. Despite an early conciliatory tone—"We value our relations with the United States and care about Americans' perception of us," Putin wrote in a November 1999 op-ed justifying Moscow's crackdown against Chechen separatists, and after 9/11 he was among the first heads of state to offer Washington support—any pretense of rapprochement soon dissipated into antagonism. In 2007, Putin addressed an international security conference in Munich and, informing the audience that he would "avoid excessive politeness," launched into a diatribe against the US-led post–Cold War system.

"What is a unipolar world?" he asked. "It is a world in which there is one master, one sovereign." He called this model not only "unacceptable" but "impossible," and criticized Washington, mired in Iraq and Afghanistan, for having "overstepped its national borders in every way." Putin assailed the NATO alliance for arraying its "frontline forces" on Russia's borders, calling that a "serious provocation." He complained that NATO and the European Union sought to supplant the United Nations (where, conveniently, Russia enjoys a Security Council veto), and that Western lectures on freedom were hypocritical cover for self-serving security policies. "Russia—we—are constantly being taught about democracy," he said. "But for some reason those who teach us do not want to learn themselves."

Moscow did not have to accept this imbalance of power, he argued: "Russia is a country with a history that spans more than a thousand years and has practically always used the privilege to carry out an independent foreign policy." The invasion of Ukraine has supposedly proved his desire to upend and remake the international order, but Putin declared those intentions, publicly and clearly, long ago.

In July 2021, Putin published an essay titled "On the Historical Unity of Russians and Ukrainians." The two nations are really one people sharing a faith, culture, and language, he asserts, and "modern Ukraine" is little more than a creation of the Soviet era. As always, he calls out nefarious foreign efforts to undermine this shared heritage, but he also laments how the Soviet Union, at its inception, mistakenly granted individual Soviet republics the right to secede. This "time bomb," he writes, went off at the end of the Cold War, and the former Soviet satellite states "found themselves abroad overnight, taken away . . . from their historical motherland."

In *Mr. Putin: Operative in the Kremlin* (2013), Fiona Hill and Clifford G. Gaddy write that Putin often deploys "useful history"—that he manipulates collective memory for personal and political goals, as a means to "cloak himself and the Russian state with an additional mantle of legitimacy." In the justifications for invading Ukraine, useful history is busy at work. As Putin tells it, it's not an invasion but a reunification; it's not a violation of international law but the return of lawful possessions that were wrested away when the Cold War ended.

There is an unsubtle progression to Putin's historical interpretations. In July, the Russian president wrote that "true sovereignty of Ukraine is possible only in partnership with Russia," which is, to say the least, a peculiar definition of sovereignty. In a speech on February 21, he went further, asserting that Ukraine "actually never had stable traditions of real statehood." Three days later, with the invasion seeming inevitable, the threat was reversed; Ukraine didn't need Russian assistance to survive, but it and its Western allies posed an existential threat to Russian survival, "to the very existence of our state and to its sovereignty."

Putin incessantly denounces the US or NATO interventions of the post–Cold War world—particularly in the Balkans, Libya, Iraq, and Syria—as intolerable aggressions. In a 2013 *New York Times* op-ed, he warned against a US strike on Syria, urging deference to the United Nations. "Under current international law, force is permitted only in self-defense, or by the decision of the Security Council," he wrote. No wonder that, when deploying force himself, from Chechnya at the turn of the century to Ukraine today, Putin reliably invokes national self-defense. "The current events have nothing to do with a desire to infringe on the interests of Ukraine and the Ukrainian people," he stated on February 24. "They are connected with defending Russia from those who have taken Ukraine hostage." The formula is simple: when you swing it, it's a sword; when I swing it, it's a shield.

Putin relies on standard populist rhetoric to justify his attack on Ukraine—corrupt Ukrainian elites, beholden to foreign influences, are looting the country and turning the people against their Russian brethren, he claims—and he blithely combines World War II–era threats (Nazis overrunning Ukraine) with those of the Cold War (Ukraine acquiring nukes). Talk about useful history. But his speeches on the eve of invasion made his underlying preoccupation clear, with Putin expending enormous time and vitriol on the United States. He sneered at the "low cultural standards" and "feeling of absolute superiority" of post–Cold War America, while emphasizing the "empire of lies" in contemporary US politics. In particular, he reminded the world that the United States employed "the pretext of allegedly reliable information" about weapons of mass destruction to invade Iraq. He did so even while warning that Ukraine, as a puppet regime of the West, might deploy WMDs (which it agreed to give up in 1994 in exchange for protection from Russian invasion) against Russia. "Acquiring tactical nuclear weapons will be much easier for Ukraine than for some other states I am not going to mention here," he declared. "We cannot but react to this real danger." It's not his only American echo. Putin sounds downright Trumpy when warning that Russia will respond to any foreign interference in Ukraine, "and the consequences will be such as you have never seen in your entire history."

It's almost like, while invading Ukraine, he's trolling Washington— because both are his targets.

Of course, the writings of a former KGB officer should not be taken at face value; the purpose is to obscure as much as to reveal, the content is propaganda more than truth. Putin is a terrible communicator to begin with; according to *First Person*, his KGB instructors found him withdrawn and tight-lipped, and even his former wife understood him so poorly that, when he was proposing marriage, she thought he was breaking things off. But as with all political writing, propaganda is enlightening because it reveals something about how its purveyors wish to be perceived. Read in wartime, Putin's accounts offer glimpses of the fighter he hopes the world will see in him, and the one he imagines himself to be.

Putin shares two stories in *First Person* that depict him as a risk-taker. He tells his interviewer that when he attended the KGB's intelligence school, a supervisor noted his "lowered sense of danger" in one of his evaluations. "That was considered a very serious flaw," Putin recalls. "You have to be pumped up in critical situations in order to react well. Fear is like pain. It's an indicator. . . . I had to work on my sense of danger for a long time." Message: he does not fear risk as ordinary people do.

He also recounts a time he was driving a car with a judo coach during his university days and saw a truck loaded with hay coming in the other direction. Putin reached out his window to grab some hay as he drove past, and he accidentally veered off course. "I turned the wheel sharply in the other direction," Putin says, "and my rickety Zaporozhets went up on two wheels." Somehow, they landed safely rather than crashing into a ditch. Only when they reached their destination did his astonished coach finally speak. "You take risks," he said, and walked away. "What drew me to that truck?" Putin later wonders. "It must have been the sweet smell of the hay." Message: Putin takes what he wants, regardless of the dangers to himself or others.

Yet a third story in *First Person*, from Putin's childhood, places him in a less daring light. There were rats in the apartment building where his family lived, and Putin and his friends would chase them with sticks. One day, he spotted a large rat and trapped it in a corner—but then it suddenly turned and jumped toward him. "I was surprised and frightened," Putin recalls. "Now the rat was chasing me. It jumped across the landing and down the stairs. Luckily, I was a little faster and I managed to slam the door shut in its nose." What's the message here? That when Putin thinks he's beaten a weaker foe, all it takes is his rival lashing out to get him to run away?

It's an easy and tempting analogy. The apparent renewed unity of the transatlantic alliance against Putin's assault on Ukraine, and the early resistance of Ukrainian forces and politicians, would seem to serve as a deterrent to a wider, longer war. But with Putin, it could just as well prompt further escalation. "If you become jittery, they will think that they are stronger," he states in *First Person*, describing his attitude toward Russia's enemies. "Only one thing works in such circumstances—to go on the offensive. You must hit first, and hit so hard that your opponent will not rise to his feet."

For Putin, power must not be paralyzed. It must be wielded.

March 2022

LIBERALS VERSUS
AUTHORITARIANS

WHEN WARRING CULTURES AND DISTANT poles are the metaphors for our politics, genteel calls for moderation may seem quaint. When authoritarian impulses are ascendant, wishing for self-restraint can feel foolish, a denial of reality and an abdication of responsibility.

But what if moderation and restraint—the acceptance of limits in political life—are not just the right thing, but really all that is left to try?

"We are now in the midst of the most sustained global assault on liberal democratic values since the 1930s," Gideon Rachman writes in *The Age of the Strongman*, his survey of illiberal political leaders in countries such as Brazil, China, Hungary, Russia, Turkey, and the United States. It is not exactly a novel account—the death-of-democracy bookshelf is quite crowded—and it covers the greatest hits of aspiring autocrats: the cult of personality, the us-versus-them populism, the disdain for law, the manipulation of racial and xenophobic resentments. It is most intriguing, perhaps, for placing one country, and one leader, virtually alone on the other side of the fight. "A crucial question for the Biden era," Rachman writes, "is whether the new president will be able to restore the prestige of the American liberal democratic model—and so halt the global march of strongman politics."

The question becomes even more crucial when that restoration must take effect within the United States as well as beyond it, when liberalism, the doctrine that limits the powers of government and upholds the rights of individuals, is under assault not just by competing ideologies but by those long living under its protection. In *Liberalism and Its Discontents*, Francis Fukuyama restates the case for liberalism even as he considers its critics on the nationalist right, who despise its cultural and secularist manifestations, and on the progressive left, who abhor its economic inequalities and its privileging of individual over group identities. "The answer to these discontents is not to abandon liberalism as such," Fukuyama argues, "but to moderate it."

It is a tricky thing to march into battle under a banner of moderation, to make impassioned pleas on behalf of dispassion and incrementalism. Fukuyama freely acknowledges the "legitimate criticisms" of liberalism from right and left, but still contends that the benefits flowing from liberal values—reduced violence, enhanced personal autonomy, and economic growth—are worth the price. Besides, he asks, "what superior principle and form of government should replace liberalism?"

The question sounds like a throwback to Fukuyama's end-of-history days, as though the answer is obvious: that there is no superior alternative, that liberal democracy remains the end of our ideological evolution. But authoritarian leaders are choosing their own adventure, standing together "in revolt against the liberal consensus that reigned supreme after 1989," Rachman writes. "Their success is a symptom of our crisis of liberalism."

It should not surprise that these works pose uncomfortable questions and offer dissatisfying answers. That is the way of liberalism, too.

Writers too easily rely on new decades and new centuries as inflections in the historical timeline, but in the case of Rachman's strongman age, it sort of works. "It is all too symbolic," he writes, that Russian president Vladimir Putin took over the office from Boris Yeltsin on New Year's Eve in 1999. In the new century, Putin would become the model for a new generation of authoritarian leaders.

Putin moved to influence, then control, mass media. He assailed Western powers for allegedly stoking revolutionary fervor in the neighborhood. He depicted Russia as not just a country but a civilization and then enhanced the powers of the state—that is, his own power, and his own permanence in office—in its supposed defense. He was not the first to do so, of course, but "for right-wing and nationalist politicians," Rachman writes, "Putin has become something of an icon." The war in Ukraine may erode that status, although Rachman emphasizes that strongmen capitalize on foreign military adventures to strengthen their influence at home.

In *The Age of the Strongman*, authoritarian leaders form a chummy club. Donald Trump's giddy admiration for Putin was evident before, during, and after his presidency. Chinese president Xi Jinping shares Putin's belief that the demise of the Soviet empire was a catastrophe and worries that such a fall could come his way, too. In Trumpian style, Brazilian president Jair Bolsonaro entrusts family members with significant official roles. And, not unlike Rodrigo Duterte, the outgoing president of the Philippines, he aggravates middle-class fears about crime. Poland's Jarosław Kaczyński, leader of the right-wing Law and Justice party and former prime minister, deploys conspiracy theories as freely as Trump does, while Bolsonaro's swearing-in featured Hungary's nationalist president, Viktor Orbán, as a guest of honor. When Fox News host Tucker Carlson takes his show on the road to Hungary and the Conservative Political Action Conference holds a shindig in Budapest, the affinities are too clear to contest.

Why have so many such leaders arisen? Rachman points to the declining life expectancy and increasing poverty in Russia during the 1990s that left the public disenchanted with post-Soviet experiments, boosting the appeal of a leader "who promised to turn back the clock to better days." Similarly, the global financial crisis of 2008 broke the assumption that economic well-being would continue flowing from the liberal model, with its free movement of money, people, and ideas. Authoritarian leaders promised to "get tough" with outsiders and played on worries that the dominant majority would be brushed aside. "It is when economic grievances are linked to broader fears—such as immigration, crime, or national decline—that strongman leaders really come into their own," Rachman explains. They alone can fix it.

Fukuyama layers on a more theoretical explanation. Liberalism, ascendant for so long, went too far, lapsing into a "counterproductive extreme." On the right, it devolved into neoliberalism, whereby "property rights and consumer welfare were worshipped, and all aspects of state action and social solidarity denigrated." On the left, Fukuyama writes, the personal autonomy that liberalism advances "evolved into modern identity politics, versions of which then began to undermine the premises of liberalism itself."

But if liberalism has gone too far, so have its critics, Fukuyama contends. Religious conservative thinkers decry the "moral laxity" of liberalism and flirt with overt authoritarian governance to restore "religiously-rooted" standards of behavior, he writes. Progressive thinkers, meanwhile, have transformed what Fukuyama considers a more valid version of identity politics—extending equality to groups that were historically denied its full benefits—into a new iteration that elevates group rights and experiences over the commonalities binding a people, and a nation, together.

It is one thing to critique liberalism for failing to live up to its own principles; it is another to say that those principles themselves are no longer worth affirming. These threats to liberalism are not symmetrical, Fukuyama emphasizes. The assault from the right is more immediate and endangers core democratic practices involving voting rights and the transparency and legitimacy of the electoral process. The attacks on the left are mainly in the cultural realm and often proceed more incrementally, even if they elicit a further backlash from the right. Just about every critique of liberalism, Fukuyama concludes, "begins with a number of true observations, but then is carried to unsupportable extremes."

Yet he endorses the legitimacy of those critiques. Liberal societies, Fukuyama admits, can be excessively consumerist, permissive, tolerant of inequality, dominated by political and cultural elites, and slow to respond to the needs and demands of citizens. (The procedural and institutional obsessions of liberal governance almost render that slowness obligatory.) To say that we simply have no better system may be true, but it is hardly encouraging, and it won't do much to maintain a constituency for that system. Fukuyama's conclusion about liberalism's critics—they have a point but go too far—is similar to his assessment of liberalism itself: a worthy project that believed its own hype, producing its modern "discontents." Some discontents do come from malcontents, but not all.

These two books are familiar in distinct ways. Rachman's is one more in the spoken-word poetry of titles on its subject (*How Democracies Die . . . On*

Tyranny; *How Democracy Ends . . . Surviving Autocracy*), whereas Fukuyama's distills insights from many of his past works on political order, identity, and liberalism. (It is his shortest book but manages to incorporate much from the others, and even Hegel makes his obligatory cameo.) One book is a state of play. The other, a culmination.

Rachman lingers on the dual challenges for Biden: a Republican Party still dominated by Trump and "increasingly assertive" rivals in Moscow and Beijing. These two fronts are linked, he argues, because "America will not be able to defend freedom overseas, if it cannot save its own democracy." He worries Washington will have to pick and choose, allying with less than savory characters against bigger foes. (It would not be the first time.) Rachman believes that the Age of the Strongman will eventually pass, but this belief seems anchored in his hopes more than his analyses, and he remains aware of the damage that can be inflicted in the interim.

Fukuyama's solution is twofold. First, to promote a sense of national identity not focused on "fixed characteristics" such as race or faith but on patriotism and love for a liberal, open society of which citizens, whatever their politics, should be justly proud. He worries that the left too easily cedes this ground to right-wing nationalists. Next, he urges moderation in our politics, both from classical liberals such as himself and from the discontented. "Sometimes fulfillment comes from the acceptance of limits," Fukuyama writes in his final lines. "Recovering a sense of moderation, both individual and communal, is therefore the key to the revival—indeed, to the survival—of liberalism itself."

That moderation would involve conservatives learning to embrace, rather than reject, the nation's demographic shifts, once they realized that many voters, including recent immigrants, could be enticed more by conservative policies than by right-wing identity politics. It would mean the left grasping that "there are strong limits to the appeal of the cultural part of the [progressive] agenda," Fukuyama writes, and that dismissing large segments of society as beyond moral redemption is not a path to expanding that appeal.

Fukuyama wants everyone to calm down, and that's an attractive proposition. If only politics came with a common understanding of which moves and positions are too extreme to be productive, and which stands are in fact principled and necessary. But choosing which hills to die on and which to gently hike down is a matter of individual choice. And that is the promise of liberalism as well.

May 2022

A HISTORY OF AMERICA'S COMING WAR WITH CHINA

IT IS UNFAIR, BUT TALES of war tend to be more exciting than stories of peace. The same is true, perhaps more so, for warnings of wars to come versus assurances of goodwill. Dire scenarios of risk and escalation are almost always more captivating than those dissenting voices that explain how to avoid a fight. It is a narrative advantage that hawks enjoy over doves, realists over idealists, and those believing in nightmares over those who dream of the alternative.

The 360-degree rivalry between the United States and China has yielded a barrage of recent books about the possibility of armed conflict breaking out, with plenty of advice on how to forestall it. If "Who lost China?" was an American preoccupation of the early Cold War, "Who lost *to* China?" threatens to become its contemporary variant. After five decades of engagement between Washington and Beijing, a period that featured both America's unipolar triumphalism and China's ascent to economic superpower status, the two countries are on a "collision course" for war, many of these books assert, even if the rationales are varied and at times contradictory.

In these works, the antagonists are bound for strife because China has become too strong or because it is weakening; because America is too hubristic or too insecure; because leaders make bad decisions or because the forces of politics, ideology, and history overpower individual agency. A sampling of their titles—*Destined for War, Danger Zone, 2034: A Novel of the Next World War,* and *The Avoidable War*—reveals the range and limits of the debate.

I don't know if the United States and China will end up at war. But in these books, the battle is already raging. So far, the war stories are winning.

———

The US-China book club is insular and self-referential, and the one work that all the authors appear obliged to quote is 2017's *Destined for War: Can*

America and China Escape Thucydides's Trap? by Graham Allison, a political scientist at Harvard. He recalls the war between ascendant Athens and ruling Sparta in the fifth century BC and echoes Thucydides, the ancient historian and former Athenian general, who argued that "it was the rise of Athens and the fear that this instilled in Sparta that made war inevitable." Sub in China for Athens and the United States for Sparta, and you get the gist.

Allison, best known for *Essence of Decision*, his 1971 study of the Cuban missile crisis, does not regard a US-China war as inevitable. But in his book he does consider it more likely than not. "When a rising power threatens to displace a ruling power, the resulting structural stress makes a violent clash the rule, not the exception," he writes. He revisits sixteen encounters between dominant and ascendant powers—Portugal and Spain fighting over trade and empire, the Dutch and British contesting the seas, Germany challenging twentieth-century European powers and other confrontations—and finds that in twelve of them, the outcome was war.

As China continues amassing economic and political clout and an American-led global order appears less sustainable, it becomes "frighteningly easy to develop scenarios in which American and Chinese soldiers are killing each other," Allison warns. When there is mistrust at the top, when worldviews are irreconcilable, and when each side regards its own leadership as preordained, any nudge will do. "Could a collision between American and Chinese warships in the South China Sea, a drive toward national independence in Taiwan, jockeying between China and Japan over islands on which no one wants to live, instability in North Korea, or even a spiraling economic dispute provide the spark to a war between China and the US that neither wants?" he asks. In *Destined for War*, this is a rhetorical question.

Such storylines are the lifeblood of the US-China literature. Hal Brands and Michael Beckley, senior fellows at the American Enterprise Institute, begin *Danger Zone: The Coming Conflict with China* (2022) with a surprise Chinese invasion of Taiwan set in early 2025. US forces in the western Pacific are too scattered to respond effectively, and soon enough an ailing President Biden is pondering a low-yield nuclear strike against Chinese forces in mainland ports and airfields. "How did the United States and China come to the brink of World War III?" Brands and Beckley ask. Too easily.

In *The Avoidable War: The Dangers of a Catastrophic Conflict Between the US and Xi Jinping's China* (2022), Kevin Rudd, a former prime minister of Australia and a longtime scholar of China, imagines ten distinct plotlines, many revolving around the fate of Taiwan. For instance, what if China seeks to take the island by force and Washington opts not to respond? That would be America's "Munich moment," Rudd writes, eviscerating any American moral authority. Even worse would be the United States reacting with military force but then losing the fight, which would "signal the end of the American century." Half the scenarios in his book, Rudd notes, "involve one form or another of major armed conflict." And he's the most dovish of the lot.

An extended war story is found in *2034*, a work of fiction written by Elliot Ackerman, a novelist and former marine special operations officer who served in Iraq and Afghanistan, and James Stavridis, a retired four-star admiral and former supreme allied commander of NATO. Published in 2021, *2034* is basically a beach read about how we get to nuclear war. The authors imagine a seemingly chance standoff in the South China Sea between a flotilla of US destroyers and a Chinese trawler toting high-tech intelligence equipment, which in a matter of months escalates into a world war that leaves major cities in ashes, tens of millions of people dead, and neither Washington nor Beijing in charge. One of the main characters, a Chinese official with deep US ties, recalls taking a class at Harvard, "a seminar pompously titled The History of War taught by a Hellenophile professor." If it's a dig at the ubiquitous Allison, it might also work as a homage, because in *2034* China and the United States are ensnared by Thucydides.

In *The Avoidable War*, Rudd cautions that the incentives for Beijing and Washington to escalate hostilities, whether to save lives or save face, "could prove irresistible." Ackerman and Stavridis follow that script. In their novel, a recklessly hawkish US national security adviser—with the perfect last name of Wisecarver—and a smugly overconfident Chinese defense minister keep going until cities like San Diego and Shanghai are no more and India emerges as a global power, both in terms of its military capabilities and its mediating authority. (The UN Security Council even relocates from New York to New Delhi.) "This conflict hasn't felt like a war—at least not in the traditional sense—but rather a series of escalations," an influential former Indian official declares near the end of the novel. "That's why my word is 'tragic,' not 'inevitable.' A tragedy is a disaster that could otherwise have been avoided."

By these accounts, the forecast for tragedy is favorable. Allison sees the rise of Chinese nationalism under Xi Jinping as part of the long-term project to avenge China's "century of humiliation," from the First Opium War to the end of the Chinese civil war in 1949, and restore the country's top rank. Both the United States and China view themselves in exceptional terms, Allison explains, as nations of destiny. Washington aims to sustain the Pax Americana, whereas China believes that the so-called rules-based international order is just code for America making rules and China following orders—an oppressive scheme to contain and sabotage China's pent-up national greatness.

The extent and durability of that greatness are matters of disagreement in these books. Allison contends that the economic balance of power "has tilted so dramatically in China's favor" that American pretensions to continued hegemony are unrealistic. But Brands and Beckley, writing five years later, see a middling Middle Kingdom, a nation that for all its "saber rattling" (an obligatory activity in foreign policy tomes) is threatened by enemies abroad and an aging population and faltering economy at home. "China will be a falling power far sooner than most people think," Brands and Beckley declare. "Where others see rapid Chinese growth, we see massive debt and Soviet-level inefficiency. Where others see gleaming infrastructure, we see ghost cities and bridges to nowhere. Where others see the world's largest population, we see a looming demographic catastrophe."

Except that those interpretations do not render China any less dangerous to US interests or security. Just the opposite, Brands and Beckley argue. As China sees its window of opportunity closing rapidly, it could decide to make a move in pursuit of its goals—taking Taiwan, expanding its sphere of influence, achieving global preeminence. Thus the 2020s is the decade when US-China competition "will hit its moment of maximum danger."

Note how Allison believes war is possible because China is on an inexorable path to growth and influence, whereas Brands and Beckley worry about conflict precisely because Chinese power may be waning. This is the occupational hazard of national security thought leadership: Once you've decided conflict is likely, any set of conditions can credibly justify that belief.

The notion of the American dream is inseparable from the national identity of the United States, no matter that it can mean different things to different Americans. But there is also a Chinese dream, articulated, somewhat amorphously, by one individual: Xi, who is also the general secretary of the Chinese Communist Party and the chairman of the Central Military Commission.

The US-China books devote much attention to the motives and intentions of China's leader. Allison describes Xi's Chinese dream as a combination of power, prosperity, and pride, "equal parts Theodore Roosevelt's muscular vision of an American century and Franklin Roosevelt's dynamic New Deal." Rudd devotes eleven chapters of his book to Xi's ambitions and worldview, including his relentless focus on retaining power; his push for national unity, particularly regarding Taiwan; his need to maintain China's economic expansion; his drive to modernize the military, especially China's naval strength; and his effort to challenge Western-style liberal norms.

These goals may appear more attainable to Xi thanks to the "theory of American declinism" that gained currency among China's foreign policy elites during the Obama years, Rudd writes, particularly after the post-9/11 wars and the Great Recession. The corollary of that theory, of course, is that the time for China's primacy has arrived. In *2034* the same view comes alive in a melodramatic monologue by China's defense minister. "Our strength is what it has always been—our judicious patience," he declares, in contrast to the Americans, who "change their governments and their policies as often as the seasons" and who "are governed by their emotions, by their blithe morality and belief in their precious indispensability." In a thousand years, the United States "won't even be remembered as a country," he states. "It will simply be remembered as a moment. A fleeting moment." In the novel,

China seizes its moment to try to end America's moment. Instead, both moments come to an end.

In *Party of One: The Rise of Xi Jinping and China's Superpower Future* (2023), Chun Han Wong, a correspondent for the *Wall Street Journal*, notes that the Chinese president has no deep animosity toward the United States and in fact has some affection for American culture. When Xi was vice president, Wong writes, he sent his daughter to study at Harvard, and he has shared his affection for American movies like *Saving Private Ryan*. Of course, a Chinese president's fascination with a film about brutality, heroism, and loss in a past world war may signal something less encouraging than the strength of America's soft power.

Wong explains how Xi has hardened his control over the Chinese Communist Party with anti-corruption purges and has deployed state security and surveillance to suppress any threats to China's stability and, more to the point, to his power. The president is an "ardent nationalist," Wong writes, one who is "stoking a sense of Chinese civilizational pride" among his country's leadership and people. Xi has made a more robust military "a centerpiece of his China dream, demanding that the armed forces be 'ready to fight and win wars.' " It doesn't take much sleuthing to imagine who the opponent in such wars might be. Xi's assertions of a rising East and a diminishing West "has become an article of faith within the party and beyond," Wong writes. "Questioning such views is almost tantamount to disloyalty."

Brands and Beckley are less fixated on Xi; they see China's revisionist project as long predating China's latest leader. "America has a China problem, not a Xi Jinping problem," they write. But they might find validation in Wong's reporting. By centralizing so much power and control in himself and by governing through fear, Xi "may have become the weakest link in his quest to build a Chinese superpower," Wong writes. Scared of disappointing Xi, the state bureaucracy becomes paralyzed, while the party is so animated by a single personality that any potential successor could struggle to lead it.

"Xi's China is brash but brittle, intrepid yet insecure," Wong concludes. "It is a would-be superpower in a hurry, eager to take on the world while wary of what may come."

———

Throughout these books on China and the United States, scenarios of war abound, while paths to peace are less obvious. Allison pines for the era of Washington wise men like George Kennan, George Marshall, Paul Nitze, and other Cold War luminaries. The United States requires not one more "China strategy," Allison admonishes, but serious reflection on American objectives in a world with a rival that could become more powerful than the United States. "Is military primacy essential for ensuring vital national interests?" Allison asks. "Can the US thrive in a world in which China writes the rules?" We need the big thinkers, he writes, because "destiny dealt the hands, but men play the cards."

Brands and Beckley are wise to point out, contra Allison's Thucydides trap, that countries can be rising and falling at the same time and that moments of great geopolitical peril happen not only when a country is on the rise but also when its ambition and desperation come together. Unfortunately, their practical proposals are obscured by the self-help buzzwords of the national security set. "The key is to take calculated risks—and avoid reckless ones," they advise. And "Danger-zone strategy is about getting to the long game—and ensuring you can win it." Brands and Beckley even call for Washington to deploy "strategic MacGyverism—using the tools we have or can quickly summon to defuse geopolitical bombs that are about to explode." (Translation: wing it and hope that someone super smart will step in to fix any crisis.)

Adding "strategic" to any foreign-policy lingo immediately gives it a loftier vibe, of course, and Rudd is a master of this approach. In *The Avoidable War*, he invokes strategic perceptions, strategic adversaries, strategic equations, strategic logic, strategic thinking, strategic community, strategic direction, strategic off-ramps, strategic language, strategic literacy, strategic red lines, strategic cooperation, strategic engagement, strategic temperature, and a joint strategic narrative—and that's just in the introduction.

No surprise, Rudd's plan to avoid this avoidable war is something he calls "managed strategic competition." It involves close and ongoing communication between Beijing and Washington to understand each other's "irreducible strategic red lines," thus lessening the chance of conflict through misunderstandings or surprises. (Rudd likens it to Washington and Moscow's efforts to improve communication after the Cuban missile crisis.) Under managed strategic competition, both sides could then channel their competitive urges into economics, technology, and ideology and their cooperative needs into arenas such as climate change and arms control.

Washington may be employing some form of Rudd's playbook. Antony Blinken, the secretary of state, Janet Yellen, the secretary of the Treasury, and John Kerry, the special envoy for climate change, visited China this week. "We believe that the world is big enough for both of our countries to thrive," Yellen said at a news conference after her meetings. Except thriving is no longer either side's sole objective. Thriving under whose leadership and under whose terms? The Biden administration has imposed restrictions on the sale of semiconductor technology to China and is planning additional measures, whereas Chinese hackers recently penetrated the email account of the secretary of commerce, Gina Raimondo, who has been critical of China's business policies—all reminders that economic tensions have ways of spilling beyond the purely commercial realm.

Even Rudd admits that his preferred approach may just temporarily forestall an eventual conflict. He also acknowledges that managed strategic competition would require "unprecedented bipartisan consensus" among the American political class to ensure continuity regardless of the party in power. Normally, the need for bipartisanship only guarantees the failure of any Washington initiative, but China has been one of the few areas of some consistency across the Trump and Biden administrations. In a much-discussed *Foreign Affairs* essay titled "The China Trap," Jessica Chen Weiss, a former senior adviser with the State Department's policy planning staff in the Biden administration, notes that the US president "endorsed the assessment that China's growing influence must be checked" and that on Capitol Hill "vehement opposition to China may be the sole thing Democrats and Republicans can agree on."

The trap Weiss foresees is not China tricking the United States into conflict, as occurs in *2034*. Rather, it is that Washington, understanding nothing but a zero-sum world, will accept that conflict with China is inevitable or necessary. In other words, bipartisanship may be required for peace, but it can also lead to war.

Weiss proposes meaningful US discussions with China's leaders not merely about how best to communicate during a crisis "but also about plausible terms of coexistence and the future of the international system—a future that Beijing will necessarily have some role in shaping." She calls for "an inclusive and affirmative global vision," which sounds nice but is never explained in detail. "The United States cannot cede so much influence to Beijing that international rules and institutions no longer reflect U.S. interests and values," Weiss argues. "But the greater risk today is that overzealous efforts to counter China's influence will undermine the system itself." It is the kind of distinction that can be parsed only in hindsight: make sure you go far enough, but just don't go too far.

In one of the disquisitions on world affairs and national character that crop up throughout *2034*, a Chinese official concludes that the United States suffers not from a lack of intelligence about other countries' intentions but from a lack of imagination about how those intentions translate into actions. Judging from these various books, however, it seems that American and Western thinkers are perfectly capable of exercising their imaginations. That might be part of the problem. Writing in the journal *Liberties*, Ackerman wonders if a new world war becomes likelier when the generation that remembers the last one dies out. "Without memories to restrain us, we become reliant on our imaginations," he writes. So far, though, the imagined scenarios for war are more persuasive than those for peace.

These need not be the only stories we tell. "China is like that long book you've always been meaning to read," a US intelligence official tells Brands and Beckley, "but you always end up waiting until next summer." This is the summer I finally picked up that book. I hope there will be more to come, books in which the stories of peace have at least a fighting chance.

July 2023

III. BELONGING

READING TOCQUEVILLE AT
JUST THE RIGHT TIME

I PICKED QUITE A YEAR to become an American.

In late 2014, I rose to my feet in a Baltimore auditorium, alongside two dozen other immigrants from Africa, Asia, Europe, and the Americas, and swore an oath to defend a nation. In return, that nation has surprised and challenged me every day since.

My first full year as a citizen of the United States was also the year Donald Trump made nativism a viable political project. It was the year college activists battled racism with their own peculiar intolerance. It was the year Rachel Dolezal was redefined, Atticus Finch rewritten, Caitlyn Jenner revealed. It was the year police shootings became viral, mass shootings became daily, and same-sex marriage became law. It was a year America did little else, it seemed, than fight over values, identity, premises.

It's exhausting, being American. Seriously, you do this every year?

I'm not a recent arrival. I graduated from college here, got married here, built a family here. But only with citizenship did I grasp the distance I'd always kept. I left my native Peru behind twenty-seven years ago, but whenever this country seemed too painful or complicated, I'd shake my head sagely. *Estos gringos locos.* Except now everything about the place—its virtues and excesses, its history and future—is all mine, too. For the first time, I feel the glorious burden that is the United States.

To carry it, I need help. Yes, I passed the citizenship test, even practicing the list of one hundred questions with my kids. But for the advanced coursework, my instinct was to turn to a book. What could I read that would guide me through the chaos that is democracy in America?

Fortunately, there's a book called *Democracy in America*—written more than 175 years ago by, of all people, some know-it-all foreigner.

It's embarrassing to admit that I'd never read Alexis de Tocqueville's classic until now, but I'm glad I picked this year to do it. Few books have been so often cited and imitated, so I won't presume to offer more insight than this: *Democracy in America* is an ideal book to read as a new citizen. Yes, it's really long and stuffed with annoying, self-referential French digressions. (I can say that sort of thing now, I'm American!) But it also explains perfectly to a brand-new compatriot so much of the essential minutiae of life here, so much of what America is and was, so much of what it risks losing.

Democracy in America, for example, explains why Americans always want you to join things and sign stuff. As soon as they welcome you to the whole, the parts start claiming you. It could be your race or ethnicity or sexual identity. Or your hobby, your school, your politics, your team. Where do you belong? Which identity is strong enough to get you to commit and be counted? "American" is just the beginning. The drop-down menu never ends.

Tocqueville obsesses over this freedom of association. "In America, citizens of the minority associate primarily to ascertain their numerical strength and thereby weaken the moral ascendancy of the majority," he writes. "The second purpose of association is to promote competition among ideas in order to discover which arguments are most likely to make an impression on the majority, for the minority always hopes to attract enough additional support to become the majority and as such to wield power."

I first grasped this when I arrived here after high school and collegiate groups tried to mark their territory. Would I join the Hispanic Americans organization? The international students? Pick! Now I get to vote, but I have to register with a party. In America, you're always taking sides. "There is only one nation on earth where daily use is made of the unlimited freedom to associate for political ends," Tocqueville writes. Americans not only use it daily but obsess over whether that's enough. Bowling alone is frowned upon.

Democracy in America also notes that Americans go temporarily insane every election cycle. New citizens will be relieved or unnerved to learn that the 2016 campaign is not entirely unusual. Trump's candidacy is an extreme instance; his proposals on immigration, terrorism, and religion have eviscerated the boundaries of acceptable political speech, or maybe reflected the state of that speech more accurately than ever.

"A presidential election in the United States may be looked upon as a time of national crisis," Tocqueville writes. "Long before the date arrives, the election becomes everyone's major, not to say sole, preoccupation. The ardor of the various factions intensifies, and whatever artificial passions the imagination can create in a happy and tranquil country make their presence felt. . . . As the election draws near, intrigues intensify, and agitation increases and spreads. The citizens divide into several camps, each behind its candidate. A fever grips the entire nation. The election becomes the daily grist of the public papers, the subject of private conversations, the aim of all activity."

Normalcy returns, he contends, once a verdict is rendered. "This ardor dissipates, calm is restored, and the river, having briefly overflowed its banks, returns peacefully to its bed. But is it not astonishing that such a storm could have arisen?" Yes. Every time.

Democracy in America captures the fights between security and liberty, a battleground long before Edward Snowden and the National Security Agency, religious tests and Syrian refugees. "What good does it do me, after all," Tocqueville asks, "if an ever-watchful authority keeps an eye out to ensure that my pleasures will be tranquil and races ahead of me to ward off all danger, sparing me the need even to think about such things, if that authority, even as it removes the smallest thorns from my path, is also absolute master of my liberty and my life?"

For Tocqueville, that authority threatens whenever it expands its scope. "Administrative centralization serves only to sap the strength of nations that are subjected to it, because it steadily weakens their civic spirit," he writes. Tocqueville shows more deference to the governing structures of towns, counties, and states than that of Washington. "What is most striking about public administration in the United States is its extraordinarily decentralized character," he asserts. The existence of a massive federal bureaucracy would alarm him, whatever its good intentions. "No central power, no matter how enlightened or intelligent one imagines it to be," Tocqueville writes, "can by itself embrace all the details of the life of a great people. It cannot, because such a labor is beyond human strength. If it tries to build and operate such a complex machine on its own, it will either content itself with something far short of its goal or exhaust itself in futile efforts."

So, new citizens, anytime you hear Americans screaming about the proper size of government—that happens a lot here—this helps explain why.

Even as you pledge allegiance to the flag, it is hard to always feel welcome in the republic for which it stands. "As Americans mingle, they assimilate," Tocqueville assures. "Differences created by climate, origin, and institutions diminish." But he doesn't think those differences are all that vast; and in his time, he may have been right. "All the immigrants spoke the same language," he writes, and "all were children of the same people." And he praises America's homogeneity—of interests, origins, language, and education—as an enabler of federalism. "I doubt that there is any nation in Europe, however small, whose various parts are not less homogeneous than the people of America." Americans today speak of diversity with reverence, but also with the comfort of an eternal aspiration.

This is made evident in the book's lengthy discussion of black Americans, one that resonates now with arguments over reparations, policing, and the Black Lives Matter movement. "The Negro in the United States ... is caught between two societies," Tocqueville writes. "He remains isolated between two peoples, sold by one and repudiated by the other." Even freed slaves, he argues, as well as those born after slavery, would remain "deprived of rights. . . . They are exposed to the tyranny of laws and the intolerance of mores. ... They have memories of slavery working against them, and they cannot claim ownership of any part of land." Written nearly two centuries ago, these arguments could grace the pages of the *Atlantic* today.

Finally, *Democracy in America* explains why, from time to time, wherever a crowd of Americans is gathered, new citizens will hear a chant that grows with a strength untethered to its relevance, a mantra that cannot be reasoned with.

"USA! USA!"

No, Tocqueville did not mention this particular cheer, but he knows the type. "Nothing inhibits ordinary social discourse more than the irritable patriotism of the American," he complains. "A foreigner may be prepared to praise a great deal in the United States, but some things he would like to criticize, and this the American absolutely refuses to allow. America is therefore a land of liberty where, in order not to offend anyone, a foreigner must not speak freely about individuals or the state, the people or the government, public or private enterprises, indeed about anything he finds there, except perhaps the climate and soil." (Climate? Oh, Alexis, if you only knew.)

Americans today are engaged in a great contest of offense-taking. Students want their pain validated; conservative Christians lament a war on their faith; liberals despair at the demagoguery of the Republican front-runner; the GOP presidential field is outraged by every action of the liberal president. America sounds like the nineteenth-century France Tocqueville describes, where "in the heat of struggle, people have been driven beyond the natural limits of their own opinions by the opinions and excesses of their adversaries, to the point where they have lost sight of their objectives and begun to speak in ways that have little to do with their true feelings."

But new citizens should not fear that they've joined a nation gone soft or mad. I prefer Tocqueville's diagnosis of the American character: "No one can work harder at being happy than Americans do," he explains. ". . . Americans do not converse; they argue. They do not talk; they lecture."

What I witnessed this year, then, was a great tradition. America challenges while it seduces. "The United States, it seems, is unmatched when it comes to arousing and sustaining our curiosity," Tocqueville concludes. "Fortunes, ideas, and laws are in constant flux there. Even immutable nature sometimes seems mutable, so great are the transformations she daily endures."

So, welcome. Now start reading this book.

December 2015

THE RADICAL CHIC OF
TA-NEHISI COATES

IN EARLY 2014, BEFORE FERGUSON, before Eric Garner, Tamir Rice, and Walter Scott, before Emanuel AME Church, Ta-Nehisi Coates got caught up in a skirmish over who should be deemed America's "foremost public intellectual." Coates nominated MSNBC's Melissa Harris-Perry; *Politico*'s Dylan Byers dissented. Rapid-fire posts were exchanged, accusations of racism and anti-intellectualism traded. As Twitter wars go, it was a Grenada.

The episode is worth recalling only because, within a year and a half, Coates had won that title for himself, and it wasn't close. In an America consumed by debates over racism, police violence, and domestic terror, it is Coates to whom so many of us turn to affirm, challenge, or, more often, to mold our views from the clay. "Among public intellectuals in the U.S.," writes media critic Jay Rosen, "he's the man now." When the Confederate battle flag on the statehouse grounds in Columbia, South Carolina, seemed the only thing the news media could discuss, my *Washington Post* colleague Ishaan Tharoor put it simply: "Just shut up and read @tanehisicoates." You hear many variations on that advice.

Coates is more than the writer whose thinking and focus best match the moment. With his 2014 *Atlantic* cover essay "The Case for Reparations," which explores the US history of redlining and housing discrimination, and with the critical rapture surrounding his book *Between the World and Me*, he has become liberal America's conscience on race. "Did you read the latest Ta-Nehisi Coates piece?" is shorthand for "Have you absorbed and shared the latest and best and correct thinking on racism, white privilege, institutional violence, and structural inequality?" If you don't have the time or inclination or experience to figure it out yourself, you outsource it to Ta-Nehisi Coates.

The structure of *Between the World and Me* speaks to this role. Coates's book is written as a letter to the author's teenage son, conveying the personal and historical struggle to "live free in this black body," a body that faces the constant, exhausting threat of state-sanctioned violence. But the book also reads like an open letter to white America, to the well-meaning sorts who at some point might have said, "Yes, things are bad, but they're getting better, right?" It is to them that Coates is delivering this stern, fatherly talk.

And the audience is rapt. "*Between the World and Me* is, in important ways, a book written toward white Americans, and I say this as one of them," writes *Slate* critic Jack Hamilton. "White Americans may need to read this book more urgently and carefully than anyone, and their own sons and daughters need to read it as well."

In one of the earliest assessments, *New Yorker* editor David Remnick described *Between the World and Me* as an "extraordinary" book and likened Coates to James Baldwin. (Actually, everyone else has, too.) Reviewers have hailed it as "a classic of our time" (*Publishers Weekly*), "something to behold" (the *Washington Post*), "a love letter written in a moral emergency" (*Slate*), and "precisely the document this country needs right now" (the *New Republic*). This is more than admiration. It is an affirmation of enlightenment. *New York Times* film critic A. O. Scott went as far as one could go, calling Coates's writing "essential, like water or air." We cannot live without Ta-Nehisi Coates.

What does such veneration—especially from a news media that Coates has attacked as indifferent to black America or inclined to view black America as a criminal justice problem—mean for Coates's arguments about the enduring influence of white supremacy? Does the praise disprove him, or to the contrary, does it only suggest that, in an age when liberal elites line up to lament their white privilege, the structures of inequality are resilient enough to accommodate, even glorify, this most radical critic?

In his 2009 memoir, *The Beautiful Struggle*, Coates tells the story of his childhood in West Baltimore and his relationship with his father, "Conscious Man," a librarian and ex–Black Panther, publisher of obscure black texts, father of seven children by four women, a man who "never shirked when his bill came due." He sought to instill consciousness in the young Ta-Nehisi, awareness of a community's historical struggle. "He covered the crib with Knowledge, until rooms overflowed with books whose titles promised militant action and the return to glory," Coates wrote of his father. The son absorbed the lessons, listening to Malcolm X's "The Ballot or the Bullet" on his Walkman, becoming "a plague" on his father's books. "My Consciousness grew, until I was obsessed with having been birthed in the wrong year," Coates wrote in the earlier memoir. "All the great wars had been fought, and I was left to rummage through the myths of my fathers."

Coates has found his new wars, mainly by realizing that the old ones never really went away. *Between the World and Me* seeks to impart that consciousness not just to his son but to all of us: that the violence done to black Americans is not accidental but by design, "the product of democratic will"; that white America's dream of nice houses, good schools, and Memorial Day cookouts is built on centuries of plunder of African American bodies, through lynching and redlining, bullets and chokeholds; and that "sentimental firsts"—the first black this or that—are little consolation. "Never forget that we were enslaved in this country longer than we have been free," he writes.

The more radical Coates's critique of America, the more tightly America embraces him. Challengers are soon shouted down, whether *Politico*'s Byers or *New York* magazine's Jonathan Chait, who in 2014 debated Coates in a series of thoughtful posts on culture, poverty, and personal responsibility, and was deemed the loser. Those who posit any shortcomings in Coates's analysis—as when *BuzzFeed*'s Shani O. Hilton argued that in his worldview, "the black male experience is still used as a stand in for the black experience"—do so almost lovingly. Even conservative critics, such as *National Review*'s Kevin D. Williamson, must spend nearly as much time extolling Coates as tackling his arguments, or like Shelby Steele in a painful appearance on ABC's *This Week*, they seem to capitulate even before the battle has been joined.

So, it feels almost blasphemous to note, for instance, that the prose in *Between the World and Me* can stray from overwhelming to overwritten, with sentences such as: "Poetry was the processing of my thoughts until the slag of justification fell away and I was left with the cold steel truths of life." Or to suggest that *The Beautiful Struggle*, the book Coates wrote when no one was watching, is a more bracing, more intimate work than *Between the World and Me*, which for all its power feels written with the presumption of a high Amazon ranking.

"Our media vocabulary is full of hot takes, big ideas, takeaways, grand theories of everything," Coates writes in the later book. "But some time ago I rejected magic in all its forms." His followers have not. If racism is America's oldest sin, reading Coates has become its newest absolution. It is of no consequence that he thinks little of his white readers. "When people who are not black are interested in what I do, frankly, I'm always surprised," Coates told Benjamin Wallace-Wells of *New York* magazine. "I don't know if it's my low expectations for white people or what."

Wallace-Wells concludes that Coates is that rare radical writer who "radicalizes the Establishment." But if so, how lasting might that radicalization prove, and to what effect? The acclaim for "The Case for Reparations" came not just despite the unlikelihood of any reparations actually coming to pass; as with many causes, its very improbability may have made it especially easy to embrace. All consciousness, few demands. Perfect for a white America that Coates diagnoses as "obsessed with the politics of personal exoneration."

The decision to move up the publication of *Between the World and Me* is instructive. Originally slated for early September, the book was released in July instead, because of the surge of outrage and interest that followed the Charleston, South Carolina, massacre. "It spoke to this moment," Christopher Jackson, executive editor of Spiegel & Grau, told the *Wall Street Journal*.

The irony is that, if you read this book, it is obvious that the moment for *Between the World and Me* is far more than July 2015. It is also last summer. And last century. And long before then, and long to come. There is no "moment." Racism requires no news hook; it already has too many. Yet the move by Coates's publisher seems to betray a worry that there is something fleeting or merely fashionable here, that even a writer with the reach and talent of Coates may have difficulty retaining his appeal. Or worse, that he will grow increasingly radicalized before a lovely, enlightened audience that continues to read, continues to applaud, and continues to do nothing.

And there's little beauty in that struggle.

July 2015

THE PROJECT OF THE
1619 PROJECT

THE *NEW YORK TIMES*'S CELEBRATED 1619 Project is as intriguing for the second half of its title as for the first. What is the project of this sprawling project; what are not just its principal conclusions and messages but also its underlying methods and objectives? For a work of journalism—or history, or perhaps something in between—grounded in the specificity of a single date, there is also an elusiveness, almost a malleability, pervading the effort. Part of the challenge in assessing it involves the multiple formats in which the project has been showcased: The *New York Times Magazine* special issue published on August 18, 2019, with print and online versions; a broadsheet edition appearing the same day; a podcast spin-off; a new, lengthy book version; an illustrated children's book; plus the many responses, updates, and essays published by the *Times* defending, amending, or otherwise explaining the project.

Together these elements form a powerful and memorable work, one that launched a seismic national debate over the legacy of slavery and enduring racial injustice in America. It is also a work with a variety of competing impulses, ones that can at times confuse and conflict. This is evident in *The 1619 Project: A New Origin Story*, a book that softens some of the edges of the prior magazine collection but also transcends its original mission as a historical corrective, informing readers what they now must do or else risk personal complicity in the painful story they have just been told.

The elusiveness begins where the project begins—in 1619, with the first ship carrying enslaved Africans to reach the English American colonies, and that moment's proper status in the history of the United States. In his note introducing the special issue, *New York Times Magazine* editor Jake Silverstein first depicts the project as something of a thought experiment, a counterfactual to the common notion of 1776 as the year of the nation's birth. "What if, however, we were to tell you that this fact, which is taught in our schools and unanimously celebrated every Fourth of July, is wrong, and that the country's true birth date, the moment that its defining contradictions first came into the world, was in late August of 1619?" Three sentences later, the question mark is gone, the tone more declarative. The barbaric system of slavery introduced that month is not just the United States' "original sin," Silverstein asserts; it is "the country's very origin." The project's broadsheet supplement widens that perspective, declaring that "the goal of the 1619 Project is to reframe American history, making explicit that slavery is the foundation on which this country is built." From what-if to no-matter-what, all on the same day.

This does not settle matters. In October 2020, in an article titled "On Recent Criticism of The 1619 Project," Silverstein indicated that the notion of 1619 as the country's birth year should be regarded as a "metaphor" and not read literally. This is why, he explained, the *Times* had deleted a description of 1619 as our "true founding" that previously appeared in the project's online presentation. But then, in a November 2021 essay titled "The 1619 Project and the Long Battle Over U.S. History," Silverstein wrote that the date indeed "could be considered" the moment of the United States' "inception."

In the new book version, Nikole Hannah-Jones, the *Times* journalist who conceived of the overall effort and wrote its lead magazine essay, offers a few interpretations. In the preface, she cautions that the project is "not the only origin story of this country—there must be many." Then, in the opening chapter, Hannah-Jones repeats the text of her original magazine essay and refers to black Americans as the country's "true 'founding fathers,' " as deserving of that designation "as those men cast in alabaster in the nation's capital." Some four-hundred-plus pages later, in a concluding chapter, she writes that the origin story in the 1619 Project is "truer" than the one we've known.

What might an assiduous reader conclude from all this? That 1619 is a thought experiment, or a metaphor, or the nation's true origin, but definitely not its founding, yet possibly its inception, or just one origin story among many—but still the truer one? For all the controversy the project has elicited, this muddle over the starting point is an argument that the 1619 Project is also having with itself.

These distinctions matter because, with this subject, framing is everything. History, Hannah-Jones writes in the book, is not just about learning what happened. "It is also, just as important, how we *think* about what happened." Had this effort been labeled "The Slavery Project" and made similar arguments about the enduring impact of black enslavement and racism in American life, it would have been influential but probably would not have reverberated as widely. Reframing America's start from July 1776 to August 1619—from the "wrong" date to the "truer" story—and placing those landmarks in conversation with each other is what forces you to stop and think, to peer within competing frames.

Silverstein echoed this idea in "The 1619 Project and the Long Battle Over U.S. History." History is not "a fixed thing," he wrote, emphasizing instead the "dynamic, contested and frankly pretty thrilling process" by which historical understanding is remade. He was talking about historiography, he explained, the study of how history is written and how it evolves—history's own history.

The 1619 Project, from magazine to book and all the forms in between, displays its own dynamic and contested historiography. Its evolution is sometimes forthright, sometimes subtle, and sometimes grudging, as it determines what it wants to say.

The book *The 1619 Project* features expanded versions of the original 2019 essays, along with additional short fiction and poems complementing each chapter. There are also entirely new contributors, many of them historians. (This is a welcome upgrade after the original special issue sought to reframe history yet did not include many practitioners of the discipline.) There is an almost relentless coherence to the new book. Many of the authors begin with a story of violence or racism or inequality, then assert that such injustices find their roots in colonial times or the post-Reconstruction era, and then spend the rest of the essay identifying the ties between those periods and ours. The approach is slightly formulaic but no less effective for its formula.

"Since the nation's founding, our legal and political architecture has privileged the safety and self-defense of white people over that of black people," historian Carol Anderson writes in her essay "Self-Defense," one of the strongest new contributions. Anderson traces the history of the Second Amendment, emphasizing how it did not concede the right of black Americans to bear arms because "the enslaved were not considered citizens," and how it was widely understood that the suppression of black uprisings was among the purposes of the amendment's "well regulated militia." This chapter speaks to another, titled "Fear," authored by historian Leslie Alexander and legal scholar Michelle Alexander. They describe how, after Reconstruction, local police forces throughout the South "were often made up of former slave patrollers and members of the Ku Klux Klan" who targeted black citizens for "daring to behave as though they were free." Reflecting on the police murder of George Floyd, the coauthors write that the "kindling" had long been laid for the protests that the nation saw in 2020. "Nothing has proved more threatening to our democracy, or more devastating to Black communities, than white fear of Black freedom dreams."

Several essayists from the original magazine edition have expanded or otherwise edited their works for the new book. Whether they are broadening or qualifying their arguments, the results are both instructive and uneven.

Consider sociologist Matthew Desmond's chapter, "Capitalism." In his original magazine essay, Desmond argued that many labor-management and record-keeping practices of modern American capitalism originated on plantations, with lasting consequences for the nation's growth and industry. He indicated, for instance, that the vast increases in the productivity of America's cotton fields—an average enslaved field worker in 1862 picked 400 percent more cotton than one had in 1801—flowed from the meticulous efforts to manage every detail and moment of those workers' lives. "Bodies and tasks were aligned with rigorous exactitude," Desmond wrote in the essay, describing the "uncompromising pursuit of measurement and scientific accounting displayed in slave plantations."

Critics of this essay pointed out that some financial and management practices Desmond mentions, such as double-entry bookkeeping, predated the slave-plantation era. More consequentially, they argued that Desmond's discussion of cotton productivity bypassed the real explanation for the increase. In the new book, Desmond addresses this, but only to a point. Following a detailed discussion of the management of enslaved labor, he again cites the boost in productivity. Then he adds this caveat: "Historians and economists have attributed this surge in productivity to several factors—for example, Alan Olmstead and Paul Rhode found that improved cotton varieties enabled hands to pick more cotton per day—but advanced techniques that improved upon ways to manage land and labor surely played their part as well."

Note what is happening: a different explanation is introduced for an important point of fact, but the overall narrative remains—because "surely" it still holds. Readers should always be open to new historical interpretations, but when revising history, "surely" does not reassure. When facts complicate a story, they shouldn't be tucked in an aside but taken up as part of that dynamic and contested process of discovery that Silverstein so praised.

Other entries in the book improve on the original contributions in distinct ways. Civil rights lawyer Bryan Stevenson's chapter, "Punishment," argues persuasively that mass incarceration and law enforcement brutality against black Americans can be traced to the legacy of slavery and to a loophole in the Thirteenth Amendment, which ended involuntary servitude "except as a punishment for crime whereof the party shall have been duly convicted." His writing here grows to include a discussion of recent juvenile-justice cases before the Supreme Court, including one that Stevenson himself argued, and he more fully establishes the "unbroken links" between slavery, Black Codes, convict leasing, white lynch mobs, and the injustices of our time. "Black people still bear the burden of presumptive guilt," he concludes.

In "Inheritance," perhaps the most memorable of the chapters, journalist Trymaine Lee recounts at greater length the infuriating tragedy of Elmore Bolling, a black businessman in Alabama who was killed (six pistol shots and one shotgun blast to the back) by two white men in December 1947. His offense: succeeding while black. Bolling leased land on which he had a large house, a general store, and a gas station, and he also ran a delivery service and catering company. The *Chicago Defender* reported at the time that his killers were "jealous over the business success of a Negro." Bolling had stressed the importance of education and business savvy to his children, but his two oldest— fourteen and fifteen at the time of his murder—would struggle through menial jobs for much of their lives, while the twelve-year-old son who saw his father's body lying in a ditch later spent part of his adulthood in a psychiatric institution. The children collected no inheritance, Josephine Bolling McCall, one of Elmore's daughters, explains to Lee; "it was all taken away," she said. Lee places this family's story in the context of the post-Reconstruction dismantling of federal protections and support for newly emancipated black Americans.

Times critic Wesley Morris's magazine essay on the impact of black musicians on American culture—and the brutal impact of blackface minstrelsy on the black American soul—was one of the sharpest contributions to the original 1619 Project collection (and his rendition in Episode 3 of the *1619* podcast is well worth the thirty-four minutes). "Decades of jams written, produced, and performed by Black artists sustain parties in places that sustain no actual Black people," he writes in the book. The ingenuity and intuition of art constitute the "very core" of American culture, "in part because white people won't stop putting it there." Something about this white American desire for cultural blackness "warps and perverts its source, lampoons and cheapens it even in adoration," he laments. "Loving Black culture has never demanded a corresponding love for Black people. And loving Black culture has tended to result in loving the life out of it."

This last passage is almost identical in the magazine and the book, yet in the next paragraphs of the book chapter, something unexpected occurs. "But not always," Morris writes. He pivots into new territory, an argument too lengthy and thoughtful to be dismissed as a reluctant caveat. "The ongoing disputes over whose stuff is whose obscures a more important irony: music has midwifed the only true integration this country has known," Morris writes. He emphasizes that American musical history "effervesces with work made by white people *alongside* Black people," with white artists working "in Black traditions with admiration and respect." Whereas the magazine essay decried a kind of cultural gentrification through which "black people have often been rendered unnecessary to attempt blackness," in his book chapter Morris also highlights the "crucial distinction between what's appreciative and what's appropriative."

This is fertile soil in the debates over artistic and cultural appropriation. And the new version of Morris's argument loses none of its power for acknowledging that the relationship between black and white artists and artistry can be more complicated—less, well, black and white—than previously suggested. Morris isn't just demanding that readers rethink their world; he is reconsidering it along with them.

The opening 2019 magazine essay by Nikole Hannah-Jones, "The Idea of America," was awarded the Pulitzer Prize for commentary. (I am a member of the Pulitzer Prize Board but was recused from the discussion of that category because of a competing finalist from the *Washington Post*.) The essay combined personal reflections and historical interpretations, and one of its most moving moments, when a young Hannah-Jones is asked by a teacher to draw the flag of her ancestral land, and she hesitates because she does not know what it is, has been transformed into a beautiful children's book, *Born on the Water*. In the essay, Hannah-Jones recalls feeling embarrassed by her father's insistence on flying the American flag outside their Iowa home and how she came to understand the impulse only years later. Black Americans' struggles for freedom and equality have pushed this country to live up to its ideals, she wrote in the magazine, and therefore "no people has a greater claim to that flag than us." The flag she should have drawn as a child, she realized, was the Stars and Stripes.

The essay also received high-profile criticisms, including from a group of historians whose letter requesting corrections was published in the *Times*, along with a lengthy response from Silverstein defending the work. In her preface to the book, Hannah-Jones characterizes the historians' critique, but her portrayal does not always match their letter as published by the *Times*.

("They did not agree with our framing, which treated slavery and anti-Blackness as foundational to America," she writes. "We applaud all efforts to address the enduring centrality of slavery and racism to our history," the historians had written.) Their main criticisms included two of Hannah-Jones's statements in the original essay: first, that "one of the primary reasons the colonists decided to declare their independence from Britain was because they wanted to protect the institution of slavery," and second, that in the long struggle for equal rights, "for the most part, black Americans fought back alone."

Hannah-Jones addresses both criticisms in the book, in part by reframing the disputes. On the matter of whether upholding slavery was a primary impetus behind the revolution, she writes in the preface that the sentence "had never been meant to imply that every single colonist shared this motivation." As a result, she explains, the online version of her essay had been amended to refer to "some of the colonists," and that is also how the line is rendered in the book. (An editor's note by Silverstein, published more than six months after the original magazine package, explained this "clarification" in similar terms.)

I will not presume to represent a typical *Times* reader, but I never interpreted that original passage as suggesting that every single colonist shared this motivation; rather, I reasonably assumed it referred to a majority or a sizable minority. The *Times*'s two-word "update" to the project ("some of" the colonists) sidestepped the central issue: What was the range of motivations animating the revolution, and among them, how powerful was the desire to protect slavery? This was a clarification that clarified little.

In the opening chapter of the book, titled "Democracy," Hannah-Jones adds two explanations supporting her interpretation of colonial motives. One involves the Dunmore Proclamation of November 1775, in which the royal governor of Virginia offered freedom to enslaved people if they joined the British side of the fight. (The declaration went unmentioned in Hannah-Jones's original essay and did not appear in the magazine's timeline of important events in African American life; now, it is featured in the book's expanded timeline.) She writes that the proclamation "would alter the course of the Revolution," appropriate phrasing given that the revolution was well underway by the time of the proclamation.

How influential was this episode in the fight for independence? Here Hannah-Jones narrows the story. She stresses that the proclamation "infuriated white Virginians" and that when you think about it, the revolution was mainly a Virginia thing, anyway. "Schoolchildren learn that the Boston Tea Party sparked the Revolution and that Philadelphia was home to the Continental Congress, the place where intrepid men penned the Declaration and Constitution," she writes. "But while our nation's founding documents were written *in* Philadelphia, they were mainly written *by* Virginians . . . No place shaped the Revolution and the country it birthed more than Virginia." It is a subtle but effective shift: rather than expand history to encompass the range of the colonists' rationales, Hannah-Jones limits the universe of colonists who matter. Now, Virginia is *real* colonial America.

In an *Atlantic* article published in late 2019, Hannah-Jones was quoted defending her original essay's contention that black Americans fought for freedom largely on their own. "It is not saying that black people only fought alone," she said. "It is saying that *most of the time* we did." In the book's preface, she depicts the historians' criticism as a matter of taste, or perhaps pique: "They did not like our assertion that Black Americans . . . have waged their battles mostly alone," she writes. Then, in the opening chapter of the book, Hannah-Jones repeats the identical line from the essay, but with a telling phrase added (italicized here): "For the most part, Black Americans fought back alone, *never getting a majority of white Americans to join and support their freedom struggles.*"

"Alone" now means "without majority support." The word is not omitted or replaced, but rather redefined, allowing the original phrasing and framing to endure. Is this tweak an admission that the historians' criticism had merit? Hannah-Jones's discussion of their letter in the book's preface suggests no such reconsideration. But if the landscape within it shifts, should not a frame bend, shudder, or occasionally crack?

The 1619 Project has taken pains to affirm its intellectual rigor. In "The 1619 Project and the Long Battle Over U.S. History," Silverstein was appreciative of the feedback the original magazine issue received, which helped "deepen and improve" the project, and he explained that the new book "was submitted to a peer-review process." The acknowledgments section of the book provides more detail: "In preparing this book, we sought the counsel of numerous historians as peer reviewers. All of the essays were reviewed in their entirety by scholars with subject-area expertise." It then thanks more than two dozen scholars by name. The list is impressive, no doubt, but soliciting feedback on your work from people you've selected is not quite what it means to undergo an independent peer review process, the appropriation of academic language notwithstanding.

The book, with its fifty pages of footnotes, is by necessity more academic in presentation than the original magazine edition. In its concluding sections, however, *The 1619 Project* displays its most significant evolution, moving away from its strictly historical inquiry. In a chapter titled "Progress," historian Ibram X. Kendi writes that the popular notion of America making steady, if slow, headway toward greater racial justice is "ahistorical, mythical, and incomplete." The "mantra" of incremental improvement can undermine efforts to promote real equality. Kendi cites Chief Justice John Roberts's majority opinion in *Shelby County v. Holder* (2013), which held that the country's progress against discrimination meant that certain states and counties no longer needed federal approval before amending their voting laws, as the Voting Rights Act required. (The decision unleashed a series of state-level initiatives creating obstacles to voting.) "Saying that the nation *has* progressed racially is usually a statement of ideology," Kendi writes, "one that has been used all too often to obscure the opposite reality of *racist* progress." The failures of the Reconstruction era led to the "Second Reconstruction" of the twentieth-century civil rights movement, a cause and effect that Kendi says is too often "left out of the story."

Kendi then introduces something else he says is left out of the story—that America requires a "Third Reconstruction" to address the unfulfilled promise of the second. Here the 1619 Project's project becomes explicitly political. Hannah-Jones fills in the details in the book's final chapter, "Justice," where she identifies the racial wealth gap as the most serious challenge for black Americans. "White Americans' centuries-long economic head start," she writes, is what "most effectively maintains racial caste today." To narrow that gap, the country must embark on "a vast social transformation produced by the adoption of bold national policies."

Among these are a slate of priorities such as "a livable wage; universal healthcare, childcare, and college; and student loan debt relief," Hannah-Jones writes. They also include cash reparations for black Americans—specifically, for those who can document having identified as black for at least ten years prior to any reparations process and who can "trace at least one ancestor back to American slavery." Also suggested is a commitment to enforce civil rights laws regarding housing, education, and employment, as well as "targeted investments" in black communities across the country.

And so the *New York Times*'s 1619 Project is now enlisted in the service of a policy agenda and political worldview. The book's concluding chapter underscores that link. "It is one thing to say you do not support reparations because you did not know the history, that you did not understand how things done long ago helped create the conditions in which millions of Black Americans live today," Hannah-Jones writes. "But you now have reached the end of this book, and nationalized amnesia can no longer provide the excuse. None of us can be held responsible for the wrongs of our ancestors. But if today we choose not to do the right and necessary thing, *that* burden we own."

It would be comforting if history always came with a policy road map, a detailed agenda that quickly placed us on its right side. Still, the 1619 Project's activist turn need not necessarily affect how one regards the American origin story it presents. As Hannah-Jones writes in the first line of the book's final chapter, "Origin stories function, to a degree, as myths designed to create a shared sense of history and purpose." In this book, the 1619 Project makes both its history and its purpose clear.

November 2021

ALWAYS COLUMBINE

FIVE DAYS AFTER THE APRIL 1999 massacre at Columbine High School, and just hours after they cremated the remains of their son Dylan—cremation was the only option, really, because a grave site would certainly be vandalized— Sue and Tom Klebold returned to their Colorado home. It had been a crime scene for several days, but now the detectives were gone, the media vigil over. A single lamp Tom had left on still burned in the front window. Using sheets, thumbtacks, and masking tape, they went from room to room, blocking any windows or sight lines into the house. "Only when we were sealed in this patchwork cocoon," Sue Klebold writes, "did we finally turn on another light at the very back of the house."

When your seventeen-year-old son has just perpetrated what was then the deadliest school shooting in US history, killing twelve students and one teacher and wounding twenty-four others before he and classmate Eric Harris turned their weapons on themselves, you're not eager for prying eyes. The Klebolds tried to block out a world that had already found them guilty.

With *A Mother's Reckoning*, Sue Klebold takes those sheets down. Reading this book as a critic is hard; reading it as a parent is devastating. I imagine snippets of my own young children in Dylan Klebold, shades of my parenting in Sue and Tom. I suspect that many families will find their own parallels. This book's insights are painful and necessary, its contradictions inevitable. It is an apology to the loved ones of the victims; an account of the Klebold family's life in the days and months following the shooting; an assembly of warning signs missed. Most of all, it is a mother's love letter to her son, for whom she mourned no less deeply than the parents of the children he killed mourned for their own. "To the rest of the world, Dylan was a monster; but I had lost my child."

That child, born on a September 11th and named for a poet who raged against the dying of the light, was a good kid, Sue explains. "He was easy to raise, a pleasure to be with, a child who had always made us proud." Dylan loved Legos and origami, was in a middle school gifted program, and worked sound equipment for school plays. They called him their Sunshine Boy. It was their older son, Byron, who gave them headaches.

Sue scours Dylan's childhood for warnings. Dylan was unforgiving of himself when he failed at anything, "and his humiliation sometimes turned to anger," she recalls. When he didn't make the high school baseball team, he retreated into computers. As some of Dylan's buddies found girlfriends, he drifted into a closer friendship with Eric Harris, whose sadism would play off of Dylan's depression.

A Mother's Reckoning features searing scenes: when Sue, upon learning that Dylan was involved in the shooting, finds herself praying for his death, "the greatest mercy" she could imagine. When she and Tom and Byron reassure each other that they won't commit suicide. When the three hold hands at the funeral home, and together they grasp Dylan's cold fingers. ("We were finally by his side, a family again.") When, less than two months after the shooting, the family is allowed to visit the school library, where many of the kids had died. Sue recognized her son's lanky shape marked on the floor. "My tears splashed the floor," she writes. ". . . I knelt beside the shape resembling my son and touched the carpet that held him when he fell."

She understands why people blame her. "HOW COULD YOU NOT KNOW??!" read one of thousands of letters. How could she not realize that their son was stockpiling weapons? How could she not glimpse the violence within him? Did she not love him? Didn't Sue ever hug him?

Sue knows she will always be seen as "the woman who raised a murderer," but she insists that she and Tom were loving, engaged parents. Though they recognized that Dylan had problems, "we simply—and drastically and lethally—underestimated the depth and severity of his pain and everything he was capable of doing to make it stop."

Trouble escalated during Dylan's junior year. He was suspended for lifting locker combinations from the school's computer system; he quit his job at a pizza place; he endured bullying. He became irritable, unmotivated. Most serious, Dylan and Eric were arrested for stealing electronic equipment from a parked van. "I practically threw up when I saw Dylan paraded past me in handcuffs," Sue recalls. The boys entered a diversion program for first-time juvenile offenders, involving counseling and community service. For a while, the mothers agreed to keep them apart.

In his senior year, Sue writes, Dylan seemed to improve. He got a job, applied to college, and was released early from the diversion program. "Dylan is a bright young man who has a great deal of potential," the counselor wrote, three months before the massacre.

Six months after the Columbine shooting, authorities showed the Klebolds videos that Eric and Dylan had made—the notorious "Basement Tapes"—in which both spoke in violent and racist terms, drinking alcohol and brandishing weapons. The Klebolds also received Dylan's journals, drawn from school notebooks and scraps of paper, revealing his despair. "Thinking of suicide gives me hope that i'll be in my place wherever i go after this life—that ill finally not be at war w. myself, the world, the universe—my mind, body, everywhere, everything at PEACE—me—my soul (existence)," he wrote. And later: "oooh god i want to die sooo bad ... such a sad desolate lonely unsalvageable I feel I am ... not fair, NOT FAIR!!!"

Sue repeatedly asserts that Dylan was responsible for his actions, but she highlights multiple factors enabling his descent. "We cannot dedicate ourselves to preventing violence if we do not take into account the role depression and brain dysfunction can play in the decision to commit it," she writes. There is also Dylan's co-conspirator. "For years after the attack, I resisted blaming Eric for Dylan's participation," Sue writes. "Given what I have learned about psychopathy, I now feel differently. I find the violence and hatred seething off the page in Eric's journals almost unreadably dark." Or as Andrew Solomon, author of *The Noonday Demon*, suggests in the book's introduction: "Eric was a failed Hitler; Dylan was a failed Holden Caulfield."

Sue also blames herself, in part. "Dylan did not learn violence in our home," she stresses. Her fault was not amorality or indifference, she says, but ignorance. "Dylan did show outward signals of depression," Sue writes. "... If we had known enough to understand what those signs meant, I believe that we would have been able to prevent Columbine."

Some signals flash so bright they seem hard to miss. During Dylan's senior year, his English teacher told Sue and Tom that one of his papers was disturbing. They asked Dylan about it, but didn't follow up. A year after his death, they read it: It was about a man dressed in black who kills the popular kids in school. Even now, Sue isn't sure how she would have reacted: "I cannot help but wonder if, as an artist myself, I would have seen it as a danger sign if I had read it before his death. Artistic expression, even when it's unpleasant, can be a healthy way of coping with feelings."

Stories of victims are prevalent in our reckoning with mass shootings. They carry greater moral force, or less moral ambiguity, than those of perpetrators. But Sue Klebold is both the mother of a killer and of one of his victims, too. "Coming to understand Dylan's death as a suicide opened the door to a new way of thinking for me about everything he had done," she says. "Whatever else he had intended, Dylan had gone to the school to die."

The author has remade herself as a suicide-prevention activist, and the book seeks to help families recognize red flags. "How does a concerned parent parse out the difference between garden-variety adolescent behavior … [and] real indicators of depression?" she asks. Look for shifting moods and sleep patterns; know that depression in teens may appear less as sadness than anger; implement mental health screenings in schools.

But beyond her recommendations, this book is littered with regret. "I wish I had listened more instead of lecturing; I wish I had sat in silence with him instead of filling the void with my own words and thoughts," Sue writes. "I wish I had acknowledged his feelings instead of trying to talk him out of them."

It's not that she didn't love him. "I loved him while I was holding his pudgy hand on our way to get frozen yogurt after kindergarten; while reading Dr. Seuss's exuberant *There's a Wocket in My Pocket!* to him for the thousandth time. … I loved him while we were sharing a bowl of popcorn and watching *Flight of the Phoenix* together, a month before he died," she writes.

It's that love wasn't enough.

February 2016

JOSH HAWLEY AND
THE PROBLEM WITH MEN

IT'S THE PROBLEM THAT HAS too many names.

Toxic masculinity. The feminization of America. The epidemic of father-lessness. The crisis of boys. The end of men. There are many competing ex-planations and many competing solutions for the plight of the contemporary American male. The state of manhood has become one more front in our culture wars, a debate that keeps breaking down along political lines, even as men themselves just keep breaking down.

By now the elements of that breakdown are well known: Boys in the United States are less prepared than young girls when they begin school and less likely to graduate from high school or finish college. Young men are fall-ing out of the labor force. So-called deaths of despair—by suicide and drug overdose—are nearly three times as common among men as women. One out of every five fathers does not live with his children. In 1990, 3 percent of men reported having no close friends; in 2021, 15 percent do.

Such indicators are everywhere in Richard Reeves's *Of Boys and Men* (2022), which has become a go-to text on the matter. "The problem with men is typically framed as a problem of men," Reeves writes. "It is men who must be fixed, one man or boy at a time. This individualist approach is wrong."

A scholar of class and inequality, Reeves instead sees men encumbered by structural problems in our society, and he has various fixes in mind. He wants to delay boys' entry into kindergarten by one year, in part because their brains develop more slowly than those of girls. He wants to see more male teachers in kindergarten through twelfth grade, because they serve as role models for boys and help improve their academic performance. And at a time when automation and freer trade have transformed job markets, Reeves wants to create more opportunities for men in what he calls HEAL jobs—

health, education, administration, literacy—which are typically dominated by women.

These are sensible ideas, yet I wonder if they are up to the challenges Reeves himself convincingly outlines. Will more male middle-school science teachers or an extra year of pre-K address the "gnawing sense of purposelessness" afflicting men today, in the words of one writer Reeves cites, or expand the "narrower range of sources of meaning and identity" from which they suffer? The "dramatic rebalancing" of economic and cultural power between the sexes in recent decades "has rendered old modes of masculinity, especially as family breadwinner, obsolete," Reeves writes. "But nothing has yet replaced them."

Josh Hawley, the senior US senator from Missouri, has some thoughts on what could replace them. His *Manhood: The Masculine Virtues America Needs* draws on biblical influences—the stories of Adam, Abraham, David, and Solomon in particular—to combat the malaise of American men, so addled by video games and pornography and troubled by depression and drug abuse that they cannot discern their calling. "They have no template," Hawley worries, "no vision for what it is to be a man."

Men are called to cultivate and protect and expand the Eden that is Earth, Hawley writes, to confront evil, embrace servanthood, privilege duty over pleasure, discipline their bodies, and order their souls. They must "start families and build homes and leave legacies of character that will span generations." The senator is unapologetic about finding solace in the past. "American men, it is time to wake up," he writes in his final chapter. "It is time to become free men, as your fathers and grandfathers were."

But it is far from clear that our fathers and grandfathers had it all figured out. Lamentations on the condition of men have a long history in American cultural debates, dating back to well before Hawley, the forty-three-year-old, was born. In 1958, *Esquire* magazine featured an essay by Arthur Schlesinger Jr. called "The Crisis of American Masculinity," which almost reads like it could have been published today. "What has happened to the American male?" Schlesinger asked. "For a long time, he seemed utterly confident in his manhood, sure of his masculine role in society." However, by the mid-twentieth century, Schlesinger wrote, men had come to see their maleness "not as a fact but as a problem."

The poet Robert Bly, in his bestselling *Iron John: A Book About Men* (1990), traced the grief of modern man from the Industrial Revolution, which separated men from their families and from nature, to the Information Revolution, which left office-bound men too enervated to teach their children well. "So many roles that men have depended on for hundreds of years have dissolved or vanished," Bly wrote. Writing a generation after Schlesinger and one before Reeves and Hawley, Bly concluded that adult men found themselves ashamed, and young boys found themselves confused.

For Schlesinger, the answer was not to reassert some John Wayne macho attitude to counter growing female empowerment but to rebuild a sense of individual identity to fight back against the stifling bureaucracy and economic centralization of postwar America. In other words, lose the gray flannel suit and "organization man" ethos and instead develop a sense of the irreverent, of the artistic, of the moral, of the political—this was the way, according to Schlesinger, for men, for people, to resist uniformity. In Bly's view, part of the answer was to re-create ancient rites of male initiation and restore mentoring between young men and their elders, a relationship that instructs boys to channel, but not suppress, their instincts.

It is easy to raise an eyebrow at Hawley's book—a lengthy lecture on masculinity feels a bit like overcompensation when it comes from the guy whose raised-fist salute to pro-Trump protesters on January 6 was followed by a senatorial sprint through the Capitol hallways to avoid the rioters—but there is much to take seriously in its pages. He calls for the subordination of the self to the needs of those we love. He argues for the dignity of all work, no matter whether it is denigrated as a "dead-end" job. He recognizes fatherhood as a daily reminder of the ways we are flawed. And he urges young men to assume greater responsibility for their own lives ("Ditching porn is a good place to start," Hawley writes) as a step toward glimpsing that missing vision of manhood. To dismiss or mock such views merely because they come from Josh Hawley is to let partisan commitments overwhelm intellectual ones.

Now, if Hawley had just written a book about the very real struggles facing young men in America, appending his preferred recommendations for how to live a more fulfilling life, *Manhood* could have been a worthwhile effort. Even more so had Hawley further explained why "no menace to this nation is greater than the collapse of American manhood" and how, absent the restoration of masculinity, "we will be no longer a self-governing nation because we will not have the character for it." For these warnings to be more than rhetorical flourishes, they deserve greater exploration.

But Hawley does neither of those things. Instead, he turns *Manhood* into a familiar assault on a godless, judgmental, pleasure-seeking left, which, he contends, is attempting to subdue men and transform them into complacent, androgynous, dependent consumers. "Much of today's left seems to welcome men who are passive and tame, who will do as they are told and sit in their cubicles, eyes affixed to their screens," Hawley writes. The left's "woke religion" purports to supplant the God of the Bible, and demands that we "renounce manhood, womanhood, Christianity, and other supposed markers of 'social power' and submit to the corrective tutelage of the liberal elite."

In Hawley's telling, the left regards men as the source of their own problems. "In the power centers they control, places like the press, the academy, and politics, they blame masculinity for America's woes," the senator writes. Hawley is not necessarily wrong when he complains about the mixed messages aimed at young men today—Your identity is yours to shape and claim, but why are you so toxic and oppressive?—but he seems not to notice the contradiction at the heart of his book: Hawley spends chapter upon chapter telling young men to stop blaming others for their troubles, urging them to take personal responsibility for their lives and failings . . . and then he proceeds to give those same young men someone to blame for their fate.

Which is it, Senator? Do American men need to man up like their forefathers or hunker down in ideological silos like their political leaders? If you are promoting manhood, why wallow in victimhood? This is a book that raises its fist, then runs for cover.

Though he does not mention Reeves by name (except in his endnotes), Hawley takes issue with "experts safely ensconced in their think tanks" who call for more men to enter professions like teaching and social work. "There is nothing wrong with those careers, of course," Hawley assures—after all, home health aides vote, too—but he seems concerned that such jobs just aren't manly enough. "Men are historically less interested in these fields and less educationally prepared to take them on," Hawley writes. And besides, "is it really too much to ask that our economy work for men as they are, rather than as the left wants them to be?"

Reeves does take on Hawley by name in *Of Boys and Men*, recalling a 2021 speech the senator delivered at the National Conservatism Conference, in which he outlined the challenges facing men and assailed the left's effort to define masculinity as toxic. (I, for one, would be delighted if "toxic" and "woke" canceled each other out and we never heard from either again.) "When it came to solutions, Hawley came up largely empty-handed," Reeves writes. He also accuses the right more broadly of riling up male grievance for political ends and for wanting to "turn back the clock" on economic relations between men and women. Since the publication of Hawley's book, Reeves has also posted a lengthy rebuttal to the senator's suggestion that men don't want to take on so-called HEAL occupations, under the somewhat self-referential title "What Josh Hawley gets wrong about me."

There are plenty of meaningful disagreements among these writers—and they are right to hash them out—but I was struck by one broad concurrence. A senator, a scholar, and a poet all agree that manhood does not spring fully formed from a mother's womb or commence with a recognizable biological transformation, such as puberty, that turns boys into men. Instead, it must be constantly molded and reaffirmed.

"Manhood is something attained, not born to," Hawley writes. "It is an attainment of character."

"Manhood doesn't happen by itself," Bly writes. "It doesn't just happen because we eat Wheaties."

"Manhood is fragile," Reeves writes, adding that "the making of masculinity is an important cultural task in any society."

The unity of these visions is conceptual; their differences are practical. Whether manhood is constructed through biblical interpretations, nurtured through rituals and mentorship, or reimagined in periods of cultural and economic upheaval is less vital than the simple notion that it is created.

This forging of manhood is not without risks; if men and boys are groping for a sense of purpose and meaning they will find it, whether in a temple or a basement, from a mentor or an influencer, through a ritual or an addiction. Reeves is right that men's collective struggles should not be interpreted as a problem inherent to one gender, as though every man is flawed and must be sent back for repairs. But if we conceive of manhood as something created or achieved—not given, inherited, or immovable—then this collective crisis of boys and men is also an opportunity for individual self-definition. It can be about every man, each of us, deciding what it means to be one. It doesn't have to be about manning up or settling down.

June 2023

IV. ENDURING

THE CHALLENGES
OF IMPEACHMENT

Some mode of displacing an unfit magistrate is rendered indispensable by the fallibility of those who choose, as well as the corruptibility of the man chosen.

—George Mason, Constitutional Convention, June 1787

We're going to go in there. We're going to impeach the motherf—er.

—Rep. Rashida Tlaib, Democrat of Michigan, January 3, 2019

THE CONTRAST BETWEEN THESE TWO statements reveals everything about the challenge of exercising Article II, Section 4 of the Constitution and attempting to remove President Trump from office. By now, the "unfit" condition of this magistrate is clear, as is his disdain for the principles and traditions of American public life. But the fitness of Congress, the sole branch empowered to impeach and convict the president, also bears scrutiny.

Is the least-trusted institution in America—rated lower than big banks, the news media, and the presidency itself—ready to investigate and try a president in a way that conveys legitimacy and inspires broad confidence? And could the American public, already so divided and cynical, regard whatever outcome emerges from that process as fair?

These questions loom over the numerous guides and retrospectives on presidential impeachment—authored by historians, law professors, journalists, and assorted commentators—that have appeared in the two years since Trump swore the oath of office. (For some reason, many publishers imagined that a refresher might come in handy.) Partisanship, they contend, poisons impeachment, both the process and its legacy. This is the paradox: when a demagogic or authoritarian leader comes to power by stoking cultural division and partisan hatreds, the need for impeachment grows, but so does the difficulty of seeing it through.

George Mason, James Madison & Co. would hardly have been surprised by the boom in impeachment talk during the Trump administration. They feared a president who might "pervert his administration" into a scheme for personal enrichment or "betray his trust to foreign powers." Mason asked: "Shall the man who has practiced corruption, and by that means procured his appointment in the first instance, be suffered to escape punishment by repeating his guilt?"

Yet impeachment is the nuclear option of American politics, "nullifying the will of voters," historian Jeffrey Engel emphasizes in *Impeachment: An American History.* So the drafters of the Constitution spent months considering who would ultimately wield that power. Should it be the Senate or the Supreme Court? A vote of state legislatures or governors? The final choice of the House of Representatives (a simple majority vote for impeachment) and the Senate (a two-thirds majority for conviction) flowed from contrasting imperatives, Laurence Tribe and Joshua Matz explain in *To End a Presidency,* a thorough look at the history and legalities of impeachment. The House, directly elected and more susceptible to the passions of the moment, "could credibly claim unique authority to speak for the American people," whereas the Senate could strive for greater impartiality, wisdom, and rigor.

Placing this power in Congress rather than with the courts makes impeachment more a political process than a legal one. But calling it political does not denigrate impeachment; it elevates it. Impeachment *should* be political, reflecting the nature of impeachable offenses and the judgments that should be brought to bear when considering it. The endlessly parsed phrase "high Crimes and Misdemeanors" does not cover policy differences, unpopularity, personal animus, or simple "maladministration" on the part of the president, a term the framers considered but dismissed as so vague that it would leave presidents at the mercy of Congress. In fact, an impeachable offense need not involve the commission of a crime. Rather, it must feature misdeeds that "so seriously threaten the order of political society as to make pestilent and dangerous the continuance in power of their perpetrator," wrote the late legal scholar Charles L. Black Jr. in his classic study *Impeachment: A Handbook*, published in 1974 and reissued in 2018. Impeachment ought to follow egregious abuses of power that constitute, in Engel's description, wrongdoing "against the entire American people."

In *Impeachment: A Citizen's Guide*, law professor Cass Sunstein acknowledges the political dimensions of impeachment but emphasizes the exacting standards and judgment that should be brought to bear. "It is in part because the standard is high that political opponents of presidents have so rarely resorted to the impeachment mechanism," he writes. "Despised presidents, and bad presidents, have hardly ever been impeached, which is a tribute to the Rule of Law." The problem is not that the process could be political but that it could easily become too partisan, another weapon in a permanent campaign. "When an impeachment is purely partisan, or appears that way, it is presumptively illegitimate," Tribe and Matz warn.

Indeed, the impeachment efforts historians remember as least legitimate are precisely those, such as the case of President Bill Clinton, that were most partisan. "For both Clinton and his foes, the impeachment battle was not so much a search for facts or even a debate about what this generation of Americans believed constituted high crimes and misdemeanors than it was another political contest to be won or lost," writes *New York Times* reporter Peter Baker, a contributor to *Impeachment: An American History*. By contrast, the House Judiciary Committee's action against President Richard Nixon reflected a judicious and painstaking effort, one that would eventually compel Nixon to resign rather than face impeachment in the House—where the Judiciary Committee had approved three articles of impeachment on a bipartisan basis—as well as likely conviction in the Senate at the hands of both Republicans and Democrats.

"What has changed is ourselves," writes Columbia law professor Philip Bobbitt, in an essay appearing alongside Black's rereleased impeachment study. "We no longer have the confidence in the leadership of Congress that we had in the Nixon era." In 1973, some 42 percent of Americans expressed "a great deal" or "quite a lot" of confidence in Congress, according to Gallup polls. By 2018, that endorsement had dropped to 11 percent.

The presidents enduring impeachment proceedings hardly help matters, typically painting the efforts as purely partisan. "The law case will be decided by the PR case," Nixon argued to his chief of staff in the heat of the Watergate saga; he also complained that his lawyer, James St. Clair, treated the impeachment inquiry "too much as a trial" rather than a raw partisan fight. Historian Timothy Naftali, founding director of the Nixon Presidential Library and a contributor to *Impeachment: An American History*, emphasizes how that view nearly succeeded, largely because, for a long time, "the Republican partisan mind refused to absorb the incriminating nature of the [White House] tapes."

Similarly, during the Clinton impeachment, Democrats attempted to turn every skirmish with the Republicans and the special counsel into a party-line war. "The more partisan the impeachment effort looked, the less legitimate it would seem in the eyes of the public," Baker writes. "While they decried partisanship, the Democrats intentionally tried to promote it." Even the Starr report's descriptions of Clinton's personal encounters with Monica Lewinsky managed to help the president, by making his rivals seem more obsessed with sex than with the Constitution. "For Clinton, the release of the report was a public humiliation but a political boon," Baker explains.

Clinton's behavior in the Lewinsky scandal, though sordid, abusive, and duplicitous, offers a less obvious collection of impeachable offenses than Nixon's electoral sabotage, abuses of power, and obstruction of justice. Yet Clinton's inquisitors seemed to display deeper personal aversion toward their target than did Nixon's antagonists. Just compare Rep. Peter Rodino (D-NJ), the chairman of the House Judiciary Committee during Watergate, who worked to build bipartisanship and appealed to what he called "the middle," with the hard-charging House majority whip during the Clinton era, Rep. Tom DeLay (R-TX), who referred to the impeachment effort as "The Campaign."

Trump has at times offered a positive case against impeachment. "How do you impeach somebody that's doing a great job?" he asked last fall. But more often, he assails the accusations and investigations against him as hoaxes, witch hunts, or desperate moves by "angry Dems," all in an attempt to preemptively delegitimize any grounds for tossing him out. In this light, comments such as Tlaib's "motherf—er" moment only affirm his argument.

Indeed, the more partisan the books against him, the less persuasive they feel. *Trump Must Go: The Top 100 Reasons to Dump Trump (and One to Keep Him)*, by liberal commentator Bill Press, exemplifies the genre. Press mixes the prospect of Russian collusion with the president's personality quirks (such as Trump's Twitter addiction), speculation about his health ("he may be certifiably mentally ill"), and policy disagreements (on issues from marijuana to the national debt) to argue that Trump needs to leave office now. Even the alleged "pee tape" of Russia dossier lore, "which none of us have seen, but which many of us just know exists," makes a cameo.

When scholars argue that the removal of a president must be bipartisan, they are expressing less an opinion than a historical fact. Nixon still enjoyed the support of roughly a quarter of American voters when he resigned, and he could have counted on some ten to fifteen Republican votes in the Senate, writes Williams College legal scholar Alan Hirsch in *Impeaching the President*. But the public would have accepted his removal, Hirsch explains, because significant numbers of Republicans in both chambers supported it. Similarly, it was the partnership between Sens. Tom Daschle, a South Dakota Democrat, and Trent Lott, a Mississippi Republican, that made the conclusion of Clinton's Senate trial a somewhat bipartisan undertaking.

In some ways, the Trump era combines the most toxic elements of the Nixon and Clinton episodes: the likelihood of impeachment-level wrongdoing, as well as inflamed—and deeply personal—partisan opposition. In such an environment, impeachment proceedings could harden, not ease, our national divisions. "Virtually every source of dysfunction in our democracy—hyperpartisanship, dark money, fake news, manufactured outrage, cultural warfare—could be magnified tenfold by an impeachment," Tribe and Matz write.

Of course, that doesn't mean it's a bad idea.

Perhaps the most instructive case—and one undergoing something of a historical revision—is the 1868 impeachment of President Andrew Johnson. In his contribution to *Impeachment: An American History*, historian Jon Meacham highlights the parallels with our era: "an obstinate president; a divided Congress; a nation that seemed intractably tribal; fears that the grand American experiment in democracy was coming to an end; and, as a capstone, a battle over the legitimacy of the president."

The impeachment of Johnson, a Democratic vice president thrust into the Oval Office after Abraham Lincoln's assassination, has often been remembered as a partisan exercise, and in many ways it was. The Republican-led Congress despised Johnson, deriding him as "Acting President," "His Accidency," and "His Vulgarity." And Johnson's precipitating offense—violating the Tenure of Office Act by firing the secretary of war without Senate approval—was a technicality, a trap, not a serious constitutional violation. Impeached in the House, he survived in the Senate by a single vote, in part because some senators feared his potential successor, the controversial Ohio Republican Benjamin Wade.

But scholars today also stress the legitimate reasons for seeking Johnson's ouster. In a nation just emerging from an existential conflict over slavery, Johnson opposed the Fourteenth Amendment granting citizenship to former slaves and vetoed major civil rights legislation. When Congress overrode him, the president refused to enforce the law properly. He was, in many respects, still fighting for the cause of the defeated South. "Johnson's virulent use of executive power to sabotage Reconstruction posed a mortal threat to the nation—and to civil and political rights—as reconstituted after the Civil War," Tribe and Matz write. "These were not ordinary policy disagreements."

In a comprehensive *Atlantic* essay making a case for Trump's impeachment, historian and journalist Yoni Appelbaum looks back on the Johnson episode and sees justice, not partisanship. Johnson wanted to "restore America as it had been" before the war, he writes, shorn of slavery but with little else changed. "If his impeachment was partisan, it was because one party had been formed to defend the freedom of man, and the other had not yet reconciled itself to that proposition." Although Johnson served out his term, the close call damaged his political prospects so badly that he did not stand for a second term. "The chorus of experts who now present Johnson's impeachment as an exercise in raw partisanship are not learning from history," Appelbaum concludes, "but, rather, erasing it."

Today, it is tempting to imagine that Trump's impeachment and removal would take the country back to a saner, simpler time. This illusion ignores the forces that brought Trump to power as well as the risks of impeachment itself. "I confess to a very strong sense of the dreadfulness of the step of removal, of the deep wounding such a step must inflict on the country," Black writes. Engel warns that impeachment "disrupts the American political landscape as few other events do, leaving scars for generations." A failed impeachment drive could encourage a president's most dangerous impulses, and even if it succeeds, impeachment only kicks out an offending leader, "it doesn't fix the democratic decline that brought [him] to power," Tribe and Matz emphasize. "It doesn't undo the havoc he wreaked while in office. And it doesn't forestall the trauma of expelling him." They worry that core supporters of the impeached leader would consider his removal "a gussied-up coup d'état" and walk away from the American project, drift toward revolutionary politics, or even commit violence—"especially if the ousted president refuses to depart gracefully and instead terrorizes the polity that rejected him." And a graceful exit is hard to imagine under current management.

Yet not undertaking impeachment can be momentous as well. Sunstein fears a wholly partisan impeachment effort but is just as concerned about the failure to impeach when justified. "If a president systematically overreaches in his use of executive authority, or puts civil rights and civil liberties seriously at risk, he is likely to have, or to be able to get, the backing of a lot of Americans—at the very least, a big chunk of the electorate. Will We the People end up doing anything in response? I don't know. That's worth worrying about."

Even if the new Democratic majority in the House decides to move forward on impeachment, the Senate remains in Republican hands, and reaching sixty-seven senators seems unlikely. Except when recalling the Nixon era: "Nixon's saga reveals that when support for an embattled presidency fades, it cascades," Engel writes. "Why did so many Americans change their minds so quickly? Because the facts changed."

That is why truth, if lawmakers do begin an impeachment process, not partisan fury, must remain the foremost value—and that means offering a full accounting of Trump's offenses. There is a compulsion on the part of some of the president's critics to hinge everything on the work of special counsel Robert Mueller, the Godot of the Trump era, as if specific legal misdeeds were the only issue. "Proof that a crime occurred can feel comfortingly objective," Tribe and Matz write. "It relieves us of the need to exercise judgment and casts a technical gloss over bitterly divisive political questions."

Obstruction of justice, violation of the emoluments clause, the betrayal of trust to a foreign adversary—any one of these is a significant misdeed that should be core to any impeachment process. Yet they all reflect Trump's greatest offense against the American public and the American experiment: his lack of interest in faithfully executing the office of the president. His biggest lie, out of so many, occurred when he swore the oath and then, in his inaugural address, pledged to be a leader for all Americans. Trump governs for his own interests and those of his family, and for the cheers of his base. His opponents righteously declare that he is "not my president," forgetting that Trump made that choice for them long ago.

January 2019

STACEY ABRAMS'S LEAP OF FAITH

BETWEEN THE DAY I BEGAN reading Stacey Abrams's *Our Time Is Now* and the day I finished, multiple new facts about our time became clear: That in our time, more than one hundred thousand Americans are dead from a pandemic. That in our time, more than forty million Americans are newly unemployed. That in our time, a white Minneapolis police officer can pin his knee on a black man's neck, unimpeded, for more than eight minutes. And that in our time, more than one hundred US cities are erupting in protest.

All this is our time, and America feels like it is running out of it. Abrams, the former Georgia state legislator who narrowly lost the 2018 governor's race and is considered a long-shot veep contender for the 2020 Democratic ticket, writes of our time, but also of others that never stop echoing. She begins in 1968, a year when another man sought to win a presidential election by calling for law and order. The author's grandmother was preparing to cast her first-ever ballot in her home state, Mississippi. It was three years since the Voting Rights Act had passed, but Wilter Abrams remained in her bedroom, "paralyzed by fear," Abrams writes. After all, laws had changed before, but life hadn't always followed, not for black families such as theirs. "I'm afraid of the dogs and the police," she told her husband. "I don't want to vote."

Angered, Abrams's grandfather reminded his wife of the sacrifices they and their children had made to reach this moment. She finally gathered her courage and headed to the polls. Her grandmother understood the meaning of the Voting Rights Act, Abrams explains: "But she also knew not to expect immediate change, and she was right."

The tensions between patience and urgency, between fear and resolve, between the promise of someday and the demands of right now, are at the heart of *Our Time Is Now*. Abrams covers plenty of territory—identity politics, voting rights, and the frustrations and revelations of her gubernatorial race—but above all, she writes about the grinding work required to make real the compact of democratic participation.

She looks back on constitutional amendments ending slavery and expanding suffrage, landmark court decisions such as *Brown v. Board of Education*, and vital legislation such as the Voting Rights Act, but she recognizes each as a step, not an end. "We often see these historical moments as flash points with instant gratification; however, with most movements, the new laws, the new rules, only herald possibility," Abrams writes. "More must be done to make it so."

For Abrams, that "more" is the fight against voter suppression, and not only because she contends that it played a significant role in her 2018 defeat. *Our Time Is Now* mixes the author's experiences as a lawmaker, candidate, and activist with America's long history of slowly expanding—and sometimes receding—voting rights. Voting can be "a leap of faith," Abrams writes. It is faith not just in a candidate or a party but in a system, one that can be twisted and obstructed at multiple steps along the way.

The first step, voter registration, is an "opaque and confusing" process, Abrams writes, varying wildly from state to state. She describes how registration drives by outside groups are blocked and vilified; how discriminatory "exact match" policies mean that just a missing hyphen or misplaced apostrophe in someone's name can torpedo an application. Even if you are registered, frequent purging of the voter rolls has become "an effective tool to strip eligible voters of their rights." Sometimes the mere fact of not having voted recently suffices to purge a voter—as if constitutional rights just disappear because of the failure to exercise them. "I don't lose my Second Amendment right if I choose not to go hunting," Abrams points out, "and I still have freedom of religion if I skip church now and then."

Even if voters are registered and manage to remain so, their right to be heard is curtailed by limits on absentee ballots, restrictive voter-ID laws, the closure or narrow hours of polling sites, and the difficulty of making provisional ballots actually count. Such measures affect minority groups, who are more likely to sign up to vote through third-party registration drives and may face fewer options—for transportation and time off work—to get to the polls. "Modern-day suppression," Abrams argues, "has swapped rabid dogs and cops with billy clubs for restrictive voter ID and tangled rules for participation." Partisans who imagine that the demographic transformation of America will magically deliver some new electoral coalition are far too optimistic, she concludes, still living a 2008 high. "Demography is not destiny," Abrams writes. "It is opportunity."

The villain of her story is Gov. Brian Kemp, the Republican who defeated Abrams in 2018 and who, as Georgia's secretary of state at the time, was a candidate in an election he was charged with overseeing. Abrams did not offer a conventional concession to her opponent, she explains, because she believed doing so "would validate the system that slashed voters from the rolls, ensured thousands could not cast ballots, and blocked thousands more from being counted." Instead, in a speech more than a week after the election, she merely acknowledged that she had no remaining legal remedy. "The system worked as manipulated," she writes.

But Abrams looks beyond Kemp; state-level GOP officials across the country "have waged war on voter access," she contends, "their targets uniformly being people of color, naturalized citizens, and students—all populations more likely to vote Democratic." The scare tactic of voter fraud is used to justify various barriers, although "the reality of voter theft stands out much more clearly." President Trump has explained that he opposes expanding voting by mail during the coronavirus pandemic, on the overtly partisan grounds that it would hurt Republican candidates.

This book appears precisely when voting is being hailed as an alternative form of activism and expression. Hoping to contain the tensions in her city last weekend, the mayor of Atlanta delivered an impassioned speech. "If you want change in America, go and register to vote!" Keisha Lance Bottoms urged. "Show up at the polls on June ninth [the state primary]. Do it in November. That is the change we need in this country." The plea is consistent with Abrams's appeals. Yet the book highlights the varied obstacles that aspiring voters face, not just procedural or partisan but psychological, too. "One of the most pernicious and salient effects of voter suppression," she writes, "is that it not only blocks a voter from casting a ballot but convinces others to not bother trying."

Abrams's 2018 campaign made efforts to reach out to the "unlikely voter," those who vote only sporadically, those who are easily ignored by campaigns in favor of coveted swing voters. When courted and engaged, unlikely voters "can transform the political landscape," Abrams writes, but she understands that they are most susceptible to feeling alienated from the entire process—especially when they are made to feel as if the failure to vote is always their fault.

Abrams has been up-front about her desire to become Joe Biden's pick as the party's vice presidential nominee this year. In her book, she nationalizes the implications of her Georgia campaign, highlighting her ability to attract all kinds of voters, unlikely or otherwise. She stresses her success with Latino, Asian, and African American voters, but also emphasizes how white suburban women and college-educated white Americans overall were energized by her campaign. Abrams also devotes a chapter to international affairs, lest she be pegged as a foreign policy lightweight. ("I intentionally worked to build a robust understanding of international complexities," she writes, a bit dutifully.) And though she embraces identity politics in a straightforward way—Americans should be able to pick "between more than two heterosexual white men," she writes—Abrams knows it is only the beginning, not the end, of her pitch. "We found that my personal story and identity alone could not woo voters, especially black women. ... More than who I was, voters of all ages and all races wanted to know what I would do."

We could do worse than electing officials who answer that query by devoting themselves to the protection of Americans' right to vote. But *Our Time Is Now* is more than just another campaign book. Despite the immediacy of her title, Abrams also takes the long view. She urges fellow Democrats to focus on elections for state legislatures, secretaries of state, attorneys general, school boards, county commissions—"the unmentioned corridors of power we too often cede." And she stresses that boosting participation in the US Census can help reshape and expand representation in America. "Instead of treating the census as a once-a-decade activity, we should use education and voting to directly connect the census to the issues that matter," she writes. Abrams is focused not just on this year's census process but on getting more people counted ten years from now, too: "Otherwise, in 2030, we will once again find ourselves playing catch-up, despite a ten-year head start."

These are not the priorities of someone fixated on her short-term political prospects, no matter how brightly such ambitions may burn. "Those who cannot vote have no say in the operation of government, which creates a permanent state of powerlessness," Abrams writes. Yes, she would like to wield power on their behalf, and in the cause of progressive ends. But Abrams mainly wants to level the playing field of voting. She wants a fair fight, as she puts it again and again.

"No assault on democracy will ever be limited to its targets," Abrams writes. It's the sentence in this book that I can't forget. Not when, like Wilter Abrams five decades ago, Americans making their voices heard still have reason to fear the police and those "most vicious dogs" the president threatens to unleash. Not when that is still our time.

June 2020

OF SCANDALS AND WARNINGS

"No group of prosecutors and supporting personnel ever have labored under greater public scrutiny," the special counsel report declares on its opening page. "Every decision seemed to be a delicate one and previously uncharted courses frequently had to be faced. Each action occurred in the midst of a national turmoil."

It was 1975, and the Watergate Special Prosecution Force had just issued a lengthy report after twenty-eight months spent investigating Richard Nixon's administration and campaign. Let it not be said we've never been here before.

They form an odd American literary genre: reports by special counsels and select congressional committees on presidential wrongdoing. They carry the weight of official history yet are contested on arrival, even before. Their authors are prosecutors and lawmakers, so the texts can veer from dense to prosaic to dramatic. The documents identify possible crimes and other misdeeds at the highest level, yet their political implications tend to overpower all else.

Robert S. Mueller's report on Russian interference in the 2016 election—which he delivered to Attorney General William P. Barr on Friday—does not just complete two years of investigation, indictment, prosecution, and, of course, incessant speculation and anticipation. It will also take its place alongside works on presidential scandals past. And Mueller will join the ranks of Sam Ervin, Archibald Cox, Leon Jaworski, Lawrence E. Walsh, and Kenneth Starr.

The Watergate, Iran-Contra, and Clinton-Lewinsky special investigations reflect the struggles of our government to hold itself accountable; they exist because normal checks and balances failed. Yet, beyond their marshaling of facts and revelations of malfeasance, particularly striking are these reports' warnings to future generations on how to avert the kinds of scandals they examined and, more prophetically, theories of why they recur. Embedded in all these reports are strident calls for reform, urgent pleas for citizens to defend their democracy, grudging conclusions that new laws or old guardrails alone will not protect us, and, above all, simple exhortations to elect leaders of integrity.

If these past documents feel at times like they were written for us, that's because they were. Mueller's inquest exists not just because we have failed to police ourselves. It exists because we have failed to listen.

Sam Ervin, the North Carolina Democrat and chairman-turned-hero of the Senate Select Committee on Presidential Campaign Activities, wanted readers to know that Watergate wasn't fake news. "Watergate was not invented by enemies of the Nixon administration or even by the news media," he wrote in his opening statement to the committee's massive 1974 report. "On the contrary, Watergate was perpetrated upon America by White House and political aides, whom President Nixon himself had entrusted with the management of his campaign for reelection." Such aides, Ervin noted in a dry aside, often lacked the credentials or experience befitting their posts, save for their loyalty to the president—a malady that has struck the Trump White House in concentrated form.

The report of the Ervin committee, appearing just weeks before Nixon's resignation, detailed the offenses of the Watergate era: the broad effort to destroy the integrity of the electoral process, the hush-money payments and assurances of clemency for some of the original break-in defendants, the use of federal agencies as instruments of political revenge and electoral machination, and so much more.

In his lengthy and eloquent coda to the report, Republican senator Lowell P. Weicker Jr. of Connecticut lamented the way Nixon's allies tolerated such abuses. "A Constitutional stillness was over the land," he wrote. The Nixon-era misdeeds matter not only "because they contain sensational crimes, but because they confirm a misuse of the intended functions of important institutions." Watergate, he explained, "reflects a departure from legitimate government that if allowed to persist would be of far greater significance, over time, than any short-term criminal event." Similarly, today, the popular fixation on "collusion" as the burden of proof for the Mueller report—a view President Trump has done much to encourage—could lead the public to overlook the insidious erosion of standards of official behavior, inadvertently legitimizing what was once considered illegitimate or inappropriate, even if not illegal.

The report on the Iran-Contra scandal by special counsel Lawrence Walsh is instructive here. Though Walsh concluded that Ronald Reagan's personal conduct "fell well short of criminality which could be successfully prosecuted," the president nonetheless "created the conditions which made possible the crimes committed by others." Reagan made clear to his subordinates that he wanted the contras sustained "body and soul," as he put it, despite a congressional ban on US aid to the Nicaraguan rebels. Reagan officials who were convicted or pleaded guilty later saw their verdicts overturned on what Walsh considered technicalities, while others received preemptive presidential pardons. "The failure to punish governmental lawbreakers feeds the perception that public officials are not wholly accountable for their actions," Walsh complained. "It also may lead the public to believe that no real wrongdoing took place." The general haziness with which the Iran-Contra scandal is often recalled—unlike the historical consensus around Watergate and the partisan divide enveloping the Clinton impeachment—suggests that Walsh was right.

It is precisely the actions of such subordinates, at all levels, that determine the impact of a president's worst impulses. During Watergate, the Nixon White House pressured executive agencies to fund projects, promote initiatives, and fill jobs with an eye toward the president's reelection needs; the effort was known internally as the Responsiveness Program. But the White House encountered "considerable resistance in the Federal establishment to bending the system to fit reelection purposes," the Senate Watergate report explained approvingly. (Behold the "deep state," slow-walking the 1970s!) Two decades later, Walsh would encourage that reaction. "When a President, even with good motive and intent, chooses to skirt the laws or to circumvent them, it is incumbent upon his subordinates to resist, not join in," Walsh

wrote. Their oath is to the Constitution, "not to the man temporarily occu-
pying the Oval Office."

The main instruments of special counsels are indictments and prosecu-
tions, but their reports also call for bold, innovative reforms of government.
After wrestling with whether it could indict a sitting president, the Watergate
Special Prosecution Force—yes, that was the stone-cold name of the special
prosecutor's team—suggested a constitutional amendment to resolve the matter. Its report also recommended that presidents not nominate, and the Senate
not confirm, any candidates for attorney general who had held senior roles
in the president's campaign. The memory of John Mitchell, who had served
as Nixon's campaign manager in 1968 and who later as attorney general was
implicated in the Watergate scandal, loomed large, no doubt, but the dueling
imperatives of an attorney general—as both a key cabinet member serving
the president and as the nation's top law enforcement officer—would trouble
other special counsels, too.

Walsh, for instance, noted the "irreconcilable conflict" an attorney general faced in the case of high-level wrongdoing in the executive branch. He
complained that Attorney General Edwin Meese, who appointed the Iran-
Contra special counsel in 1986, "had already become, in effect, the President's
defense lawyer," whereas Meese's successor, Richard Thornburgh, engaged
in "unprecedented and unwarranted intrusion" into Walsh's prosecution efforts. Trump, for his part, has at times expressed his desire for loyalty from
law enforcement officials, and he never seemed to forgive his first attorney
general, Jeff Sessions, who had also been a high-profile Trump campaign
surrogate and adviser, for recusing himself from the Russia investigation.

The Senate report on Watergate also called for a number of reforms, or
"remedial legislation," as its mandate required, including the creation of a
Public Attorney's Office, a sort of permanent special prosecutor appointed
by the judiciary and confirmed by the Senate, with the mandate to prosecute
criminal cases involving a conflict of interest in the executive branch. (Other
authorities, including the Watergate Special Prosecution Force, were less
than enthused about the proposal, and it eventually died.) And the committee's vice chairman, Republican senator Howard Baker of Tennessee—who

uttered the immortal "What did the president know, and when did he know it?" query during the Watergate hearings—suggested the abolition of the electoral college as well as the repeal of the Twenty-Second Amendment, so that second-term presidents could stand for reelection and thus face accountability from voters.

Whatever their merits, the proliferating reform proposals flowed from a conclusion common to many of these reports: that the normal checks and balances of the American system were no longer sufficient. In the Senate Watergate report, Senator Weicker hailed the separation of powers as "one of our foremost Constitutional doctrines" but acknowledged that the system's success is not automatic, since it "depends to a large degree on self-adherence and restraint by those in a position to upset the balance." Such restraint was in short supply in the Watergate era, and in others, too. Walsh was particularly blunt at the conclusion of his Iran-Contra report. In finding that the president, various aides, and major cabinet officers had skirted or broken the law and attempted to hide that fact, Walsh asked: "What protection do the people of the United States have against such a concerted action by such powerful officers?" When the executive branch provides false, incomplete, or misleading information to Congress, "the rightly celebrated constitutional checks and balances are inadequate, alone, to preserve the rule of law."

How then, to prevent such actions? "Law is not self-executing," Ervin admitted. "Unfortunately, at times its execution rests in the hands of those who are faithless to it." To deserve public office, then, individuals must "understand and be dedicated to the true purpose of government, which is to promote the good of the people, and entertain the abiding conviction that a public office is a public trust, which must never be abused to secure private advantage," Ervin wrote. They must also possess intellectual and moral rectitude. "The only sure antidote for future Watergates is understanding of fundamental principles and intellectual and moral integrity in the men and women who achieve or are entrusted with governmental or political power."

In periods of intense partisan and cultural division, traditional safeguards break down because traditional representation is lacking. Political parties, for instance, usually serve as a mediating force between constituen-

cies and those who govern, but "when the parties do not function well, individual citizens feel a loss of control over politics and Government," Weicker
wrote. "They find themselves powerless to influence events. Voting seems
futile; politics seems pointless. The political process crosses the line ... and
things go badly for America." That seems as true in the late 2010s as it was
in the early 1970s.

The Starr report on the Clinton-Lewinsky saga of the late 1990s reads like
the most overtly partisan of these tomes, even making the case for impeaching Clinton in its first sentence. Yet it unexpectedly offers one of the most optimistic passages. In an otherwise gross conversation it recounts between the
president and political adviser Dick Morris, Clinton fesses up to his relationship with Monica Lewinsky—"I've tried to shut my body down, sexually, I
mean ... with this girl I just slipped up"—and worries about independent
counsel Ken Starr and the whole "legal thing." Morris, hardly an exemplar of
virtue, nonetheless assures him that there is "a great capacity for forgiveness
in this country and you should consider tapping into it."

Such belief in the virtue of the people emerges throughout these
reports—an unexpected epilogue to their relentless documenting of the
seamy side of American public life. But maybe there really is no one else left
to depend upon. "This won't be the Watergate to end all Watergates," Weicker concluded. "Other men will tape the doors of America in other times.
Whether they succeed will be a matter of spirit." Ervin, for one, believed
that spirit had been roused by the horrors of the presidential abuse he helped
expose. "The American people have been re-awakened to the task democracy
imposes upon them—steadfast vigilance of the conduct of the public officials
they choose to lead them." And the Watergate Special Prosecution Force recalled how, when Nixon ordered the firing of the original special prosecutor,
Archibald Cox, "Americans rose in anger ... When vigilance erupted, institutions responded."

Has vigilance erupted today as well? Ervin described how critics of
Nixon were branded as "enemies" by the president's circle, while adminis-
tration-friendly journalists argued that the Senate committee members were

"biased and irresponsible" and that allegations of White House wrongdoing were merely the "venomous machinations of a hostile and unreliable press." The playbook is familiar. Perhaps such public-spiritedness is harder to harness, or simply less effective, with today's relentless assault on investigators and opponents.

So we look to Mueller's report, expecting so much from it—even when the lesson from Mueller's predecessors is that, in truth, they demand far more from us.

March 2019

THE UNITED HATES OF AMERICA

THE PANDEMIC AND THE ECONOMY. Race and immigration. Health care and climate change. Guns and abortion. Justice and inequality. And, of course, the almighty Supreme Court. These are the issues in our November 3 election, and *the issues*, we are told, are supposed to matter.

But what if American voters, and 2020 voters in particular, are animated by baser instincts that are far more timeless, such as hatred, tribalism, and exclusion? What if more than wanting their candidates to win, more than hoping to see their preferences implemented as policy and enshrined in law, they mainly want the other side to suffer a humiliating defeat?

The growing polarization of the United States into a nation torn by partisan identities is one of the legacies of the Trump presidency, even if it began long ago. What Bill Bishop, writing in the 2000s, called the Big Sort was a decades-long process of clustering by geography, income, and culture, producing homogeneous enclaves with self-reinforcing and mutually opposing worldviews. Under President Trump, however, polarization morphed into an overt campaigning and governing strategy, one the country has embraced as party affiliation increasingly tracks divides of culture and religion, race and place. Here, there are no win-win outcomes. Each camp finds vindication in the struggles of its rival, preferring results that are worse for all if they manage to boost the home team's relative advantage and magnify the differences between the sides.

We're way past bowling alone; now, we're gripping that bowling ball and looking for something to smash.

A decade after Bishop's work, multiple volumes in the Trump years have chronicled America's descent into this negative partisanship, a condition in which opposition overwhelms affirmation. Lilliana Mason's *Uncivil Agreement*, Amy Chua's *Political Tribes*, Ezra Klein's *Why We're Polarized*, David French's *Divided We Fall*, and Pete Buttigieg's *Trust*—and that is just a sampling of the subgenre—explain how the adjective in "United States" has come to seem aspirational, even vestigial. "More than simply disagreeing, Democrats and Republicans are feeling like very different kinds of people," Mason writes, while French worries that our very political and geographic union can no longer be taken for granted.

The authors hazard proposals for how to break free from this cycle in which a polarized electorate compels politicians to campaign in more po-larized ways, thus entrenching voters even further. Above all, many urge a restoration of citizenship as an overriding American identity, even as they recognize the difficulty of getting there when the gaps between us are ex-panding. And the popular, political, and intellectual fixation on Trump himself—and the divisions he so relishes and deepens—may make it harder still. In a country where all have lined up either as Trump's resistance or his base, it seems almost countercultural to suggest that these are not our only options, that this man need not remain the sole reference point defining us.

The challenge of a nation defined by ideas is that ideas can lose their appeal, their seeming relevance, even their understood meaning. "The great Enlightenment principles of modernity—liberalism, secularism, rationality, equality, free markets—do not provide the kind of tribal group identity that human beings crave," Chua, a professor at Yale Law School, writes in *Political Tribes*. And they crave it above all when they feel threatened by ascen-dant forces in the culture, in the campaign, on the job. "Today, no group in America feels comfortably dominant," Chua warns. "Every group feels attacked, pitted against other groups not just for jobs and spoils but for the right to define the nation's identity. In these conditions, democracy devolves into zero-sum group competition."

It can be the fear of losing status in the face of the country's racial and de-mographic transformations; or it can be the anger at never receiving enough status to avoid the threat of harm, harassment, even death at the hands of an unfair justice system. The cultural and political trenches of the Trump years—whether #MeToo and Black Lives Matter, the resurgence of racist forces, or the horrors at the southern border—all intensify the sense of zero-sum identity, Klein contends, of belonging to one camp and confronting the other. "There is nothing that makes us identify with our groups so strongly as the feeling that the power we took for granted may soon be lost or the injustices we've long borne may soon be rectified," he writes.

Trump instinctively grasps the power of these sentiments and has aggravated them whenever possible, from the birtherism lie to the demonization of Mexican immigrants to the specter of Cory Booker overrunning white suburbia. Trump's disregard for conservative mantras of family values and fiscal rectitude is often held up as proving the hypocrisy of his party, but it merely proves that in America today, identity beats policy. "Partisans dislike each other to a degree that cannot be explained by policy disagreements alone," Mason emphasizes. "When partisanship implicitly evokes racial, religious, and other social identities . . . it [is] far easier for individual partisans to dehumanize their political opponents."

In this context, efforts to unmake the Affordable Care Act or squeeze in one more associate justice are not just about the policies or principles at stake but about defeating and demoralizing the other side. It's owning the libs as domestic policy.

In his 2016 campaign, Trump was "a master marketer who astutely read the market," in Klein's words, but he did not have to be the one to serve it. "Eventually, someone was going to come along and give the Republican base what they wanted," Klein writes. And Trump has done it again in his latest campaign, running not on a proposed second-term agenda (he has none) but, in the words of *National Review*'s Rich Lowry, as a crude insult to the cultural left. "To put it in blunt terms, for many people, he's the only middle finger available," Lowry writes.

In *Divided We Fall*, French identifies a shared core in the nation's dueling narratives, a "burning conviction that the other side doesn't just want its opponents to lose political races, but rather wishes for them to exist in a state of permanent, dangerous (perhaps even deadly) subordination." For Christian conservatives, this fear manifests itself in any perceived threats to religious liberty; for progressives, it is evident in any possible erosion of abortion rights. French imagines two secessionist scenarios—a "Calexit" in which California secedes from the union over gun laws, a "Texit" in which the Lone Star State departs over abortion disputes—both of which seem eerily plausible. "We cannot assume that a continent-sized, multi-ethnic, multi-faith democracy can remain united forever," he concludes.

Trump's rhetoric and policies pick at the scabs of all such divides. His constant dismissal of the plight of "Democrat-run" cities or states during the coronavirus pandemic, for example, makes clear that our president already believes he governs a torn nation.

"Authors write whole books about devilishly complex social problems and then pretend they can be solved in a few bullet points," Klein, editor at large of *Vox*, admits in his own book. "I have more confidence in my diagnosis than my prescription." So, is there a way to even mitigate America's crippling polarization? The writers suggest possible solutions, though not with enormous certitude—the Big Sort Of.

Mason, a University of Maryland government professor whose 2018 book is cited frequently in the later volumes, posits that some overriding national goal could unite Americans—except she has trouble imagining one that works. Chua, who contends that both the bigotry of right-wing tribalism and the political correctness of left-wing tribalism are gnawing at our bonds, worries that there is "nearly no one standing up . . . for an American identity that transcends and unites the identities of all the country's many subgroups." She concludes by arguing that we need "one-on-one human engagement" and praises those Americans who "empathize with each other's humanity," but is concerned that seeing each other as one people may just be impossible right now.

For former Democratic presidential candidate Pete Buttigieg, our polarization is a crisis of trust—not just trust in one another but in our political institutions, too. "We live in a country whose most radical founding premise was that people could be trusted to govern themselves—and that the people, trusted in this way, would produce leaders who themselves are worthy of trust," he writes. Because American identity is civic rather than ethnic, a sense of personal trust and mutual belonging is indispensable.

To strengthen that trust, Buttigieg calls for a voluntary civilian service program that would put millions of diverse Americans in conversation; a more egalitarian system of taxation; and a truth commission that can confront America's racist history and present, because racism is the country's "most pernicious form of distrust." He also urges a more aggressive use of constitutional amendments to end the electoral college, pass the Equal Rights Amendment, and reform campaign financing. Buttigieg envisions a "new American social democracy" as ambitious as the New Deal and the civil rights era combined; the alternative, he writes, is a continued national decline.

Klein does not imagine we can rid ourselves of political polarization, nor would we entirely want to; some degree of polarization is needed if the parties are to offer contrasting and coherent platforms. He merely wants to help us live with it. To that end, he would eliminate the debt ceiling and the filibuster, approve statehood for DC and Puerto Rico, and do away with the "archaic" electoral college. He doesn't see such reforms as revolutionary; they would merely insulate government operations against the most serious risks of polarization, he writes. (The debt ceiling, for instance, allows the creditworthiness of the American government to be held hostage by a minority party, while a popular vote would compel the parties to seek broad, moderating coalitions.) Even so, it is not hard to imagine such reforms—as well as Buttigieg's—falling into what, in French's analysis, would feel to the right like an effort at cultural and political dominance. That doesn't make them wrong, but it does make them hard.

French, for his part, envisions a new federalism—"the eighteenth-century solution to our twenty-first-century problem," he writes—such that progressives can build progressive communities and conservatives can build conservative ones, in a live-and-let-live scenario. This is a path toward eliminating polarization by, in a sense, allowing it: "The rebirth of federalism involves standing by and *consenting* to your ideological opponents in different jurisdictions enacting policies and practices you may despise and consider unwise or unjust." With the full protection of the Bill of Rights, he argues, neither progressive nor conservative states could oppress dissenters in their ranks. French calls this a system of "protected customization."

He's not calling on us to agree—just to continue disagreeing without destroying ourselves. But even that may be too much right now. "In the short run . . . a return to federalism is not on the table," French laments. "The drive for domination is still too strong, and the hopes for domination are still high." Instead, he calls for "a renewed commitment to courage and character" on the part of the nation's political leaders.

Which brings us back to that election on Tuesday. It is tempting to conclude that Trump, with his divisiveness and his indifference to the needs of the nation as a whole, is a prime mover behind our polarization and that his departure could ease our tensions, could take us beyond a world where even the hat you choose to wear—or the mask you don't—becomes a marker of political identity. But it is also possible that, by bifurcating our disagreements, Trump is papering over them; by simplifying our discourse into pro-Trump or against him, he is inhibiting the more meaningful and painful debates before us.

Without him, Americans would suddenly have to wrestle with everything else that keeps us apart, with all the discord and estrangement within and between our parties, movements, cultures, and regions. It would be messier but perhaps more honest, more consistent with the American story, that relentless fight to determine who we are. The holding pattern in which we live—with fantasies of *after the election* or *after the pandemic* so dominant—will not last forever. Soon we'll have to find out if Trump is indeed the only middle finger available to us, or if it's just that the middle finger is the only one we still remember how to use.

October 2020

THE BIG LIE AND THE BIG JOKE

DONALD TRUMP'S SO-CALLED BIG LIE is not big because of its brazen dishonesty or its widespread influence or its unyielding grip on the Republican Party. It is not even big because of its ambition—to delegitimize a presidency, disenfranchise millions of voters, clap back against reality. No, the lie that Donald Trump won the 2020 election has grown so powerful because it is yoked to an older deception, without which it could not survive: the idea that American politics is, in essence, a joke, and that it can be treated as such without consequence.

The big lie depends on the big joke. It was enabled by it. It was enhanced by it. It is sustained by it.

When politicians publicly defend positions they privately reject, they are telling the joke. When they give up on the challenge of governing the country for the rush of triggering the enemy, they are telling the joke. When they intone that they must address the very fears they have encouraged or manufactured among their constituents, they are telling the joke. When their off-the-record smirks signal that they don't really mean what they just said or did, they are telling the joke. As the big lie spirals ever deeper into unreality, with the former president mixing election falsehoods with call-outs to violent conspiratorial fantasies, the big joke has much to answer for.

Books like *Why We Did It: A Travelogue from the Republican Road to Hell*, by a former Republican operative and campaign consultant, Tim Miller, and *Thank You for Your Servitude: Donald Trump's Washington and the Price of Submission*, by the *Atlantic*'s Mark Leibovich, place this long-running gag at the center of American politics. The big joke separates words from accountability, divorces action from responsibility, and enables all manner of lies. "Getting the joke" means understanding that nothing you say need be true, that nobody expects it to be true—at least nobody in the know. "The truth of this scam, or 'joke,' was fully evident inside the club," Leibovich writes.

"We're all friends here. Everyone knew the secret handshake, spoke the native language, and got the joke."

Without the big joke, the big lie would not merit its adjective. Its challenge to democracy would be ephemeral, not existential.

The chroniclers of Donald Trump's election lie typically seek out an origin story, a choose-your-own adventure that always leads to the Capitol steps on January 6, 2021. In *The Big Lie: Election Chaos, Political Opportunism, and the State of American Politics After 2020,* Jonathan Lemire of *Politico* pinpoints an August 2016 campaign rally in Columbus, Ohio, during which Trump first suggested that the contest against Hillary Clinton would be rigged against him. This, Lemire writes, was when "the seeds of the big lie had been planted."

Tim Alberta of the *Atlantic* starts six months earlier, when Trump accused Sen. Ted Cruz of Texas of cheating in the Iowa caucuses. "That episode was a bright red, blinking light foreshadowing everything that was to come," Alberta told PBS's *Frontline*. In *The Destructionists: The Twenty-Five Year Crack-Up of the Republican Party,* the *Washington Post* columnist Dana Milbank offers a far longer accumulation of lies from the right: the notion that Bill and Hillary Clinton were involved in the death of the White House lawyer Vince Foster, the illusions behind President George W. Bush's invasion of Iraq, the birther concoctions, the death-panel ravings—all building toward the big one. "The GOP's quarter-century war on facts had come to this: a gargantuan fabrication aimed at discrediting democracy itself," Milbank sums up. And Leibovich quotes Rep. Adam Schiff's view of how his House colleagues slowly submitted to Trump's fantasies. "It's one small lie, followed by a demand for a bigger lie and a bigger concession, a bigger moral lapse, until, you know, these folks that I admired and respected, because I believe that they believe what they were saying, had given themselves up so completely to Donald Trump."

Such accounts reflect the common understanding that the big lie is really all the little lies we told along the way—a cycle of deceit and submission, culminating in a myth so powerful that it transcends belief and becomes a fully formed worldview. Lemire notes how Trump's assertion that he had been wiretapped by President Barack Obama during the 2016 campaign seemed like a pretty gargantuan lie at the time, one that Trump tweeted "without any evidence." (Journalists love to note that the former president utters falsehoods "without evidence," an adorable euphemism for "making stuff up.") But even this one dissipates in the wake of the big lie. After "big," the term "unprecedented" may be the election lie's most common descriptor.

But it is not without precedent. After all, what was birtherism if not the same lie? Its underlying racism rendered the grotesque theory about Obama's birthplace especially repugnant, but the basic assertion is familiar: that a president whom the American people lawfully chose is not legitimate, is something less than the real thing.

The 2020 election lie is not bigger than birtherism. History should not remember the effort to delegitimize Obama's presidency as just another rung on the ladder toward the big lie. The lies are akin even in their power of persuasion. Leibovich recalls how in 2016, 72 percent of Republicans said they believed Trump's lies about Obama's background. This figure is comparable to the 71 percent of Republicans who said in late 2021 that they believed President Biden was not a fully legitimate president. And much as support for the 2020 election lie provides a loyalty test in the Trumpified Republican Party, a willingness to believe the worst of Obama was a near requirement in the party during his presidency. "A testing ground for Republican squishiness was how strongly, and how bitterly, one opposed Obama," the historian Nicole Hemmer recalls in *Partisans: The Conservative Revolutionaries Who Remade American Politics in the 1990s*, on the rise of the post-Reagan right. "To match the response of the party's base, politicians would need to reflect the emotions gripping it." And they did.

For Hemmer, the Republican Party's evolution from the party of Reagan to the party of Trump began with Pat Buchanan, the White House aide, television pundit, and authoritarian-curious presidential candidate who "fashioned grievance politics into an agenda," she writes—a program that emphasized identity, immigration, and race as its battlegrounds. For Milbank, it was Newt Gingrich, the former House speaker, and the "savage politics he pioneered" in advance of the Republican Revolution of 1994.

"There was nobody better at attacking, destroying, and undermining those in power," Milbank writes. Gingrich made compromise a thought crime and labeled his opponents as sick and traitorous, tactics that should also sound familiar.

You needn't pick between Buchanan and Gingrich—it's enough to say that Buchanan gave the modern Republican Party its substance and Gingrich provided its style. (I imagine they'd both be honored by the distinctions.) When Trump dispatched his supporters to the Capitol on January 6, telling them to "fight like hell," urging them to preserve a country that was slipping away, calling them patriots who could take back an election stolen by the radical left, he was channeling both men. The big lie is part of their legacy, too.

In his j'accuse-y yet semi-confessional *Why We Did It*, Miller, now a writer at large for the anti-Trump conservative forum The Bulwark, tries to grasp why his old colleagues followed Trump all the way to his rally at the Ellipse on January 6. "I needed to figure out where our parting had started," he writes. Miller understands the futility of seeking a single origin story—"I'm sure a student of history might be able to trace it back to the Southern Strategy or Lee Atwater or, hell, maybe even Mark Hanna (give him a Google)," Miller writes—but he does hazard some explanations. He points to Republicans' ability to compartmentalize concerns about Trump. Their unquenchable compulsion to be in the mix. Their self-serving belief that they could channel dark arts for noble purposes. Their desire to make money. (Miller acknowledges his own paid work asssting the confirmation of Scott Pruitt as Trump's Environmental Protection Agency administrator, a stint that makes Miller more of a Rarely Trumper than a Never Trumper.) Most of all, his old colleagues succumbed to Trump because they believed they were playing "some big game devoid of real-world consequences."

Miller lingers on this game—the amoral world of tactics, messaging, and opposition research, the realm of politics where facts matter less than cleverness and nothing matters more than results. He once thought of it as winning the race, being a killer, just a dishonest buck for a dishonest day's work. "Practitioners of politics could easily dismiss moralistic or technical concerns just by throwing down their trump card: 'It's all part of the Game,'" Miller writes. He has a nickname for the comrades so immersed in the game that they are oblivious to its consequences: the LOL Nothing Matters Republicans. "The LOLNMRs had decided that if someone like Trump could win, then everything that everyone does in politics is meaningless."

The big lie thrives on LOL Nothing Matters.

What Miller calls "the Game" becomes "the joke" in Leibovich's book, the depressing tale of the high-level supplicants who surrounded Trump during his presidency and continue to grovel in what they hope will be an interregnum. If the purely transactional nature of Washington power was the subject of Leibovich's 2013 bestseller, *This Town*, the mix of mendacity and subservience behind every transaction is the theme of his latest work. Reince Priebus, during his incarnation as Republican National Committee chairman before his six-month sojourn as Trump's White House chief of staff, explained to Leibovich that of course he got the joke. "This was his way of reassuring me that he understood what was really happening beyond his surface niceties about unity, tolerance, grace, or the idea that Trump could ever 'pivot,'" Leibovich writes. In other words, don't take his words seriously. "He got the joke and knew that I did, too."

The platonic ideal of the big joke was immortalized in the *Washington Post* the week after the 2020 election, uttered by an anonymous senior Republican official reflecting on Trump's election claims. "What is the downside for humoring him for this little bit of time? No one seriously thinks the results will change. He went golfing this weekend. It's not like he's plotting how to prevent Joe Biden from taking power on Jan. 20." It was wrong in so many ways—the downside would prove enormous, the believers would become legion, the plotting was underway.

The big lie is that the election was stolen; the big joke is that you can prolong that lie without consequence. The former is a quest for undeserved power; the latter is an evasion of well-deserved responsibility.

Other renditions of the big joke were more subtle. A few days after the election, a reporter asked Secretary of State Mike Pompeo if the State Department was preparing to work with the Biden team to facilitate a "smooth transition" of power. "There will be a smooth transition," Pompeo responded, making the slightest of pauses before adding, "to a second Trump administration." He then chuckled, a possible signal that he was aware of the truth, and that he "hoped that perhaps everyone understood his position," Leibovich writes.

Pompeo got the big joke about the big lie. Yet the man charged with representing American values to the world still felt he had to tell both.

Rep. Adam Kinzinger, one of ten Republican House members to vote in favor of Trump's second impeachment, says the joke is well understood among his party colleagues. "For all but a handful of members, if you put them on truth serum, they knew that the election was fully legitimate and that Donald Trump was a joke," Kinzinger told Leibovich. "The vast majority of people get the joke. I think Kevin McCarthy gets the joke. Lindsey gets the joke. The problem is that the joke isn't even funny anymore." Humoring Trump has grown humorless.

There was a time when even Trump grappled with the truth. Alyssa Farah Griffin, who served as communications director in the Trump White House, told PBS's *Frontline* that the president admitted defeat in the days after the election was called for Biden. "There was one moment where in this period he was watching Joe Biden on TV and says, 'Can you believe I lost to this (blank) guy?'"

But what once may have sounded like a rhetorical lament—can you believe I lost?—now seems like a challenge to anyone questioning the big lie. Can *you* believe I lost? There is only one acceptable answer. In his rally last weekend in Youngstown, Ohio, Trump reiterated his commitment to the lie. "I ran twice. I won twice," he declared. For a moment, when bragging about how many more votes he won in 2020 than in 2016, the veil almost fell. "We got twelve million more and we lost," Trump said, before recovering. "We didn't lose," he continued. "We lost in their imagination." It was a classic Trumpian projection: the lie is true and the truth is fake.

The big lie appeared to crescendo on January 6, 2021. The big joke, however, was retold during the early hours of January 7, when the election results were certified, with 147 Republican lawmakers—more than half of the total—having voted to overturn them. As Milbank puts it, "once you've unhitched yourself from the truth wagon, there's no limit to the places you can visit." You can use exaggerated warnings of voter fraud to justify state-level initiatives tightening ballot access. (Lemire warns that the big lie has "metastasized" from a rallying cry into the "cold, methodical process of legislation.") You can select election deniers to carry the party banner in midterm contests. And yes, you can visit the Capitol on the day the voters' will is being affirmed, trash the place, and tell yourself, as the Republican National Committee suggested, that you're engaging in "legitimate political discourse."

The RNC's statement, part of a resolution censuring Kinzinger and Rep. Liz Cheney for participating in the House's January 6 investigation, seemed to rebrand the assault as an exercise in civic virtue. The RNC soon backtracked, professing that the resolution had not endorsed the violence at the Capitol.

In a perverse sense, though, the RNC was right. Not about the rioters but about the discourse. Political debate has become so degraded that it includes every kind of offense, be it anonymous officials humoring the former president, QAnon conspiracists exalting him, or frenzied die-hards perpetrating violence on his behalf. Together, the big joke and the big lie have turned the nation's political life into a dark comedy, one staged for the benefit of aggrieved supporters who, imagining that the performance is real and acting on that belief, become its only punchline.

September 2022

MUELLER, UKRAINE,
AND JANUARY 6

IN RETROSPECT, THE MUELLER REPORT was a cry for help.

"The Office," as the special counsel so self-effacingly called itself in its report, knew its limits, or at least chose them. It could not indict a sitting president. It was generous with the benefit of the doubt when evaluating a potential "obstructive act" or gauging criminal intent by President Donald Trump. It considered mitigating, and sometimes dubious, explanations for his behavior, and was as restrained in interpreting the president's misdeeds as it was zealous in listing them.

Its conclusion on whether Trump obstructed justice became a Washington classic of needle-threading ambiguity: "While this report does not conclude that the President committed a crime, it also does not exonerate him." The Office declined to call Trump a criminal, however much it might have wanted to.

Instead, scattered throughout its 448 pages, the Mueller report includes some not-so-subtle instructions and warnings that future investigators, less inhibited, could heed when facing fresh misdeeds.

The two highest-profile congressional investigations of Trump that followed—the 2019 report by the House Intelligence Committee on Trump's pressuring of Ukraine and the 2022 report by the select committee on the January 6 attack—read like deliberate contrasts to the document produced by Robert Mueller and his team. Their presentation is dramatic, not dense; their conclusions are blunt, not oblique; their arguments are political as much as legal. And yet the Ukraine and January 6 reports seem to follow the cues, explicit or implied, that the Mueller report left behind.

Read together, these three major investigations of the Trump presidency appear in conversation with one another, ever more detailed drafts of a most unorthodox historical record—a history in which these documents are characters as much as chroniclers.

The documents try to explain the former president, and they also strain to contain him. The Mueller report inspects the guardrails that Trump bent and sometimes broke. The Ukraine report lays out the case that led to his first impeachment. The January 6 report now declares him "unfit" to return to the nation's highest office—the very office Trump is again pursuing—or to any office below it.

The effect is cumulative. While the Mueller report evaluates Trump's behavior as a series of individual, unrelated actions, it knows better, stating near the end that the president's "pattern of conduct as a whole" was vital to grasping his intentions. The Ukraine and January 6 reports took up that task, establishing links among Trump's varied transgressions.

While the Mueller report wonders whether Trump and his advisers committed certain acts "willfully"—that is, "with general knowledge of the illegality of their conduct"—the investigations into his pressuring of Ukraine and the Capitol assault seek to show that Trump knew that his actions violated the law and that his statements ran counter to the truth.

And while the Mueller report grudgingly posits that some of the president's questionable actions might have been taken with the public, rather than the private, interest in mind, the Ukraine and January 6 reports argue that with Trump, the distinction between public and private always collapsed in favor of the latter.

The Mueller report would not declare that the president deserved impeachment or had committed crimes, but it certainly didn't mind if someone else reached those conclusions. It states plainly that accusing Trump of a crime could "preempt constitutional processes for addressing presidential misconduct"—that is, the constitutional process of impeachment, which the Ukraine investigation would soon deliver.

The Mueller report also notes in its final pages that "only a successor Administration would be able to prosecute a former President," which is what the January 6 special committee, with its multiple criminal referrals, has urged the Biden administration's Justice Department to do.

The Ukraine and January 6 reports did their best to answer Mueller's call.

All three reports include quintessentially Trumpian scenes, consistent in their depictions of the former president's methods, and in keeping with numerous journalistic accounts of how he sought to manipulate people, rules, and institutions.

When the January 6 report shows Trump haranguing Mike Pence, telling the vice president that Pence would be known as a "patriot" if he helped overturn the 2020 election, it's hard not to recall the scene in the Mueller report when the president tells Jeff Sessions that the attorney general would go down as a "hero" if he reversed his recusal from the Russia investigation.

All three reports show Trump deploying the mechanisms of government for political gain. Less than four months into his term, Trump relies on a Department of Justice memo as cover to fire the FBI director; he uses the Office of Management and Budget to delay the disbursal of military aid to Ukraine in 2019; and he attempts to use fake state electoral certificates to upend the results of the 2020 vote.

Still, each investigation offers a slightly different theory of Trump. In the Mueller report, Trump and his aides come across as the gang that can't cheat straight—too haphazard to effectively coordinate with a foreign government, too ignorant of campaign finance laws to purposely violate them, often comically naive about the gravity of their plight. When Michael Flynn resigns from the White House after admitting to lying about his contacts with Russian officials, Trump consoles him with the assurance, "We'll give you a good recommendation," as if Flynn were a departing mailroom intern rather than a disgraced ex–national security adviser.

When the Trump campaign tried to conceal details surrounding its infamous Trump Tower meeting with a Russian lawyer in June 2016, the Mueller report suggests that the effort "may reflect an intention to avoid political consequences rather than any prior knowledge of illegality"— that is, that the Trump team might have felt just shame, not guilt.

The Mueller report rebuts the Trumpian notion that the president can employ his legitimate authority regardless of the illegitimacy of his purpose. "An improper motive can render an actor's conduct criminal even when the conduct would otherwise be lawful and within the actor's authority," the report states, in the patient tone of a parent explaining household rules to a child. But even in the damning sections on Trump's potential obstruction of justice (in which "the Office" all but states that it would have charged Trump if it could have), the report theorizes that the president may have been attacking the inquiries against him out of concern that they hindered his ability to govern, not because he was hiding some nefarious activity.

The Ukraine report, by contrast, regards Trump as more strategic than chaotic, and it does not wallow in some netherworld between the president's personal benefit and his public service. "The President placed his own personal and political interests above the national interests of the United States, sought to undermine the integrity of the U.S. presidential election process, and endangered U.S. national security," Rep. Adam Schiff declares in the report's preface. (And perhaps no moment is more believable than the Ukraine report's description of Trump's April 2019 conversation with the newly elected Ukrainian president, Volodymyr Zelensky, when Trump makes a point of mentioning that when he owned the Miss Universe pageant, "Ukraine was always very well represented.")

The three investigations tell different stories, but the misdeeds all run together, more overlapping than sequential. The president's effort to strongarm Zelensky's government into investigating the Biden family (ironically, under the guise of Trump's anti-corruption concerns) was an attempt to manipulate the 2020 election, while his desire for Ukraine to investigate its own supposed US election interference (on behalf of the Democrats, naturally) was part of Trump's ongoing battle to defend the glorious memory of his 2016 victory. "We were struck by the fact that the President's misconduct was not an isolated occurrence, nor was it the product of a naïve president," Schiff writes. Indeed, several weeks before Trump's famous phone conversation with Zelensky on July 25, 2019, Trump had already ordered a hold on hundreds of millions of dollars in military aid to Ukraine, which would be dangled as leverage. And the purely political nature of the enterprise was made plain when the report notes that Trump did not care if Ukraine in fact conducted any investigations. It simply had to announce them.

"Viewing the [president's] acts collectively can help to illuminate their significance," the Mueller report states. The Ukraine report shows that the conversation that Trump described as "a perfect call" was not the ask; it was the confirmation. When Trump said, "I would like you to do us a favor, though," Zelensky and his aides had already been notified what was coming. The Ukraine scandal was never about a single call, just like the January 6 report was not about a single day.

The January 6 report is the most dramatic—and certainly the most readable—of the three documents. It is vaguely journalistic in style, even adopting the narrative convention of turning memorable quotes into chapter titles, like "I Just Want to Find 11,780 Votes" and "Be There, Will Be Wild!" (Contrast this with the Mueller report's "Background Legal and Evidentiary Principles" or "Legal Defenses to the Application of Obstruction-of-Justice Statutes to the President," among its other sexy teasers.) The report on the Capitol assault also takes seriously the admonition to view the president's actions collectively, not individually; the phrase "multipart plan" appears throughout the report, with Trump as the architect.

Several observers of the Trump era have described how the president learned to maneuver his way through the executive branch and grew bolder in his abuses of it; in the January 6 report, that transition is complete. No longer the bumbling, reactive, and instinctual occupant of the Oval Office, here Trump is fully in charge—purposely spreading false information about election fraud, pressuring Pence to refuse to certify the electoral college count, leaning on state and local electoral officials to change the vote totals, summoning tens of thousands of supporters to Washington on January 6 and urging them to march to the Capitol, then standing by for hours as the violent attack was underway. "The central cause of January 6th was one man, former President Donald Trump, whom many others followed," the report concludes.

Trump told America that he alone could fix it; the January 6 report tells us that he alone could break it.

Even more so than the Ukraine report, the January 6 report repeatedly emphasizes how Trump knew, well, everything. "Donald Trump's own campaign officials told him early on that his claims of fraud were false,"

Liz Cheney, the committee vice chair, writes in her introduction. "Donald Trump's senior Justice Department officials—each appointed by Donald Trump himself—investigated the allegations and told him repeatedly that his fraud claims were false. Donald Trump's White House lawyers also told him his fraud claims were false."

There is no room here for the plausible deniability that the Mueller report entertained, for the notion that Trump didn't know better, or that, in the immortal words of Attorney General William P. Barr when he creatively interpreted the Mueller report to exonerate Trump of obstruction of justice, that the president was "frustrated and angered by his sincere belief that the investigation was undermining his presidency."

This alleged sincerity underscored the president's "noncorrupt motives," as Barr put it. In the January 6 report, any case for Trumpian sincerity is eviscerated in a six-page chart in the executive summary, which catalogues the many times the president was informed of the facts of the election yet continued to lie about them. "Just say the election was corrupt and leave the rest to me and the Republican congressmen," Trump told top Department of Justice officials in late December 2020, the report says.

Just announce an investigation into the Bidens. Just say the 2020 election was rigged. Trump's most corrupt action is always the corruption of reality.

The January 6 report devotes a chapter to explaining how the president purposely mustered a mob to Washington, how his "will be wild!" call-out on social media united rival extremist groups in a common cause, and how he urged his supporters to march on the Capitol and "fight like hell" to obstruct the affirmation of a legitimate vote.

Two days before his speech, Trump had already floated the idea to advisers that he would join the protesters at the Capitol, and he even briefly considered deploying ten thousand members of the National Guard "to protect him and his supporters from any supposed threats by left-wing counter-protesters," the report states.

This is among the most remarkable moments in the January 6 chronicle. Rather than worry about violence against lawmakers and the Capitol itself,

Trump was focused on protecting his supporters. They interpreted the president's call to join him in Washington that day as a command to save their country, violently if necessary, and they stood down only when he issued a video instructing them to do so. The January 6 report, in a dramatic but not inaccurate flourish, affirms that, during the assault on the Capitol, Trump "was not only the Commander in Chief of the U.S. military, but also of the rioters."

On that day, he chose to lead the rioters. January 6 was the closest Trump would get to holding that military parade he so longed to see in Washington. Instead of parading in front of the Capitol, his troops marched against it.

After making the case that Trump incited the assault, the January 6 report expresses shock at how little Trump did to stop it, an act of omission it labels a "dereliction of duty." Yet by the report's own logic, why would Trump have stopped the insurrectionists? "President Trump had summoned a mob, including armed extremists and conspiracy theorists, to Washington, DC on the day the joint session of Congress was to meet," the report states. "He then told that same mob to march on the U.S. Capitol and 'fight.' They clearly got the message." (Some variation of the word "fight" appeared only twice in Trump's prepared speech for his January 6 speech, but the president would utter the word twenty times throughout his remarks, the report states.) If the rioters were in fact doing his bidding, the president would have no reason to call them off once the mayhem began.

That Trump would rile people up and then sit back and watch the outcome on television was the least surprising part of the day. It was how he spent his presidency. In calling out Trump's failure to act, the January 6 report was imagining that Trump, in that moment, might have become presidential at last, shocked by what his own actions wrought into being something other than himself. In its condemnation of Trump, the report still longed for his transformation. After so many pages, so much testimony, so much analysis, it still struggled to understand him.

The challenges of interpreting and describing what another person thought, did, or intended at a particular moment—even a person as overanalyzed as Donald J. Trump—comes alive in one passage, or rather one word, of the January 6 report. The issue is not even the word itself but the form in which it is rendered.

The report cites the testimony of a White House aide, Cassidy Hutchinson, who explained how, on the morning of January 6, the president was incensed that the presence of magnetometers (used to detect weapons) was inhibiting some armed supporters from entering the Ellipse, where the president was to deliver his speech.

As always, Trump wanted a bigger crowd. Hutchinson said she heard him say something like, "I don't f—ing care that they have weapons. They're not here to hurt me. Take the f—ing mags away. Let my people in."

They're not here to hurt me. Which word should one emphasize when uttering that sentence aloud? If it is the verb "hurt," the sentiment would be somewhat benign. They are not here to *hurt* me, the president might have meant, but to praise or cheer or support me. If the emphasis falls on "me," however, the meaning is more sinister. They're not here to hurt *me*, the implication would be, but to hurt someone else. That someone else could be Mike Pence, Nancy Pelosi, an officer of the Capitol Police, or any of the lawmakers gathering to fulfill their duty and certify Joe Biden as president.

So, which was it? The January 6 report confuses matters by italicizing "me" in the document's final chapter but leaving it unitalicized in the executive summary. The video of Hutchinson's testimony shows her reciting the line quickly and neutrally, with perhaps a slight emphasis on "hurt" rather than "me."

Of course, the less ambiguous interpretation of Trump's words is that either inflection—whether "hurt" or "me"—still means the president was unconcerned about anyone's safety but his own. Perhaps "I don't f—ing care" is the most relevant phrase.

With a document surpassing eight hundred pages, it may seem too much to linger on the typeface of a single two-letter pronoun. But for accounts that can serve as both historical records and briefs for the prosecution, every word and every quote—every framing and every implication—is a choice that deserves scrutiny.

The studious restraint of the Mueller report came in for much criticism once the special counsel failed to deliver a dagger to the heart of the Trump presidency and once the document was so easily miscast by interested parties. Even its copious redactions, justified by the opaque phrase "Harm to Ongoing Matter" appearing over a sea of blotted-out text, seemed designed to frustrate. Yet for all its diffidence, there is power in the document's understated prose, in its methodical collection of evidence, in its unwillingness to overstep its bounds while investigating a president who knew few bounds himself.

The Ukraine and January 6 reports came at a time when Trump's misconduct was better understood, when Mueller-like restraint was less in fashion, and when those attempting to hold the chief executive accountable grasped every tool at hand. For all their passion and bluntness, they encountered their own constraints, limits that are likely inherent to the form, to the challenge of recording on paper and by committee the impulses not just of a man but of an era with which he became synonymous.

Expectations are heaped upon these reports, not only for what they might reveal, but for what those revelations might unleash, or what they might help repair. Such demands are excessive and probably counterproductive. It is hard enough to determine the true meaning of a lone word, to reconstruct a fleeting moment in history. It is harder still to rebuild a nation's political life, that other ongoing matter to which so much harm has been done.

February 2023

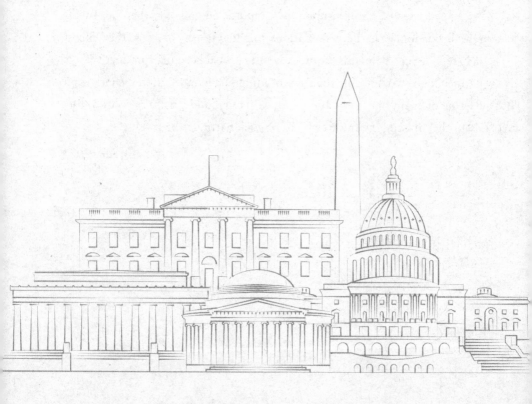

ROE, CASEY, AND DOBBS

SUPREME COURT OPINIONS ARE A series of legal interpretations, a catalogue of rights recognized, affirmed, or withdrawn. But they are also markers of a culture forever in flux, a record of how different courts and different eras have wielded influence, viewed the past, and reflected the national moment.

Such is the case with the pivotal abortion decisions of the last half century: *Roe v. Wade* (1973), which affirmed the right to abortion nationwide, *Planned Parenthood v. Casey* (1992), which accepted stricter limits on the practice while reasserting *Roe*'s central holding, and now *Dobbs v. Jackson Women's Health Organization*, which overturns the prior two decisions and leaves the regulation of abortion to state legislatures. The various rulings and dissents reveal divergent readings of history, conflicting perceptions of the role and agency of women, even contrasting attitudes toward philosophy and human nature.

Perhaps most striking, the recriminations, accusations, and counterclaims found in these documents also showcase an institution that was politicized long before a draft opinion of *Dobbs* was leaked to *Politico* in May. In his *Roe* dissent, Justice William Rehnquist acknowledged the majority opinion's historical inquiry and legal scholarship; despite his disagreements, he wrote, the opinion "commands my respect." Such niceties disappear from subsequent court decisions. The plurality opinion that decided *Casey* warned that overruling *Roe* could constitute a "surrender to political pressure" that would undermine the court's legitimacy; one justice even wrote of his "fear for the darkness" if his four colleagues who opposed *Roe* ever found one more vote. One of those four justices, in his own *Casey* dissent, disparaged the plurality's "almost czarist arrogance."

With *Dobbs*, even these characterizations seem genteel. Different factions of the high court accuse one another and their predecessors of incompetence, duplicity, hypocrisy, and untruth. The *Dobbs* majority opinion, authored by

Justice Samuel Alito, dismisses *Roe* as an "elaborate scheme" that was "concocted" to divine a constitutional right, and assails the 1973 decision with adverbial abandon, calling it "egregiously wrong," "exceptionally weak," and "deeply damaging." And while the *Dobbs* majority asserts that *Roe*'s grasp of history "ranged from the constitutionally irrelevant . . . to the plainly incorrect," it nonetheless makes selective use of US history and tradition, and takes refuge in portions of the very rulings it has now overturned.

The dissent, meanwhile, denounces the majority for betraying its principles and letting personal proclivities overpower the rule of law, and derides the majority's history lectures as "wheel-spinning" and "window dressing." With *Dobbs*, the dissent states, "the court departs from its obligation to faithfully and impartially apply the law," a conclusion it offers not with respect but, in its own words, "with sorrow."

Throughout these competing judgments and dissents, the justices bemoan how their opponents on the court have given in to insidious political impulses and pressures, whereas they alone remain uncorrupted. It is almost hard to remember that, at the outset of its opinion, the *Roe* majority declared that "our task, of course, is to resolve the issue by constitutional measurement, free of emotion and of predilection." Subsequent opinions are rife with both. If Supreme Court rulings indeed double as cultural artifacts, then it is fitting that the court has come to reflect the ideological division and political expedience of our time.

The justices sound just like the rest of us, even though their battles matter so much more.

One of the sharpest divides in the Supreme Court's abortion rulings is over history—what the record shows, what aspects are most relevant, and to what extent history should matter in determining the limits or existence of a constitutional right.

The majority opinion in *Roe* attempts to normalize legal abortion as part of the American story, with mixed results. It began by surveying the laws of ancient Greece and Rome (including the Hippocratic oath's admonition against "an abortive remedy") as well as English common law, concluding that "it now appear[s] doubtful that abortion was firmly established as a common law crime." The opinion highlighted the distinction between abortions carried out before so-called quickening—the first recognizable movements of the fetus—and those conducted later. It noted that the 1821 law barring abortion in Connecticut, the first state to enact such legislation, regarded post-quickening abortion as manslaughter but an earlier abortion only as a misdemeanor. After the Civil War, statutes regulating abortion proliferated, and by the mid-twentieth century, the *Roe* majority acknowledged, "a large majority of the jurisdictions" banned the procedure other than to save the life of the woman. Nonetheless, the opinion concluded, for a "major portion" of the nineteenth century "a woman enjoyed a substantially broader right to terminate a pregnancy than she does in most States today."

That history reads differently through different eyes. In his *Roe* dissent, Rehnquist also cited the Connecticut law, but he did so to emphasize the existence, not the leniency, of early nineteenth-century abortion restrictions. And while the *Roe* majority found the right to an abortion in the Fourteenth Amendment's due process clause, Rehnquist chided his colleagues for disregarding the intent of the drafters. When the Fourteenth Amendment was adopted in 1868, he recounts, legislatures across the country had already enacted dozens of laws limiting abortion, and those provisions went unquestioned when the amendment went into effect. "The only conclusion possible from this history," the future chief justice reasoned, "is that the drafters did not intend to have the Fourteenth Amendment withdraw from the States the power to legislate with respect to this matter." A partial dissent in *Casey*, authored by Rehnquist and joined by Justices Byron White, Antonin Scalia, and Clarence Thomas, reiterated how an "overwhelming majority" of states restricted abortion by 1973, and argued that "the historical traditions of the American people" do not support abortion as a fundamental right.

Such parsing of tradition is a critical exercise in *Dobbs* because, the majority argues, rights not explicitly mentioned in the Constitution must be "deeply rooted" in US history and tradition. Reading the various opinions thus feels like attending seminars by professors whose views of the world are irreconcilable and whose assigned readings only briefly overlap. The *Dobbs* majority opinion writes that its counterparts in *Roe* "ignored or misstated" the real history of abortion and promises to "set the record straight." For example, Alito's opinion asserts that the legal distinction between pre- and post-quickening abortions cited in *Roe* does not matter "because the rule was abandoned in the 19th century." And even if pre-quickening abortions were not criminalized, that "does not mean that anyone thought the States lacked the authority to do so." It is a deft move by the majority: it picks the period it prefers to represent tradition, and when traditions sneak off course, the majority reminds that states still could have shaped the era differently. And so tradition endures.

The justices also part company on the impact of the Supreme Court's past abortion decisions—that is, on the history of the court itself. The plurality opinion in *Casey* looked back with an excess of satisfaction on *Roe* as a rare moment when the court was able to "resolve" an antagonistic debate, calling on "the contending sides of a national controversy to end their national division by accepting a common mandate rooted in the Constitution." In his partial dissent in *Casey*, Scalia scoffed at this "unrecognizable" account of US social history. Not only did *Roe* fail to resolve the abortion debate, Scalia emphasized, "it did more than anything else to nourish it."

But after chastising the *Casey* opinion for gazing upon the politics of the post-*Roe* era so favorably, Scalia did much the same for the pre-*Roe* years, regarding them as a more tranquil and stable time when "national politics were not plagued by abortion protests, national abortion lobbying, or abortion marches on Congress," and state-by-state political compromises remained possible. "To portray *Roe* as the statesmanlike 'settlement' of a divisive issue," he wrote, ". . . is nothing less than Orwellian."

At times the majority in *Dobbs* overreaches in its attacks on *Roe*'s vision of history, in ways that are small and unnecessary. For instance, it quotes the *Roe* majority opinion as supposedly implying that nineteenth-century state laws against abortion in the United States emerged from a "Victorian social concern" regarding "illicit sexual conduct" rather than over the desire to protect fetal life. The *Roe* majority did mention that idea as an occasional explanation for such laws but immediately repudiated it, writing that "no court or commentator has taken the argument seriously." Except for Alito, who forty-nine years later resurrected the passage to discredit *Roe*.

More consequentially, the *Dobbs* majority asserts that its ruling returns the abortion debate to the state level, where it belongs and where it had long been until *Roe* showed up and ruined everything. "For the first 185 years after the adoption of the Constitution, each State was permitted to address this issue in accordance with the views of its citizens," the majority asserts. Of course, for many of those years, those considered full citizens of the nation were a much more limited set. "The men who ratified the Fourteenth Amendment and wrote the state laws of the time did not view women as full and equal citizens," the *Dobbs* dissent stresses, charging that, "because laws in 1868 deprived women of any control over their bodies, the majority approves States doing so today."

When the Supreme Court ruled on *Roe*, all nine justices were men; with *Casey*, eight of the nine were men; in the *Dobbs* decision, the court has three women and six men. The various opinions and dissents do not break down neatly along gender lines, but they do reveal much about how the high court has viewed women over the past half century—sometimes as less able to think for themselves and, thus, requiring special protection from their own bad choices, and sometimes as so empowered that additional protection was no longer necessary.

The *Roe* majority highlighted the harm inflicted upon women when they are denied the choice of continuing or ending their pregnancies, whether medical and psychological injury or the "continuing stigma of unwed motherhood." In *Casey*, the plurality opinion asserted that women are defined by far more than motherhood—no matter how long that vision has permeated American society—and that in the two decades since *Roe*, women had come to rely on the right the 1973 ruling enshrined. "The ability of women to participate equally in the economic and social life of the Nation has been facilitated by their ability to control their reproductive lives," Justices Sandra Day O'Connor, Anthony Kennedy, and David Souter contended.

Even while upholding the right to abortion, the *Casey* plurality opinion betrayed some condescension toward women intending to exercise their choice. One of the provisions in the Pennsylvania law contested in *Casey* was a requirement that pregnant women seeking abortions have access to printed materials describing fetal development and offering details on adoption agencies, medical assistance available for childbirth, and child-support requirements for fathers. This provision, O'Connor, Kennedy, and Souter concluded, supported the "legitimate purpose of reducing the risk that a woman may elect an abortion, only to discover later, with devastating psychological consequences, that her decision was not fully informed." They deemed another provision requiring a twenty-four-hour delay before the abortion is carried out to be a "reasonable measure."

In his partial concurrence and partial dissent in *Casey*, Justice John Paul Stevens argued persuasively that such compromises embodied "outmoded and unacceptable assumptions" about the ability of women to make their own decisions, and that "States may not presume that a woman has failed to reflect adequately merely because her conclusion differs from the State's preference." (Indeed, nowhere does the *Casey* opinion imagine a parallel proposal requiring that women choosing to continue their pregnancies receive detailed information on possible complications during childbirth, health risks for a newborn, or the average lifetime costs of raising children.)

Rehnquist, Scalia, White, and Thomas countered that the *Casey* plurality opinion was "unconvincing" when asserting that women had come to rely on the abortion rights enshrined in *Roe*. "Surely it is dubious to suggest that women have reached their 'places in society' in reliance upon *Roe*," they argued, "rather than as a result of their determination to obtain higher education and compete with men in the job market, and of society's increasing recognition of their ability to fill positions that were previously thought to be reserved only for men." Their logic seemed to be that women had progressed so much that the additional right of abortion is superfluous, and, incidentally, that the power to decide when or whether to have children is irrelevant to competing in the employment marketplace.

The plurality opinion in *Casey* acknowledged that it could not quantify the extent of Americans' reliance on *Roe*, but it figured it was significant and could not be dismissed. The four joint dissenters agreed that reliance upon *Roe* could not be easily specified, so chose not to try. "The joint opinion's assertion of this fact is undeveloped and totally conclusory," they wrote, and is "based solely on generalized assertions about the national psyche."

The *Dobbs* majority likewise looks back on the question of women's reliance on *Roe* and decides that the court "has neither the authority nor the expertise" to settle the matter. But it adds one more reason why establishing a generalized reliance on *Roe* is difficult: women are all just so different. Abortion regulations can have disparate effects on women depending on their "places of residence, financial resources, family situations, work and personal obligations, knowledge about fetal development and abortion, psychological and emotional disposition and condition, and the firmness of their desire to obtain abortions." Where women differ little, apparently, is in their political clout. Now that *Dobbs* has returned abortion rights to state legislatures, women on any side of the abortion dispute can shape their futures by voting, lobbying lawmakers, or running for office themselves. "Women are not without electoral or political power," the *Dobbs* majority states.

Consider the logic: Because the right to an abortion was not part of the American tradition back when women lacked political power, it cannot be a constitutional right today. And it need not be a constitutional right today because women, deprived of that right, at least have enough power to ask for it back.

The *Roe* majority held that the government has two legitimate interests regarding abortion rights. First is that abortion be performed safely for the patient, and second is the state's interest in "protecting prenatal life." The majority did not attempt to settle the question of when life begins but, rather, accepted that the latter interest is real because at least "potential life" is involved. Much of the court's debate over abortion in the past fifty years has centered on how those interests come into conflict and when one overrides the other.

In *Dobbs*, that trade-off is crystallized in two nearly identical sentences, one in the majority opinion and the other in the dissent. "The most striking feature of the dissent is the absence of any serious discussion of the legitimacy of the States' interest in protecting fetal life," the majority opinion declares. Later, deep in their dissent, the opposing justices toss that sentiment back at the majority, almost mockingly, adding quotation marks to make sure someone notices. " 'The most striking feature of the [majority] is the absence of any serious discussion' of how its ruling will affect women."

Yes, this is how a dissent briefly lapses into a diss. Even so, the passages highlight the two sides' competing priorities. The *Dobbs* majority claims that it takes no position on when life begins or when prenatal life acquires rights, but it laments that the dissenters "regard a fetus as lacking even the most basic human right—to live—at least until an arbitrary point in a pregnancy has passed." The dissent, for its part, praises the "balance" that *Roe* and *Casey* brought to the competing interests, and laments "how little [the majority] knows or cares about women's lives or about the suffering its decision will cause."

The dissenters also worry that, given the logic of *Dobbs*, constitutional guarantees such as the right to contraception or to same-sex marriage may also be at risk. After all, they too may be insufficiently "rooted in history" to hold up. The majority insists, repeatedly, that only abortion is at issue here—and that abortion is "fundamentally different" from the other rights because it "uniquely involves what *Roe* and *Casey* termed 'potential life.' " (Note the irony of the *Dobbs* majority repeatedly citing *Roe* and *Casey*, the two decisions it is overturning, to help explain why it will not do the same to additional precedents.) The majority seems exasperated, even insulted, by the suspicion that other rights could be in jeopardy. "It is hard to see how we could be clearer," Alito writes.

It's not that hard. Simply reiterating today that abortion is "different" does not preclude future iterations of the court from employing the *Dobbs* blueprint to conclude otherwise. In his concurring opinion in *Dobbs*, Justice Brett Kavanaugh promises that Supreme Court decisions allowing contraception, interracial marriage, and same-sex marriage are all still safe. "I emphasize what the Court today states," Kavanaugh assures. "Overruling *Roe* does *not* mean the overruling of those precedents, and does *not* threaten or cast doubt on those precedents." Perhaps Kavanaugh's use of italics is meant to convey seriousness of purpose—a sort of jurisprudential pinkie swear—but its already slight impact is lessened when one of the majority's signatories lays out a separate opinion targeting some of those other rights by name.

Justice Thomas, who joined the majority opinion, nonetheless declares that the court "should reconsider" some of the "demonstrably erroneous" Supreme Court opinions on same-sex marriage, contraceptive use, and gay sex—precedents that Kavanaugh and the majority insist are not in play. Thomas also appears forthright about how his personal beliefs and judicial assessments intermingle, ending his concurring opinion by citing the "immeasurable" harm of sixty-three million abortions carried out since 1973, according to a fact sheet from the National Right to Life Committee. If Alito argues by adverb and Kavanaugh argues by italics, Thomas seems to argue by Thomas—he cites himself twenty-one times in a seven-page opinion, a true testament to his judicial self-regard. The dissent in *Dobbs* highlights Thomas's opinion ("at least one Justice is planning to use the ticket of today's decision again and again and again"), but the *Dobbs* majority opinion keeps its distance from it, although it contradicts the majority's assurances. No matter. Even if Thomas does not find support on the court, his constituency and audience may reside elsewhere.

In all three cases, the decisive opinions acknowledge the complexity and divisiveness of abortion in American life. "Abortion presents a profound moral issue on which Americans hold sharply conflicting views," Alito begins in *Dobbs*. The *Roe* majority acknowledged "our awareness of the sensitive and emotional nature of the abortion controversy . . . and of the deep and seemingly absolute convictions that the subject inspires." The *Casey* plurality was the most contemplative. "At the heart of liberty is the right to define one's own concept of existence, of meaning, of the universe, and of the mystery of human life," it stated, adding that, on abortion, "reasonable people will have differences of opinion."

It is inevitable that cases of this sort elicit such pondering of life and human nature. Nonetheless, in his partial dissent in *Casey*, Scalia could not resist ridiculing his colleagues' philosophizing. In deciding that abortion is not a protected right, Scalia wrote: "I reach that conclusion not because of anything so exalted as my views concerning the 'concept of existence, of meaning, of the universe, and of the mystery of human life' " but rather because "the Constitution says absolutely nothing about it, and [because] the longstanding traditions of American society have permitted it to be legally proscribed." In his *Dobbs* opinion thirty years later, Thomas also criticized the *Casey* reflections as overly "ethereal," while the *Dobbs* majority opinion says that it's fine for people to think whatever they wish about the universe and the rest, they just can't always act "in accordance with those thoughts." In other words, enough with the big think—this question is straightforward enough.

One of the justices today seems more willing to wrestle with his thoughts, to engage for a moment in uncertainty, even ambiguity. In his separate *Dobbs* opinion, Chief Justice John Roberts Jr. agrees with the court's decision to uphold the Mississippi law at issue in the case—which prohibits abortions past fifteen weeks into a pregnancy—but does not see the need to overturn *Roe* and *Casey*. He proposes accepting the fifteen-week limit while still upholding the constitutional right to abortion, on the grounds that such a time frame provides "an adequate opportunity to exercise the right *Roe* protects." Better to reach a narrower conclusion, Roberts suggests, and leave the larger decisions "for another day."

It is a compromise that satisfies no one. The *Dobbs* majority is dismissive, stating that the chief justice's middle ground "would only put off the day when we would be forced to confront the question we now decide." Of course, that is precisely Roberts's objective. He does not pretend to have the ultimate answer; he would rather change the question. "I am not sure, for example, that a ban on terminating a pregnancy from the moment of conception must be treated the same under the Constitution as a ban after fifteen weeks," he writes. Roberts is willing to wallow in the in-between spaces that are prohibited in the political and legal debates over abortion; he is a *Casey* guy in a *Dobbs* world. The dissenting justices in *Dobbs* treat him with only slightly more kindness, noting in a parenthetical near the end of their dissent that "we believe that the Chief Justice's opinion is wrong too," but adding that they agree there is indeed a large difference between a ban at conception and one beginning at fifteen weeks.

"Both the Court's opinion and the dissent display a relentless freedom from doubt on the legal issue that I cannot share," the chief justice writes. Except doubt is not popular, and self-doubt even less so. It is a sign of how the court has become one more political battleground that the chief justice is left flailing and lonely in the institution over which he nominally presides, and that somewhere between the dismissiveness of the majority and the parenthetical of the dissent reside the remnants of a possible, but doomed, compromise. Roberts's failure is not in the specifics of his proposal or the logic of his argument. It is in daring to hope that in this moment and with this court and in this country, such an outcome ever had a chance.

July 2022

HOW FAR WILL THE
JUSTICES GO?

SOME FOUR DECADES AND TWO chief justices ago, Bob Woodward and Scott Armstrong published *The Brethren*, an unusual look inside the politics—especially the office politics—of the Supreme Court. The book's novelty, and much of the criticism it elicited when it was published in 1979, resulted from the authors' treatment of the high court as just one more Washington institution. The book exposed rivalries among the justices and self-importance among the clerks, as well as the robe-twisting that shaped major decisions on school busing, the Pentagon Papers, abortion rights, and the Nixon tapes.

In *The Brethren*, the buzzy and the meaty occupy the same chambers. Justices deride one another behind their backs—"spaghetti spine," "usurper," and "dummy" are among the typical insults—and staff members gather around a portable TV to watch the Senate Watergate hearings, with Justice Thurgood Marshall providing running commentary. ("Right on, Brother Dean.") Chief Justice Warren Burger frustrates his colleagues by waiting until the last minute to reveal his vote, thus often joining the majority and retaining the power to assign the opinion to the justice of his choice, or to himself. At times we see justices deciding their votes on political or personal rationales and then casting about for constitutional justifications. And *The Brethren* puts the "office" in office politics: When Burger extends the justices' thirty-minute lunch gatherings to a full hour, multiple dissents ensue. (Hugo Black, for instance, worries they all might start overeating.)

Joan Biskupic's new book on the high court, *Nine Black Robes*, is more analytical, less focused on insider details than on how the ideological divides of the Trump era are apparent in the decisions and demeanor of the high court. Still, it is hard to read *Nine Black Robes* without thinking about *The Brethren*. Woodward and Armstrong show how politicking inside the court led to the ascent of a moderate faction between the liberals of the Earl Warren court and the Nixon-era conservative wing. Biskupic shows how the politics surrounding the court leading to President Donald Trump's three appointments has produced a realignment in which the standard liberal-moderate-conservative lines no longer define the institution. What matters most now are the divides among the conservative justices, as they ponder how far they will go.

"The center was in control," Woodward and Armstrong write in the final sentence of *The Brethren*. "The court had no middle, no center to hold," Biskupic laments at the end of *Nine Black Robes*. Sometimes sequels are written decades apart, and by different authors.

The justices in Biskupic's account repeatedly assert that the court is not politicized. "My goal today is to convince you that this court is not comprised of a bunch of partisan hacks," Justice Amy Coney Barrett declared in a speech in 2021. (She was speaking, incidentally, at the University of Louisville's McConnell Center.) "The last thing that the court should do is to look as polarized as every other institution in America," Justice Elena Kagan said in a 2019 speech. "The only way to be seen as not that—is not to be that." Ever the institutionalist, Chief Justice John Roberts contrasted the court's work to that of the other branches. "What I would like to do, briefly, is emphasize how the judicial branch is—how it must be—very different," he said shortly after the indelible confirmation hearings for Brett Kavanaugh in 2018. "We do not sit on opposite sides of an aisle, we do not caucus in separate rooms, we do not serve one party or one interest. We serve one nation."

How the judicial branch is—how it must be—very different. Roberts's phrasing seems to acknowledge that he is stating a hope as much as fact. The Supreme Court regarding itself as apolitical is a bit like the Senate still considering itself the world's greatest deliberative body—that is, somewhere between aspiration and self-delusion. Even though politics and ideology divided the court well before Trump sat in the Oval Office, Biskupic writes, "the Trump presidency and the forceful influence of his three Supreme Court appointees propelled the judiciary into a new period of polarization."

Of course, *The Brethren* too depicts a court in which political considerations were constant. Chief Justice Burger—the only justice who the authors specifically say was not interviewed for the book—frequently worries about the implications of various decisions for the Nixon administration, and he makes a point of issuing some nonconservative opinions early in his tenure to "confuse his liberal detractors in the press," Woodward and Armstrong write. And when the court is deciding whether President Richard Nixon can invoke executive privilege to avoid handing over recordings of his White House conversations, Justice Harry Blackmun counsels Burger that the court's opinion would be more influential if written by a justice who was a Republican as well as one of Nixon's appointees. Given that William Rehnquist was recused from the case and that Burger, as chief justice, would preside over a potential Nixon impeachment trial in the Senate, that formula conveniently left only Blackmun. (Unpersuaded, Burger assigned himself the unanimous opinion in *United States v. Nixon*, in which the court ruled against the president.)

When health problems force Justice William Douglas to the sidelines, his colleagues panic over President Gerald Ford's potential pick, and how recent 5–4 opinions might end up going the other way. "They were all horrified at the prospect of half a dozen major decisions being reversed in a year's time," the authors write. "The court would appear to be a political institution, its decision less rooted in the law than in the personalities and politics of the individual justices." This concern that the court might merely appear politicized—rather than concern that it would be revealed as politicized—still reflects an abiding faith among members of the high court.

An institution less rooted in the law than in the personalities and politics of the justices is very much how Biskupic depicts the court. Before the death of Justice Ruth Bader Ginsburg, Roberts had already become the new "ideological center" of the institution. In mid-2019, she writes, "there was still some pretense that the two ideological camps were trying to work together."

But when Barrett became Trump's third appointee in late 2020, giving the conservatives a six-vote majority, the longer-serving justices Clarence Thomas and Samuel Alito were "emboldened by the ascendant conservatism," Biskupic writes. "Joined by the Trump appointees, they echoed the former president's sense of aggrievement on culture war issues, from abortion rights to vaccine mandates. Their time had come." (Much as with Trump voters, "grievance" is the obligatory reference when describing conservative justices. Biskupic claims that Alito, for one, sounds "perpetually aggrieved" and wears a "heavy cloak of grievance." Perhaps the cloak fits under the robe.)

Biskupic, a CNN Supreme Court analyst and biographer of four current and past justices, dissects the personalities on the court. Justice Thomas, previously on the "ideological fringe" and often alone in his dissents, is now in the "vanguard" of the conservative supermajority: "Both he and Alito were only in their early seventies, but they felt a sense of urgency, as if their time were limited." Justice Kavanaugh, meanwhile, comes off as painfully self-conscious, struggling to reconcile "his allegiance to conservative backers and his desire for acceptance among the legal elites who shunned him after his scandalous 2018 Senate hearings." (Biskupic points out that Kavanaugh at times adds "appeasing passages" to his opinions and dissents, just to signal that he's not a bad guy.)

So, when a chapter in *Nine Black Robes* is titled "The Triumvirate," a reader might assume that it signals a discussion of the three Trump-appointed justices, or perhaps of some powerful new coalition on the court. Instead, it concerns a trio that has wielded power over the court from outside: Sen. Mitch McConnell of Kentucky; Don McGahn, a White House counsel under Trump; and Leonard Leo, the conservative legal activist and a former vice president of the Federalist Society. "The three men understood the importance of the federal courts to a long-term policy agenda, from business interests to individual rights," Biskupic writes, and they sought "jurists appointed ostensibly as neutral arbiters but who in reality held to their own ideologies."

Each contributed to the same cause from his respective perch. McConnell blocked President Barack Obama's nomination of Merrick Garland to the Supreme Court, a move he later called "the most consequential decision of my career." McGahn shepherded Neil Gorsuch and Brett Kavanaugh onto the court and, anticipating her eventual promotion, positioned Amy Coney Barrett onto the US Court of Appeals for the Seventh Circuit. Leo, skilled in vetting judicial nominees for ideological purity and reliability, worked with McGahn and others to assemble the list of potential Supreme Court nominees that Trump, in a brilliant effort to reassure Christian conservatives, released in May 2016. It is a testament to Leo's influence—and that of the Federalist Society—that he makes a cameo in the recent *ProPublica* report about Justice Thomas's luxury vacations funded by a billionaire Republican donor. Inside the donor's private lakeside resort in upstate New York there is a painting of Thomas relaxing with the donor and a few other guests. Sitting across from the justice? Leonard Leo.

In *The Brethren*, the stamp of approval of the American Bar Association is crucial for potential Supreme Court nominations (though Nixon does ask Blackmun if his daughters, in their twenties, were "hippie types"). In *Nine Black Robes*, it is the Federalist Society's sign-off that matters most.

To chart the court's movement rightward, Biskupic focuses on recent cases expanding gun rights, prioritizing religious freedom, and curtailing the regulatory power of the state. ("There is a coherent plan here, where actually the judicial selection and the deregulatory effort are really the flip side of the same coin," McGahn told the Conservative Political Action Conference in 2018.) And Biskupic notes how, in their opinions, concurrences, and dissents, the justices don't just disagree over the finer points of legal analysis but also assail one another's motives. In a case involving policing, Gorsuch suggested that his colleagues were being deferential to Black Lives Matter activists, while in a case over sentencing of juveniles, Justice Sonia Sotomayor asserted that Kavanaugh was "fooling no one" with his "egregious" interpretation of past decisions.

While the title of *The Brethren* has a touch of irony to it, given all the bickering in those pages, those justices use the term themselves to describe their insular community, with respect and even affection. In the court that Biskupic describes decades later, all that seems to unite the members are those nine black robes.

As president, Trump was fond of possessive expressions to designate and denigrate other portions of the state—"my generals," "my Kevin"—but members of the high court have rejected his use of "my judges."

"We do not have Obama judges or Trump judges, Bush judges or Clinton judges," Roberts told the Associated Press in 2018. The court eventually signed off on the third iteration of the Trump administration's travel ban in 2018 and, most notably, helped fulfill a Trump campaign promise when it overturned *Roe v. Wade* in 2022, but it also rejected a lawsuit by Texas aimed at challenging the results of the 2020 election in several battleground states. "Trump had pulled the justices down in the dirt with him at various points over the previous four years, but not this time," Biskupic points out.

Ironically, it is a case in which the court's liberals prevailed that shows how the conservative wing has become a self-contained, Federalist Society salon. When Gorsuch wrote a 6–3 majority opinion in 2020 declaring that the 1964 Civil Rights Act protected the rights of gay and transgender employees, he based it on a so-called textualist reading focusing on the precise wording of the statute. (Title VII of the Civil Rights Act banned employment discrimination based on an individual's "race, color, religion, sex or national origin," and the majority interpreted "sex" as covering sexual orientation and gender identity.)

Gorsuch regards himself as a textualist in the mold of Antonin Scalia, but his decision did not sit well with another Scalia devotee on the court. "No one should be fooled," Alito said in a dissent. "The court's opinion is like a pirate ship. It sails under a textualist flag, but what it actually represents is a theory of statutory interpretation that Justice Scalia excoriated—the theory that courts should 'update' old statutes so that they better reflect the current values of society." According to Alito, Scalia "would have been in disbelief that the Congress of 1964 would have enacted a statute covering LGBTQ interests," Biskupic writes. Gorsuch, no slouch in the Scalia Studies Department, responded by citing a 1998 case in which Scalia had written that a statutory prohibition can "often go beyond the principal evil to cover reasonably comparable evils."

It's not just about parsing the intent of the writers of the Constitution. For this new supermajority, originalism now also seems to mean fighting over what Antonin Scalia really intended.

Biskupic offers an astute assessment of her own on how to interpret Scalia. At a Federalist Society meeting at the University of Chicago in the early

1980s, Scalia spoke of the power of like-minded people coming together with a singular, common purpose. The law professor and future justice quoted Federalist 49, written by James Madison: "The reason of man, like man himself, is timid and cautious when left alone, and acquires firmness and confidence in proportion to the number with which it is associated." Scalia mentioned that episode to Biskupic when she interviewed him for a 2009 biography, and he emphasized the loneliness of campus conservatism and the importance of intellectual fellowship.

"Rereading that Scalia comment more than a decade and a half later," Biskupic writes, "I am struck by how much it speaks to the potency of a six-justice majority over that of a five-justice bloc. The numbers have given the right wing a new confidence, beyond a single extra vote, to reconsider and overturn a half-century of rights and regulations." A conservative supermajority doesn't just affect the direction of the court. It also affects how far in that direction that majority might venture.

Biskupic is clearly troubled by the possibilities; her book has a politics of its own. She longs for the days of "unpredictable, less ideological" justices like John Paul Stevens, Byron White, Lewis Powell, and David Souter, and writes in an author's note that the court today is moving the country "backward." She looks to affirmative action, voting rights, and discrimination against same-sex couples as areas where a "greater erosion of rights" is likely.

"Three of the justices in the new conservative supermajority—Thomas, Alito, and Gorsuch—were writing daring opinions impugning decades of precedent," Biskupic writes. "The question was whether the remaining conservatives—Roberts, Kavanaugh, and Barrett—would put any brake on their zeal."

The Supreme Court's willingness to rethink precedents is an eternal preoccupation for writers and scholars of the court, and the doctrine of stare decisis has multiple index entries in both these books. One justice cited in *The Brethren*, William Rehnquist, then the youngest member of the court, made a prophetic description for his colleagues of how the battles over precedent would shift over time. Here is how Woodward and Armstrong describe it:

"It was only recently that activism on the court had become 'liberal' activism, Rehnquist reminded them. Only forty years before, the court's activists were conservatives. The balance was once again shifting back, Rehnquist said. Once it had, the liberals would be the ones calling for judicial restraint and chiding the conservatives for ignoring precedent."

And so they are.

April 2023

THE NEXT CIVIL WAR

To GLIMPSE THE COMING DISMEMBERMENT of the United States of America, just stop by your local bookstore.

How Civil Wars Start, by Barbara F. Walter, warns that the signs typically heralding such conflicts are now evident at home. *Divided We Fall*, by David French, published weeks before the 2020 election, pictures the cleaving of the United States into two culturally distinct states, united only in their mutual detestation. On the magazine racks, the *Atlantic* argues that the January 6 assault on the Capitol was merely "practice" for the more effective subversion of democracy that's underway. And from the fiction shelves, you can pick up a paperback of Omar El Akkad's *American War* (2017), a grim vision of environmental destruction, youth radicalization, internally displaced populations, and biological warfare in the United States, a vision rendered less fashionable only by its timing (here, the second American civil war is not waged until the latter half of the twenty-first century).

Into this crowd steps Canadian novelist and journalist Stephen Marche with *The Next Civil War: Dispatches from the American Future*, which takes the realities of a politically tribalistic United States—burdened by racial and economic injustice, awash with social resentments, packed with guns— and imagines its move toward all-out conflict. "The background hum of hyper-partisanship, the rage and loathing of everyday American politics, generates a widespread tolerance for violence," Marche writes. "Eventually somebody acts on it."

In this telling, the precipitating act of the next civil war is almost incidental, and Marche conjures up several options. It could be a local dispute over the closing of a small-town bridge by federal safety inspectors that escalates into an armed confrontation, forces led by a charismatic sheriff on one side and a decorated general on the other. Or the assassination of a president (no one will expect him to do it, Marche writes of the creepy young killer, yet "no one will be surprised when he does"). Or a natural disaster that upends New York City, overwhelms governmental capacities, and sends climate refugees pouring across the country. Or a drone armed with bioweapons that strikes the Capitol. "America is one spectacular act of political violence away from a national crisis," Marche writes.

Such scenario-spinning is a staple of the Civil War redux and secessionist lit. French's book imagines California breaking off over gun laws or Texas splitting away over abortion disputes, while Walter's envisions multiple bombings of state capitol buildings after the 2028 presidential election, leading to domestic terrorism and even attempts at ethnic cleansing. There is a horrifying yet normalizing quality to such discussions. The more often cable news chyrons, think tank analyses, political rhetoric, and nonfiction works elevate the discussion of a new civil war, the more inevitable such an outcome may seem, and the more fatalistic the public may feel. It's not clear that fanciful scenarios are all that necessary; in 2021, we witnessed a real-life spectacular act of political violence against the Capitol, carried live on television, while a *Washington Post*-UMD poll finds that one-third of Americans say violence against the government can be justified.

Oddly, given his book's title, Marche oscillates between certitude about a coming civil war (we are already on its "threshold," he warns, and any catalyzing event will appear "a logical outcome to the trends of the country") and the belief that we can avoid it ("none of the crises described in this book are beyond the capacity of Americans to solve," he writes, as long as we recapture the spirit of a country "devoted to reinvention"). Marche's final two chapters are titled "The End of the Republic" and "A Note on American Hope." When you're betting on the end of the American experiment, a little hedge doesn't hurt.

After all, the country has survived local-federal standoffs, domestic terrorism, natural disasters, and presidential assassinations before. Why would today be different? Marche ticks through the circumstances that, in his view, heighten the risks: extreme political and geographic polarization; the particular radicalization of the right; drought and other climate-related crises; deepening racial resentments and injustices; technological and informational silos; the proliferation of guns; and obscene levels of economic inequality. "Every society in human history with levels of inequality like those in the United States today has descended into war, revolution, or plague," Marche contends.

Given how many societies have experienced some form of war, revolution, or plague, regardless of their inequality statistics, such a warning may be less ominous than it first appears. Indeed, Marche's brisk writing sometimes falls into spirals of political and cultural buzzwords. The aftermath of a presidential assassination, for example, would produce "an ever-hardening version of soft autocracy riddled with violent grievance politics born out of a sense of institutional illegitimacy." (It's like death-of-democracy *Mad Libs*.)

Yet Marche does hit on a more fundamental tension, one that underlies so many of our divides: "Each side accuses the other of hating America, which is only another way of saying that both hate what the other means by America." Even fledgling separatists, he notes, take pains to assure that their efforts are consistent with the Constitution, with American traditions. ("It's genuinely weird," Marche admits.) A future civil war will be a fight "to preserve a coherent definition of America itself." It will be, he concludes, "a war over meaning."

And what is that meaning? "Difference is the core of the American experience," Marche argues. "Difference is its genius. There has never been a country—in history, in the world—so comfortable with difference." But now that comfort, to the extent that it ever truly existed, has become irritation, and that American genius, national zealotry. Disillusioned and angry, some citizens "don't want America's differences," Marche writes. "They can no longer tolerate America's contradictions."

Marche stresses the contradictions involving culture and race and history and national identity, of enslavers who extolled freedom and equality, or of a country that has imagined itself both a white settler republic and a multicultural democracy. These battles over meaning have animated past American conflicts—not just Marche's "next" civil war but the first one, too. Yet such contradictions are found throughout the American story. Think of the ways the country has perceived itself throughout its history, and what such notions mean today. The land of opportunity, but denying it to many. A nation of immigrants, finding new ways to be unwelcoming. American ingenuity, creating sophisticated engines of division and misinformation. The land of the free, with a system of mass incarceration. The aspirations that have defined us threaten to rip us apart.

Books on the threats to the American experiment come in waves, each new theme more treacherous than the one before. Polarization books. Democratic-decline books. Now, the new civil war literature. But we don't have to browse the latest titles to find fears of disunion. We can revisit instead some of the earliest and most lasting American prose.

George Washington's Farewell Address of September 19, 1796, was, overwhelmingly, a plea to preserve a united country. "Your Union ought to be considered as a main prop of your liberty ... the love of the one ought to endear you to the preservation of the other," he declared. Washington foresaw how the malign influence of parties and factions "agitates the Community with ill founded jealousies and false alarms, kindles the animosity of one part against another, foments occasionally riot and insurrection."

Such admonitions find resonance at a time when one major American party has grown unmoored from democratic observance, when too many of its partisans uphold false conspiracies that can propel supporters toward violence against the union. Whether it portends civil war or lesser forms of conflict, the tragedy of January 6 is not just the assault of that day and the lies that produced it, but what it signals for days to come. As our first president warned when explaining his intention to relinquish the office, "cunning, ambitious and unprincipled men will be enabled to subvert the Power of the People, and to usurp for themselves the reins of Government; destroying afterwards the very engines which have lifted them to unjust dominion."

January 2022

V. POSING

MAKING IT IN THIS TOWN

MARK LEIBOVICH TOYED WITH SEVERAL titles for his new book on self-interest, self-importance, and self-perpetuation in the nation's capital. *Suck-Up City* was one. *The Club* was another. Finally, he settled on *This Town*, a nod, he explains, to the "faux disgust" with which people here refer to their natural habitat.

It's not bad, but the longer I roamed around *This Town*, the more I thought Leibovich could have borrowed *Newsweek*'s memorable post–September 11, 2001, cover line: "Why They Hate Us." His tour through Washington only feeds the worst suspicions anyone can have about the place—a land driven by insecurity, hypocrisy, and cable hits, where friendships are transactional, blind-copying is rampant, and acts of public service appear largely accidental.

Only two things keep you turning pages between gulps of Pepto: First, in Leibovich's hands, this state of affairs is not just depressing, it's also kind of funny. Second, you want to know whether the author thinks anyone in Washington—anyone at all?—is worthy of redemption.

Leibovich, chief national correspondent for the *New York Times Magazine* and a former reporter at the *Washington Post*, is a master of the political profile, with his subjects revealing themselves in the most unflattering light. That talent becomes something of a crutch in *This Town*, which offers more a collection of scenes than a rich narrative. Still, his characters reveal essential archetypes of Washington power.

Consider longtime NBC news reporter Andrea Mitchell—a conflict of interest in human form. Married to former Federal Reserve chairman Alan Greenspan, Mitchell has specialized in covering administrations and campaigns that "overlapped considerably with her social and personal habitat," as Leibovich puts it. There are those weekend getaways at George Shultz's home. And dinner with Tipper and Al. And that surprise fiftieth-birthday party for

Condi. And what do you do when you're reporting on the 2008 financial crisis and people are pointing at your husband as a chief culprit? NBC provided a fig leaf: allowing Mitchell to cover the politics of dealing with the crisis, but not the conditions that gave rise to it. Such hair-splitting becomes inevitable, Leibovich writes, because Mitchell trying to avoid conflicts of interest is "like an owl trying to avoid trees."

Next up is Washington lawyer Bob Barnett—if he doesn't represent you, you must not be worth representing. He negotiated Hillary Clinton's $8 million book advance (not to mention the $10 million he reeled in for Bill), plus eight-figure deals for Sarah Palin in book, speaking, and television gigs. "The degree to which so many elite D.C. players stream to a single superlawyer cash redemption center is striking," Leibovich notes, "even by the parochial standards of the ant colony."

Yet Barnett longs for the very thing he delivers for his clients: a reputation upgrade. "He hates being called an 'agent,' " Leibovich explains, "with its hired-gun connotations." Barnett's desire to be considered a Washington wise man is evident in his desperate quest to join President Obama's debate prep team. When he finally broke in, before Obama's last standoff with Mitt Romney, he prefaced one of his suggestions to the president by explaining the "conventional wisdom" on an issue. Obama cracked, "Bob, you ARE the conventional wisdom."

Tammy Haddad—"a human ladle in the local self-celebration buffet"—is another only-in-Washington personality, and she embodies one of Leibovich's rules for success here: if no one's sure exactly what you do, you're doing it right. "My job is to be around the most successful people, the most up-and-coming people, and the people who have impact," Haddad told Leibovich. A former producer for *Larry King Live* and *Hardball*, Haddad is a mix of journalist, businesswoman, philanthropist, and, as Leibovich puts it, a "full-service gatherer of friends of different persuasions unified by the fact that they in some way 'matter.' "

She'll tote around a video camera (the Tam Cam!) and do ambush interviews of Washington notables. She'll broker an Obama interview for a newsweekly aboard Air Force One. And although she's best known for her exclusive brunch marking the White House Correspondents' Dinner every

April, Haddad will fete you whether you want it or not—"party rape," as the friend of one victim called it.

Haddad, no surprise, was well aware of *This Town* as a work in progress, and Leibovich shoehorns in passages of her and others discussing it. "He's writing a book about how Washington works and trying to get me to participate," the Tamster confides to Gordon Brown at a book party (presumably consensual) for the former British prime minister.

Stoked by *Politico*, speculation has centered on who will be mentioned and what scores might be settled. For this reason, *This Town* contains no index; boldface Washingtonians can't just find their pages, see how they're depicted, and read no more. These sorts of readers are the people Leibovich refers to as Leading Thinkers, Political Washington, People Who Run Your Country. (Yes, Leibovich is fond of Ironic Capitalizations Implying the Banality of Things Others Consider Important; sometimes phrases are not only ironically capitalized but *ironically italicized* as well, a move I will always think of as a Double Leibo.)

Here's how some Leading Thinkers came out: In *This Town* we're told that Chris Matthews and Matt Lauer have joked that David Gregory would rub out a few colleagues to advance his career. That Bill and Hillary Clinton are convinced that Tim Russert disliked them, and that they're not wrong. That Harry Reid has "observed privately to colleagues" that John Kerry has no friends. That West Wing types suspected Valerie Jarrett had "earpiece envy" after David Axelrod got Secret Service protection, and so arranged the same for herself. And that when a national security official suggested that Obama shouldn't skip the 2011 White House Correspondents' Dinner on the weekend of the Osama bin Laden raid because the media might get suspicious, Hillary Clinton looked up and issued her verdict: "[Expletive] the White House Correspondents' Dinner."

Leibovich notes that, outside of works like *Game Change* and Bob Woodward's tomes, political books like this one rarely achieve commercial success. *This Town* is as insidery as *Game Change*, but with lower stakes. (I suspect most Americans can make it through the day without knowing what Tammy Haddad is up to.) And it lacks the historical import of Woodward's deep dives into the White House. But it's not trying to be a book for the ages—it's a book for the moment, and it captures it well.

That moment begins with stories of frantic networking at Russert's memorial service at the Kennedy Center in June 2008, and ends with Leibovich's musings on Inauguration Day 2013. Other than the calendar, there is no clear arc to the tale, and by the 2012 campaign, *This Town* has lost some steam. If there is a focus, one that Leibovich returns to between parties, it is Team Obama's transformation from an above-it-all, apolitical wonkfest, at least in self-perception, into just another administration, where conflicts of interest are rife, lobbyists proliferate, and outgoing staffers quickly sell out (although no one in Washington sells out anymore; they monetize their government service).

Leibovich recalls Obama's attacks on lobbyists during the 2008 campaign, including the promise to keep them out of the White House. "It's not who we are," top aides intoned. But it is who they became. In a near parody of Washington's revolving door, administration honchos joined up with some of the biggest corporate villains of recent years. Leibovich highlights the "unholy triplet": Pentagon spokesman (and George W. Bush holdover) Geoff Morrell became BP's head of US communications, Treasury counselor Jake Siewert started spinning for Goldman Sachs, and OMB director Peter Orszag cashed in at Citigroup. (Morrell's deal was negotiated by Barnett. Obviously.) And whenever lobbyists joined the administration, the White House would just "acknowledge the exception, wait out the indignant blog posts and press releases, and move on," Leibovich writes. "That lobbying ban was so four years ago anyway."

This disdain for hypocrisy hints at the only semi-redeeming quality Leibovich finds in Washington. It's not honor or honesty—no one measures up—but a degree of self-awareness that you're playing a game, and not pretending otherwise.

So, he shows sympathy for Kurt Bardella, an insecure, insufferable Republican congressional press aide who passes Leibovich copies of his emails. "I loved the sheer unabashedness, even jubilance, of Kurt's networking and ladder climbing and determination," Leibovich writes. The rise, fall, and rise again of Bardella in Rep. Darrell Issa's office is among the most gripping portions of *This Town*.

A politician-turned-lobbyist such as Trent Lott also earns respect, in part because he doesn't hide his motivations. "Washington is where the money is," the former Republican majority leader told Leibovich. "That's generally what keeps people here." But Leibovich is scathing with Democrat Chris Dodd, who vowed he'd never lobby, right up until the former senator became head of the Motion Picture Association of America.

Leibovich is not all that kind to his colleagues in the Washington press corps, either, lamenting their coziness with authority and obsession with self-branding. *Politico*—"the emerging company-town organ for Political Washington"—comes in for grief as a trafficker of minutiae as a means of "driving the conversation." And Leibovich depicts *Politico*'s Mike Allen, of Playbook fame, as an "enabler" of journalistic groupthink and the media-political complex.

This broad media attack comes at a time when the Obama administration is targeting leakers, seizing journalists' phone records or labeling them "co-conspirators," and when news organizations are publishing details of top-secret government surveillance programs. Leibovich's digs seem relevant to a certain kind of Washington journalist—the frenetic political blogger, perhaps—but brunches and book parties don't seem to be easing the antagonism between the White House and the fourth estate.

Even Leibovich's critique of *Politico*, while persuasive, feels familiar. (I mean, didn't he read that great Leibovich profile of Allen in the *New York Times Magazine* in 2010?) *Politico* may have recognized the limits of a "winning the morning" strategy, recently announcing a push into long-form journalism.

So, here's a suggestion to *Politico*'s editors. Assign a revelatory Leibovich-style profile of Mark Leibovich himself, and answer the question that hovers over every page of his book: Is it really possible to be the impartial critic of a subculture that is also your own?

Too bad Leibovich can't write that story. That might be a conflict of interest, and we can't have that. Not in this town.

July 2013

WHEN POLITICIANS
ACKNOWLEDGE

THE FIRST PERSON MARCO RUBIO thanks by name in the acknowledgments of his new book, *American Dreams*, is kind of a big deal. "I thank my Lord, Jesus Christ, whose willingness to suffer and die for my sins will allow me to enjoy eternal life," the senator from Florida writes. The second person Rubio thanks: "My very wise lawyer, Bob Barnett."

Even with the Almighty on your side, it's smart to keep a Washington power broker on retainer.

Memoirs and policy books by presidential hopefuls are often predictable and dutiful works, their generic titles mirroring their originality. But at least one part of these books is consistently enjoyable and revealing: the acknowledgments sections.

There is still plenty of posturing there, and that's some of the fun. But it's also where the candidates disclose intellectual debts, hint at political favors, and unwittingly emphasize the very shortcomings they're seeking to overcome. In a crowded Republican primary field, several of the candidates have written—or at least published—books recently, and their acknowledgments can be more instructive than any policy speech, debate zinger, or surrogate's bark.

Of course, just about all the candidates thank their families right away. There are values voters to win over, people! Rand Paul (*Taking a Stand*), Ted Cruz (*A Time for Truth*), Carly Fiorina (*Rising to the Challenge*), Rick Perry (*Fed Up!*), and Mike Huckabee (*God, Guns, Grits, and Gravy*) all begin their acknowledgments with copious gratitude for spouses, children, and/or parents. Paul, however, acknowledges his own greatness as much as his family's. "To my sons William, Duncan, and Robert," the senator from Kentucky writes, "I hope the example I set for you in daily life will help you as you become adults." Ted Cruz, the Texan Cuban American by way of Canada, is quick to praise his parents as "two Americans of grit, passion, and fortitude," just in case anyone had doubts.

Rubio also expresses gratitude for his family's support, but not before a lengthier shout-out to Norman Braman, the eighty-three-year-old car-dealer billionaire who has bankrolled Rubio's past campaigns. The senator thanks Braman "not only for the advice and comments on the book, but for your friendship and wise advice to me over the years." Mentioning the cash itself would be tacky.

Acknowledgments can make plain the candidates' insecurities and self-perceived weaknesses. After thanking God and family, Scott Walker (*Unintimidated*) tries to buttress his national security credentials, not easy for a midwestern governor. "First, a salute to Major General Don Dunbar and the ten thousand men and women of the Wisconsin National Guard," he writes. "It is my sincere honor to serve as your commander in chief." (Too bad Walker's bloodiest battles have been against public employees' unions.) Rick Santorum, forever fighting "electability" concerns, spends much of his acknowledgments still bitter about the 2012 primaries; he complains that the media boxed him in as a "social issues" candidate and failed to see his bond with working-class voters. (Hence his book title, *Blue Collar Conservatives*.) And Perry, often accused of being intellectually unencumbered, emphasizes the historians and legal scholars he consulted for *Fed Up!*, published before his failed run at the Republican Party's 2012 presidential nomination. (The former Texas governor also writes that thanking his wife is a "no-brainer," an expression Perry should avoid in any sentence describing his decision-making.)

Although he is unlikely to have provided assistance other than spiritual or inspirational, Ronald Reagan makes cameos in the acknowledgments of some 2016 Republican hopefuls. Paul cites the courage of Reagan and Margaret Thatcher in challenging their parties' orthodoxies, drawing a parallel to his continued efforts to repeal the Affordable Care Act and fight Obama's "unconstitutional, lawless amnesty." And Walker thanks conservative Reagan biographer Craig Shirley for instructing him in the ways of the Gipper's 1980 campaign.

Cruz, meanwhile, inadvertently echoes a different president. The senator from Texas concludes his acknowledgments by reflecting on his immigrant father. "Only in a land like America is his story—is our story—even possible," Cruz writes. Sounds a bit like Barack Obama's "in no other country on Earth is my story even possible." Criticize a guy's rhetoric long enough and you're bound to start sounding like him.

Some candidates wonk out and list their various policy advisers. (Message: I'm serious.) In their 2013 book *Immigration Wars*, former Florida governor Jeb Bush and coauthor Clint Bolick highlight the expertise of Emilio González, a former immigration official at the Department of Homeland Security, and Tamar Jacoby, head of ImmigrationWorks USA. Also, in what must have been Bush's pre–"anchor babies" phase, the authors offer "a heartfelt thanks to the many immigrants we have had the honor to meet and know and who inspire and teach us what it means to be American." Rubio, meanwhile, names forty-five "scholars and policy experts" who form his brain trust on domestic and foreign policy, including guys from the reform conservative movement and the American Enterprise Institute. And I do mean "guys"— of the forty-five, only one is a woman. Nina Rees, president of the National Alliance for Public Charter Schools, congratulations!

Like Rubio thanking God and his Washington attorney, other candidates play the inside-outside game. Walker recaps his preferred pastimes: "In addition to hanging out with my family" (values points) "or watching sporting events" (regular guy points), "one of my favorite ways to relax is riding my 2003 Harley Davidson Road King" (cool guy points). But he slips in a mention of "my friend Reince Priebus," chairman of the Republican National Committee and former head of the Wisconsin GOP (establishment points). Walker skips Rep. Paul Ryan, a fellow Wisconsinite and the party's veep candidate in 2012. It's a noteworthy omission for a politician who lists more than two hundred people in his acknowledgments, including friends (and donors) Crystal and Jim Berg, who apparently throw fantastic pond parties.

On occasion, candidates drop out of character. In his acknowledgments, Huckabee drips folksiness like sawmill gravy on biscuits. He laments that this is the first book he's written without Jet, his beloved black Lab, and says his publisher's enthusiasm has been "better than a bowl of grits with cheese and shrimp." But when he thanks his son David, "who runs several of the companies I own," he sounds downright Trumpesque.

The Republican front-runner offers only brief acknowledgments in his 2011 book, *Time to Get Tough: Making America #1 Again*, with Donald Trump devoting a lone paragraph to his publisher and a few staffers. Relative newcomers Fiorina and Ben Carson (*One Nation*) also skimp on their acknowledgments, missing a chance to suck up, back-scratch, and repackage. They'll learn! Oddly, Sen. Lindsey Graham of South Carolina, one of the most experienced candidates of the bunch, omits an acknowledgments section altogether in his recent e-book, *My Story*. In fact, he seems to resent the entire political-book exercise.

"Everyone has a story. Not everyone has to tell it, of course, and most people have the good sense not to," Graham begins. "But if you're in my line of work, and the time arrives when you start imagining a big promotion … you are by custom expected to give a general account of your life." With a sales pitch like that, Graham has no one to thank but himself.

These books, meant to distinguish the candidates, often reinforce how small and overlapping the world of presidential contenders can be. For example, two different candidates thank the same ghostwriter (awkward!), a former speechwriter for Attorney General John Ashcroft. "Jessica Gavora was a true partner," Fiorina writes, "helping me think through the structure and the content." And for Rubio, the help seems to have been even more integral: "I am grateful to Jessica Gavora for helping me craft and organize the manuscript, interview the people who shared their life stories and meet the various deadlines on time."

Sounds like a lot of work. How about a co-byline, Senator? That's the best acknowledgment of all.

August 2015

CRITICAL CARLOS READS HEALTHY HOLLY

HI, I'M CRITICAL CARLOS, AND I want you to read books like I do! Reading is good for your brain and helps us all learn. If you read enough books, then one day, when you're big, you can become a state senator, and then the mayor of a large American city. And maybe you can write books of your own, too! The fun part is that you can make lots of money by selling one hundred thousand copies of your books, or even more, to businesses and organizations that later might need your help. Helping is nice. Everybody wins!

This week, Critical Carlos read *Healthy Holly: Exercising Is Fun!*, by Baltimore mayor Catherine Pugh. She published it all by herself. I couldn't find the book in stores or libraries. Not even Mr. Internet had any left! Fortunately, Critical Carlos knew someone in Baltimore who had a copy. (And if you're wondering why Critical Carlos is writing in the third person after starting out in the first person, good catch—*Healthy Holly* does the same thing!)

In the book, a little girl named Holly learns to exercise. She **walks** through parks, **rides** a bike, **dances** and **jumps rope** with her parents and friends. Those important verbs are in bold letters in the book, to make sure we remember all the different ways to exercise, except the author sometimes **forgets** to make the right words bold. Oops! Holly has conversations with her parents, too, except the author sometimes also forgets to put quotation marks in the right places. Oops again! *Healthy Holly* is a little sloppy!

Critical Carlos knows he might be too old to appreciate such a successful children's book. Lucky for us, Critical Carlos has three Critical Kids, ages eleven, eight, and five. Critical Carlos read the story out loud to all three of them at bedtime this week—and they sure had lots to say!

The Critical Kids are a little alarmed by the illustrations in *Healthy Holly*.

Random objects come to life throughout the pages—streetlamps, sports equipment, furniture, trash bins, clouds, even the sun! They all have faces and big smiles. "I wonder why the tennis ball is happy to be hit?" asks eleven-year-old Critical Kid. Good question! "I wonder why the clock doesn't have that many teeth," he says next, surveying Healthy Holly's living room. "Did the clock forget to brush its teeth?"

Wow, *Healthy Holly* has secret dental-health lessons, too!

A cloud in the sky "looks like a dolphin," complains eight-year-old Critical Kid. "The dad looks like he has huge boobs," she adds, pointing at various illustrations of Holly's father. He does look like he works out a lot, but Critical Carlos decides to move on quickly from this line of conversation!

The Critical Kids have other problems with the pictures, created not by Pugh but by an illustrator. They include a "shape-shifting front porch," as eleven-year-old Critical Kid puts it, as well as "a bunch of alive things that weren't supposed to be alive," says five-year-old Critical Kid. "That is so creepy."

But they are especially bothered by the way people in *Healthy Holly* talk, which apparently is not the way actual people talk in real life. Uh-oh!

"Exercising is fun," Healthy Holly's mother tells her. Holly responds: "I will be healthy. I like having fun." Eleven-year-old Critical Kid doesn't like that exchange. "The dialogue ... it doesn't sound so real," he observes. "I mean the phrase 'I like having fun.' Isn't it obvious that one likes having fun? You don't just walk up and say: 'I like having fun! I like doing things that I like!'" Ouch. Everyone's a critic at Critical Carlos's house!

"You are jumping rope," the mother tells Holly. "You are exercising." To which eight-year-old Critical Kid can only say, "Duh." You're right, Critical Kid, it is a little odd to tell a child what she is doing while she is doing it. No wonder the three Critical Kids tell Critical Carlos that reading *Healthy Holly* does not make them want to exercise more. Tough but fair!

All the characters in *Healthy Holly* are happy. That's nice, but isn't it a little weird that nothing ever seems to go wrong, even for a tiny bit? "I feel like if everyone is always happy, it takes away from the reality of the story," eleven-year-old Critical Kid says. "You could have them confused sometimes."

Good point, Critical Kid. Learning to ride a bike is hard. Remember those falls and scrapes and tears? Critical Carlos sure does! But that makes the moment when you finally keep your balance, gliding faster and faster, so much more fun and exciting!

Healthy Holly skips over all that. After Holly receives a bicycle for her birthday, "Holly's mother and father took turns teaching her to ride her bike," the book says. "Soon Holly was able to ride her bike." That's it. It sounds so easy!

Publishing children's books—and selling so many copies—is usually hard work, too. Many authors try and try for a long time. But success is so much more fun and exciting when you don't rely on bulk purchases from private corporations and state agencies, and when books arouse real interest, not just conflicts of interest, right, kids?

Who knows? Maybe the other books in the Healthy Holly series are much better. Will you be reading them? Let Critical Carlos and the Critical Kids know—because we sure won't be!

April 2019

THE SELF-REGARD OF
JAMES COMEY

JAMES B. COMEY HAS WRITTEN the Washington Book of the Moment, but he clearly does not want *A Higher Loyalty: Truth, Lies, and Leadership* to be one more Washington book of the moment, full of insider tales gauged by the grudges they settle, nuggets they unearth, and screenplays they elicit. One look at its austere cover and ponderous subtitle and you know this is meant as a lasting, highbrow work—a big-think story of values and institutions clashing with tribalism and self-interest in Washington.

Running through the book, a sort of geek chorus, is Comey's doctrine of "ethical leadership," an often preachy and sometimes profound collection of principles that he believes should govern those who govern. *A Higher Loyalty* is the brand extension of James Comey: the upright citizen turned philosopher, the lawman as thought leader. "Values—like truth, integrity, and respect for others, to name just a few—serve as external reference points for ethical leaders to make decisions," Comey writes. "Ethical leaders choose a higher loyalty to those core values over their own personal gain."

In his years as a prosecutor, Justice Department official, and FBI director, Comey attempts to live out such values, whereas President Trump embodies their antitheses. "This president is unethical, and untethered to truth and institutional values," he writes. "His leadership is transactional, ego driven, and about personal loyalty." Yet Comey understands that side-by-side comparisons are not a true measure of leadership, that leaders should be assessed against their own best performances and highest aspirations. "Ethical leaders do not run from criticism, especially self-criticism," he writes, "and they don't hide from uncomfortable questions."

So, let's pose one: Does Comey live up to the standards of ethics and leadership he outlines in this book?

In *A Higher Loyalty*, Comey provides lots of scenes, backstory, and details of his government service. What was he thinking during those one-on-ones with President Trump? Check. Why did he announce, eleven days before the 2016 election, that he was reopening the bureau's investigation into Hillary Clinton's emails? Check. How did it feel to learn he had lost his job by seeing the news on television? Check. And what does he really make of Attorney General Jeff Sessions ("overmatched"), former attorney general Loretta Lynch ("politically compromised"), and Barack Obama ("extraordinary listener")? Check, check, check.

Yet one of the distinctions of *A Higher Loyalty* is that the newsiest elements appear fairly deep in the book. First, there is plenty about Comey's childhood, his early career as a prosecutor in New York, and his time in Washington as a top Justice Department official during the George W. Bush administration. This is a real memoir, with recollections and dilemmas building methodically, sometimes dramatically, toward his ethical leadership ideals. But even as chapters fly by without a mention of the current president, Trump is everywhere.

He lurks in Comey's schoolboy battles with bullies, for instance. "All bullies are largely the same," he writes. "They threaten the weak to feed some insecurity that rages inside them." Or in his days battling mafia families as US attorney in Manhattan, a time that came back to him once he encountered Team Trump. "As I found myself thrust into the Trump orbit, I once again was having flashbacks to my earlier career as a prosecutor against the Mob. The silent circle of assent. The boss in complete control. The loyalty oaths. The us-versus-them worldview. The lying about all things."

When Comey cops to petty misdeeds, however, the self-criticism—and self-regard—is almost comical. At six foot eight, he used to lie about having played basketball for William & Mary, and he still feels bad about it. (After finishing law school, he reached out to friends and fessed up.) He once regifted a necktie to Director of National Intelligence James Clapper. "Because we considered ourselves people of integrity," Comey explains solemnly, "I disclosed it was a regift as I handed him the tie." And he congratulates himself for not exercising director's prerogative and cutting in line at the FBI cafeteria. "I thought it was very important to show people that I'm not better than anyone else."

But when the stakes rise, self-examination diminishes. On his decision to publicly denounce Clinton's handling of classified information in her private emails in July 2016, Comey's misgivings are cosmetic. He wishes he had organized the statement differently and explained early that no charges were warranted, and he wishes he had not characterized Clinton's actions as "extremely careless"—even if "thoughtful lawyers" could understand what he meant. (Too bad thoughtful lawyers weren't his only audience.)

The point of the statement was to level with the public. "We had offered transparency, tried to show the American people competence, honesty, and independence," Comey explains. For all his talk of twentieth-century Protestant theologian Reinhold Niebuhr—in the introduction, Comey quotes Niebuhr's statement that "man's capacity for justice makes democracy possible, but man's inclination to injustice makes democracy necessary"—the more relevant guru here may be Ray Dalio, founder of the hedge fund Bridgewater Associates. Comey served as its general counsel from 2010 to 2013 and grew to appreciate Dalio's belief in "a culture of complete transparency and honesty," he writes. "Transparency is almost always the best course."

But when Comey decided to inform Congress that he was resuming the investigation in late October because additional Clinton-related emails had been found on the laptop of former representative Anthony Weiner, transparency was not Comey's only motivation; his political assumptions also played a role. "Assuming, as nearly everyone did, that Hillary Clinton would be elected president of the United States in less than two weeks, what would happen to the FBI, the Justice Department, or her own presidency if it later was revealed, after the fact, that she was still the subject of an FBI investigation?" It is possible, Comey acknowledges, that "my concern about making her an illegitimate president by concealing the restarted investigation bore greater weight than it would have if the election appeared closer or if Donald Trump were ahead in all polls."

It's a startling admission for a man devoted to "serving institutions I love precisely because they play no role in politics, because they operate independently of the passions of the electoral process." His interpretation of those passions may have led to one of the most consequential decisions of the 2016 race. He's supposed to go by the book, not by the poll.

Comey's own ethical leadership suffers most in the book's treatment of his onetime boss, Loretta Lynch. He criticizes Lynch for asking him to describe the FBI's Clinton investigation as a "matter" rather than as an investigation—an "overtly political" request, he explains. Fine. But then he says that his decision to excoriate Clinton's actions resulted in part from his concern about some unverified classified materials that emerged in early 2016 and that, if publicly known, "would undoubtedly have been used by political opponents to cast serious doubt on the attorney general's independence in connection with the Clinton investigation." He insists that he personally never saw Lynch interfere, but he remains "bothered" by the existence of this classified information, which someday could be used to "question the independence of the FBI."

Of course, it is also bothersome that the former FBI director would cite vague information to imply wrongdoing by the nation's top law-enforcement official, with the very nature of the information making it hard for her to respond. (The *Washington Post* reported that in 2016 the FBI received a Russian intelligence document citing an email in which Lynch supposedly assured the Clinton campaign that the investigation would not go too deep, but that the document was unreliable.) For Comey to suggest that the attorney general "appeared politically compromised" without offering supportive evidence does not seem particularly ethical. And it does not seem like leadership.

You don't serve as deputy attorney general and FBI director without being a Washington operator, and Comey has a good eye for life in the swamp. "I had gotten used to watching the world pass by through the small dark bulletproof side windows," he remarks, nicely capturing the isolation and constraints of officialdom. When he first meets Obama, he is struck by his thinness, confidence, and focus; when he first meets Trump, Comey realizes that he looks shorter than on television and—zinger alert—that his hands are smaller than Comey's, though not "unusually so." And in the book's funniest moment, he recalls President George W. Bush raising his hand to interrupt an Oval Office briefing so he could gaze out the window and watch Marine One blow snow all over the waiting press corps on the South Lawn. "Without any expression on his face at all, Bush turned back to me, dropping his hand. 'Okay, go,' he said."

Such moments help *A Higher Loyalty* because it's hard for Comey to make hard news with this book; the territory has been so well covered by copious reporting on his memos and his congressional testimony. Whatever we learn about Trump here emerges from Comey's personal impressions and first-person anecdotes. After Comey briefed the president-elect on the infamous dossier compiled by former British intelligence officer Christopher Steele, Trump became obsessed with its more salacious accusations. "I'm a germophobe," he says to Comey. "There's no way I would let people pee on each other around me. No way." And when Comey and top intelligence officials informed the Trump team about Russian interference in the 2016 election, Trump's only question was self-serving: "But you found there was no impact on the result, right?"

Comey revisits his own big career moments—prosecuting mobsters, standing up to Vice President Dick Cheney and his consigliere David Addington over counterterrorism policies—with understandable pride. Yet he constantly worries he is too self-centered. "I can be stubborn, prideful, overconfident, and driven by ego," he admits. "I've struggled with those my whole life."

That struggle continues in this book. Comey isn't just the kind of writer who quotes Shakespeare but the kind who quotes himself quoting Shakespeare. He rejects the notion that "I am in love with my own righteousness" yet notes that "I have long worried about my ego." (Consider the egotism of being preoccupied by your egotism.) "I am convinced that if I could do it all again, I would do the same thing" given what he knew at the time, Comey says of the emails controversy, even if "reasonable people" might have handled it differently. And he apologizes to Clinton in the least apologetic way possible: "I have read she has felt anger toward me personally, and I'm sorry for that. I'm sorry that I couldn't do a better job explaining to her and her supporters why I made the decisions I made." (Ironically, it's a very Clintonian apology.)

For all his contempt for Trump—he decries "the forest fire that is the Trump presidency"—Comey concludes that the president's behavior, while disturbing and dangerous, "may fall short of being illegal." But he's not acting here as a lawyer or investigator; this is Comey the philosopher. He laments Trump's lack of self-reflection or self-awareness. "Listening to others who disagree with me and are willing to criticize me is essential to piercing the seduction of certainty," Comey writes. "Doubt, I've learned, is wisdom . . . Those leaders who never think they are wrong, who never question their judgments or perspectives, are a danger to the organizations and people they lead."

Trump is the most severe example of that tendency in this book. But he is not the only one.

April 2018

PROFILES IN THINKING
ABOUT COURAGE

THERE IS A GOOD REASON the anonymous Trump administration official who published an opinion essay in the *New York Times* in 2018 describing an internal resistance to the president has managed to remain anonymous. The op-ed, for all the speculation and controversy it generated, yielded few identifying details. The author claimed to be part of a group fighting for America's democratic institutions while "thwarting Mr. Trump's more misguided impulses," but readers did not learn what sort of work the unknown writer did or what, if anything, had been thwarted.

The essay also featured copious op-ed clichés: Comfort was cold, divides were bitter, observers were astute, heroes were not sung. And aisles, as always, should be reached across. With such material, identifying the writer—especially one residing anywhere in the federal government—was difficult. (Like many non-astute observers, I assumed that the name would leak quickly. It did not.)*

Now, Anonymous has written a 259-page book, *A Warning*, promising to "cut through the noise" of this presidency and making the case that, yes, Trump "still lacks the guiding principles needed to govern our nation." Trump is "reckless" and his management style "erratic." The president's qualities include "inattentiveness," "impulsiveness," and "intellectual laziness." He displays misogynistic behavior, embraces conspiracy theories, bullies subordinates, abuses his powers, doesn't listen to briefings, and regards criticism as treason. Anonymous also concedes that the thesis of the original op-ed—that the alleged adults in the room could curb Trump's worst instincts—has

---

* In October 2020, Miles Taylor, former chief of staff at the Department of Homeland Security, publicly confirmed that he was the anonymous author of the *New York Times* op-ed.

proved false. "Americans should not expect that his advisors can fix the situation," Anonymous acknowledges. "We cannot."

However accurate and sobering such characterizations may be, they all belong in the category of things we already know. Unfortunately, much of *A Warning* reads like a longer version of the op-ed, purposely vague and avoiding big revelations in order to preserve the author's anonymity. The writer admits as much. "Many recollections will have to remain in my memory until the right time, lest the debate devolve into one about my identity." Anonymous decries the "contemptible Washington parlor game" of guessing that identity and insists that the name is secret so the focus can be on the substance of the message, not on the messenger. "Some will call this 'cowardice,'" Anonymous writes. "My feelings are not hurt by the accusation. Nor am I unprepared to attach my name to criticism of President Trump. I may do so, in due course."

But what is the right time, if not now? When will that course ever be more due? The House of Representatives is embarked on an impeachment inquiry against the president. Civil servants are stepping forward to testify—in public, with names and faces—about what they saw, heard, and did. The writer's decision is not necessarily cowardly, but it is self-defeating. Anonymity is often granted to acquire additional information, but in this book, it excuses giving less. *A Warning* tells us plenty about what Anonymous thinks, not enough about what Anonymous knows. And without learning more about the writer, it's tough to know what to make of either.

In the absence of facts, readers are barraged by similes. Trump is "like a twelve-year-old in an air-traffic control tower, pushing the buttons of government indiscriminately," Anonymous writes. Alternatively, "the Trump White House is like an Etch A Sketch. Every morning the president wakes up, shakes it, and draws something." Trump's words sound like "those of a two-bit bartender at a rundown barrelhouse." His deceptions are "like a game of Twister gone wrong; the truth was so tied up in knots, no one knew what the hell we were talking about anymore." And most vivid, working for Trump is "like showing up at the nursing home at daybreak to find your elderly uncle running pantsless across the courtyard and cursing loudly about the cafeteria food, as worried attendants try to catch him."

There are moments of detail and revelation, but they usually affirm points long understood about the president. When discussing whether to challenge Saudi leaders on the murder of journalist Jamal Khashoggi, Trump launches into a discussion of oil prices. ("Do you know how stupid it would be to pick this fight? Oil would go up to one hundred fifty dollars a barrel. Jesus.") The president mocks women migrating to this country, feigning a Spanish-language accent. ("We get these women coming in with like seven children. They are saying, 'Oh, please help! My husband left me!' They are useless.") He asks his legal team to draft a bill slashing the number of federal judges. ("Let's get rid of the f—ing judges.") And you know Trump is about to propose something unethical when he scans the room for notetakers. ("What the f— are you doing? Are you f—ing taking notes?")

This is the fate of so many of the Chaos Chronicles—the insider books that tell us what it's really, truly like in the Trump administration. Their explosive anecdotes about the president—*He wrote up an enemies list! Cabinet secretaries think he's stupid! Top aides steal sensitive documents off his desk! He wants to build a border moat with alligators! Yes, alligators!*—manage to be shocking and alarming yet, by this point in the Trump presidency, almost entirely unsurprising.

What frustrates about reading *A Warning* is that its author is not a journalist or a former official but someone still working in the administration at a high level and ostensibly in a position to not just chronicle conditions but to affect them. Instead, the book offers an endless encore of senior officials expressing concern to one another. A sampling of the lyrics:

"We were baffled."

"Officials held their breath."

"NSC leaders were nonplussed."

"We all watched with a sense of doom."

"We were all unnerved."

"This is completely bats—."

"Man oh man what the f— is he doing?"

"There is literally no one in charge here."

I recall one occasion when Anonymous describes doing something proactive. The head of an agency had spoken on Capitol Hill about a US foreign adversary; the description was accurate but contradicted the president's stated views. Trump was threatening to dismiss the official. Anonymous and a colleague "scrambled to make sure Trump didn't take to Twitter to announce a new firing," the author recounts. "Doing so, we argued, would make him look like he was trying to manipulate the intelligence process at a time when that would be very bad for him, especially with the Mueller investigation unfinished. Thankfully, he kept his powder dry, but only temporarily."

More often in *A Warning*, actions are not taken; they are almost taken. In a particularly dire circumstance, several top officials consider resigning together, a "midnight self-massacre" that would draw attention to Trump's mismanagement. "The move was deemed too risky because it would shake public confidence," Anonymous explains. At any moment, the author writes, there are at least a handful of top aides "on the brink" of quitting. (The brink is a popular hangout for Trump officials.) Anonymous also wonders if Trump's response to the Charlottesville protests in 2017, when the president drew a moral equivalence between white nationalists and those opposing them, would have been the time for such a gesture. "Maybe that was a lost moment, when a rush to the exits would have meant something."

It's like Profiles in Thinking About Courage.

The author describes a process of disillusion, from joining the administration in the hope that Trump could be a successful conservative president, to proclaiming the internal resistance in the *Times*, to concluding that the effort had failed and watching comrades—the "Steady Staters"—steadily depart. "What remains are more defenders than do-gooders in the political ranks; obsequious pleasers outnumber thoughtful public servants."

It is not clear why, if Anonymous has concluded that the quiet resistance is powerless, the author remains in the administration. If no longer resisting, what is Anonymous doing in there? "Anyone aiding the Trump administration is, or was, one of his Apologists," Anonymous admits. "They've all waited too long to speak out and haven't spoken forcefully enough. Myself included." That is the tragedy of Trump's adults in the room; the longer you're in that room, the less of an adult you become.

The title of the book would seem to indicate a warning about the president, but the author's real warning is more generic. We have to "restore the soul" of our politics, Anonymous writes. "If, however, we shrink from the task, our names will be recorded by history as those who didn't pass the torch but let its light expire. That is my warning."

Sincere, earnest, and true, no doubt, but also the kind of sentiment appearing daily in the nation's opinion pages. We don't need a secret administration insider to tell us to pass the torch of liberty; we need that person to explain how the torch is being doused.

Anonymous, who promises to "strenuously deny" authorship should anyone ask, explains that "certain details have been withheld or modified without changing the facts to preserve the anonymity of those involved." ("Modified without changing the facts" is a great Washington formulation.) "Anyone whose sole purpose in reading this book is to uncover names, including my own, will find they are wasting their time."

But, unlike a newspaper op-ed, a full-length book is tough to write without leaving fingerprints. So, I might be getting played, but here is my tentative profile of Anonymous, gleaned from the text:

Anonymous is not a well-known figure. Anonymous does not work in the White House but in a high-profile cabinet agency. Anonymous is an establishment Republican who believes in free trade, small government, and the international liberal order. Anonymous did not support Trump during the 2016 primaries but was career-minded enough to avoid major criticisms of the candidate. Anonymous probably served in the George W. Bush administration, particularly during the second term. Anonymous has experience at the intersection of law and national security, and is serving in that second tier of senior-level jobs that can lead to more prominent roles in future Republican administrations. Anonymous is an institutionalist, obsessed with process and orderly decision-making. Under Trump, Anonymous has worked within walking distance of the White House. Anonymous is an Ivy League lawyer and has some writing background, perhaps as a former speechwriter, law clerk, or even a long-ago student journalist. Anonymous is personally familiar with top military brass but is unlikely to have served in uniform.

Anonymous expresses admiration for John McCain, though notes unspecified disagreements with the late senator. He praises former White House counsel Don McGahn for standing up to Trump and Treasury Secretary Steven Mnuchin for his efforts to ease trade disputes. Anonymous is scathing about Trump's Homeland Security officials, who "left a stain on their reputations, their department, and the country" with the family-separation policy on the US-Mexico border. Anonymous is probably a Gen Xer with a Twitter presence, but not an active one, perhaps a lurker or the holder of a private account. Anonymous is a self-described "student of history," incessantly citing Greek and Roman philosophers, Founding Fathers, past presidents and historians—the kind of person who belongs to legal or historical societies. Anonymous is a sports fan. And Anonymous probably earned a comfortable living in the private sector during the Obama years, making it easier to forgo the book advance, donate royalties, and risk losing a government job if outed as the author.

A parlor game? Maybe. But without a clearer sense of who Anonymous is and what this person has seen, done, and is still doing, *A Warning* does not cut through the noise. It just creates more of it.

November 2019

DOWN AND OUT IN TRUMP WORLD

ONE OF THE SADDEST AND cringiest moments—out of many—in Stephanie Grisham's memoir of her years in the Trump White House occurs at Mar-a-Lago, in the middle of the Stormy Daniels scandal. Grisham, then communications director for first lady Melania Trump, felt sorry for her boss and proposed that the two take a walk along the beach. Grisham hoped to "comfort her as a friend," she writes, to "hang out woman to woman," to give Melania a chance to unburden herself.

"And there will be photographers?" the first lady asked. Melania, Grisham realized, assumed it was just another press event that her aide was setting up. She did not acknowledge, or even recognize, the overture of friendship. "I felt like such an ass to have offered," Grisham admits.

In that exchange, Grisham committed a mistake that so many Trump acolytes make, and one she would repeat in her years working for the first lady and the president. She thought she belonged. "Everyone just loves you," Donald Trump assured Grisham when he named her White House press secretary. She came to believe that she was "a trusted and valued member of Trump World." Right up until she wasn't.

It's not easy writing a White House tell-all when it feels like so much about this White House has already been told. The substantive revelations in Grisham's *I'll Take Your Questions Now* are matters of detail, coloring in a picture whose contours have long been clear. Yes, Trump had a volcanic temper, sucked up to Vladimir Putin, and ogled young female staffers. Yes, Jared Kushner was in over his head and didn't seem to know it. Yes, Ivanka Trump was addicted to television cameras. Yes, Melania Trump was glamorous—"she even smelled incredible," Grisham gushes—and resentful of her media coverage, often telling Grisham "don't replay" (meaning "don't reply") to reporters' inquiries. So much of this book feels like a replay of familiar stories, even if told from a slightly different vantage point.

Grisham's most revelatory moments are not about the principals but about herself—and why she stuck around to witness so much that she says she came to revile. "Let's face it, somebody had to work in the Donald Trump White House," she deadpans. But Grisham, who resigned on January 6, with the assault on the Capitol underway, asks herself: "Why did I wait so long? I had stayed through *Access Hollywood*, impeachment, family separation, Charlottesville, accusations of rape and misconduct, and a million other things"— all moments that could have been *the* moment.

Her often self-serving answers can be oblivious and at times painfully self-aware. Grisham seems to imagine herself an adult in the room, saying she "lost count" of all the times she succeeded in getting the president to "dial back his rhetoric, to calm one situation or another." But based on this book, such moments were not terribly frequent or consequential. It shouldn't be hard to keep count.

Grisham had carved out a living in political communications—or "comms," in that grating Washington shorthand—including work with the 2012 Romney campaign and as press secretary for Arizona's attorney general before making her way to Trump's 2016 operation as a low-level press wrangler. Trump wasn't necessarily her first choice among the Republican candidates, "but once I was in it, I was in it." She found him refreshing and liked that he "challenged dumb rules." Besides, she'd always dreamed of being a White House press secretary, even putting up pictures of the executive mansion in her past workplaces to remind her of her goal.

But over time, working for Trump became a "classic abuse relationship," with the president as "the distant, erratic father we all wanted to please." She recalls a visit to an intensive care unit after a mass shooting in Dayton, when the president became angry because no press cameras had been there when the medical staff cheered for him. "What a waste," he grumbled. Upon seeing local Democratic politicians criticize the visit on television, Trump unleashed on Grisham aboard Air Force One, his face nearly purple with anger. "Why are you even on this plane? What do I have a whole team of people for if there is no one f—ing defending me?"

She was on the plane, in part, because she felt she had few options. "I was a single mom with no trust fund. If I had quit earlier, where would I have gone?" The usual lucrative path of former White House press secretaries, lined with corporate boards and speaking gigs, would not necessarily be available to Trump White House alums. Even during the impeachment saga—the first one—Grisham did not see the point of resigning. "Ask generals Mattis or Kelly, even Ambassador Bolton, if that had had any effect on how Donald Trump operated," she points out. So she stayed. "The Trumps were all I had," she writes. "At least that was what I believed for a long time."

The book is divided roughly equally between Grisham's work with the president and with the first lady, including a rough patch when she tried to work for both at once. The experience left her "heady with power," she explains, another reason she struggled to let go. Yet she never functioned as a conventional press secretary, let alone a powerful one. Grisham did not deliver a briefing and often noted that Trump was "his own best spokesperson." Meaning his real one.

Instead she wielded power in the service of petty schemes and resentments. Grisham's "sly little move" of surreptitiously rearranging seating cards so that Melania, not Ivanka, would have a better camera angle during a presidential speech in Saudi Arabia is what passes for high drama. And after the first lady visited an orphanage in Kenya and was photographed holding an African baby, Grisham was troubled to find that Ivanka had visited a hurricane recovery site in North Carolina around the same time—and was photographed holding an African American child. "Was that a coincidence?" Grisham grouses. More consequentially, Grisham and Melania succeed in getting a National Security Council adviser fired for launching an investigation into some members of the first lady's staff, including Grisham. Looking back, Grisham congratulates herself a bit. "Bold? Definitely. Unprofessional? Perhaps."

She laments how the news media fixated on the first lady's attire, even as she devotes inordinate time to explaining the "look book," a collection of drawings and mock-ups of outfits that Melania might wear for different events, managed by her personal stylist. "The look book became a big part of my life," Grisham writes. She devotes a chapter to the infamous "I Really

Don't Care, Do U?" jacket that the first lady wore on her way to visit a children's detention facility near the US-Mexico border in Texas. "To be honest, I don't know what she was thinking," Grisham writes. But she blames the news media for the mess. "All the headlines focused, of course, on the jacket rather than on the purpose of her trip to the border," she complains, even though it was the jarring contrast between the jacket's message and the purpose of the visit that made the thing so bizarre.

There are memorable descriptions in this book—I'll always remember Grisham's writing that the first lady "wore studied indifference as though it were armor"—as well as some real high-school-report-style clunkers. "The continent of Africa is vast, and as in North America, each country has its own set of problems and issues," Grisham informs readers. But she is often more noteworthy for what she does not say. Given her role as a press secretary, Grisham is surprisingly silent on the president's attacks on the press. "It is not my intention to use this book to trash the press, nor is it to defend some of our administration's behaviors and actions against them," she writes. "Truth be told, I think both parties were at fault for many things." Truth be told, that is incredibly weak.

Grisham was inclined to question the president's attitudes toward journalists mainly if she feared he would make her look bad in front of them—when he asked her to do a dramatic reenactment of the Ukraine call in a news briefing, or when he insisted that a press staffer tell reporters that Stormy Daniels had "a horse face," or when he demanded that Grisham tweet a statement denigrating former White House chief of staff John Kelly. She declined the first order, ignored the second but carried out the third, and she apologizes to Kelly for it in her book.

Grisham says there was a "little voice" in her head during the Trump presidency, telling her "it was all so wrong." Yet, before January 6, that voice spoke up only at particular moments—when Mitt Romney was humiliated in his quest to become Trump's secretary of state, and when a personal friend of Grisham's was fired from the White House, supposedly over an indiscreet Grindr account. That is, when people she liked or admired were personally affected. And her disenchantment with the White House gained strength when she realized that chief of staff Mark Meadows, whom she loathed, was seeking to demote her.

But then came January 6, "a day of reckoning for me," Grisham writes. She texted the first lady and asked if she wanted to publicly condemn the violence. Melania responded "No," just that single word. "It broke me," Grisham recalls. She waited a minute, then sent an email to the first lady, officially resigning. After talking or texting nearly every day for years, she and Melania have not spoken since that day. That silence "took some getting used to," Grisham admits.

Even now, she remains conflicted over the Trump family. "I liked them and I disliked them and I miss them and I hope I never see them again," Grisham writes. It's an occupational hazard of Trump World exiles. Some part of them still hopes to belong.

October 2021

THE GENERIC INTELLECTUALISM OF BEN SASSE

AMONG THE HUNDREDS OF BOOKS I read during my years as a critic for the *Washington Post*, only three proved so paralyzingly pointless that, upon reaching the last page, I found I had nothing to say. One was an unnecessary memoir, another a dispiriting manifesto. The third book was *Them: Why We Hate Each Other—and How to Heal*, by Sen. Ben Sasse.

It's not that *Them* is a terrible book; I have read and reviewed worse. Bad books can be valuable, even delightful, to read and critique, as long as their shortcomings lead to worthwhile questions or send readers down unexpected paths. But *Them*, published in 2018, offers few such consolations. Sasse, the junior senator from Nebraska and now the sole finalist to become president of the University of Florida,* delivered a generic, forgettable work: packed with big-think buzzwords rehashing old arguments, clichés and metaphors passing for analysis, thought-leader-ese masquerading as vision. It was not compelling enough to dislike in public. At least not then.

I was reminded of *Them* when I read the Republican senator's brief statement on his potential move to Gainesville—a possibility that has elicited campus protests and varying reactions from state and national leaders. Sasse wrote that the University of Florida is "the most interesting university in America right now," and that he would be delighted to help it become the nation's "most dynamic, bold, future-oriented university." Interesting. Dynamic. Bold. The future! It sounded a lot like *Them*. Nothing the book or statement says seems wrong, but only because they both say so little.

The central message of *Them* is that community life in the United States is in decline because of various cultural, technological, and political

---

*   Sasse became the university's president in February 2023.

forces, and that the isolation and anger replacing them threaten American democracy. This phenomenon has been documented and discussed at length for decades, yet the senator approaches it with a big-reveal vibe. "Something is really wrong here," he writes. "Something deeper is going on." Americans have a "nagging sense that something bigger is wrong." The mayhem of the 2016 presidential election was "only the consequence of deeper problems."

The problems may be deep, but Sasse clings to the surface of things. "America seems to be tearing apart at the seams," he writes, so much so that "there are, today, effectively, two different Americas." (Somewhere, John Edwards is tearing out his $400 hair.) The term "disruption" appears throughout the book, a reliable sign that an author was vaguely tech-savvy a decade ago. Facebook and Twitter are frowned upon, naturally, while italics are deployed throughout the text to give concepts a weighty air. "Our world is nudging us toward *rootlessness*, when only a recovery of *rootedness* can heal us," Sasse writes, while the word "connections" is occasionally rendered as "*connections*," which I gather makes it more significant. Sasse has a weakness for the melodramatic single-sentence paragraph. "We're hyperconnected, and we're disconnected." Or: "We live—and work—in unusual times." And, in case you hadn't heard: "America is an idea."

Them relies on the roster of social scientists and assorted thinkers you'd expect to see in a work of this kind. Kudos to the senator for reading so many luminaries of the America-is-coming-apart genre, but their presence only underscores the book's secondhand feel. (Chapter 1 relies so heavily on Robert Putnam that the senator could have skipped it and just encouraged readers to pick up *Bowling Alone* and *Our Kids*.) Sasse summons the ghosts of the American Revolution, but in the most Founders 101 way possible. Ben Franklin makes an appearance to say, "A republic, if you can keep it," whereas James Madison shows up to remind us that "if men were angels, no government would be necessary." I learned more from *Hamilton*, and I never even saw it with the original cast.

I may have expected too much from this book; my impressions are likely colored by my disappointment. In addition to his time in the Senate, Sasse is a scholar (he has a PhD in history) and an educator (he is the former president of Midland University in Nebraska), and with his early willingness to question Donald Trump's candidacy he seemed a promising and thoughtful new voice on the shrinking center-right. Published just weeks before the 2018 midterms—when Trump was promising to make the election all about migrant caravans and Brett Kavanaugh's Supreme Court confirmation—*Them* was an opportunity for this lawmaker-teacher-historian to offer a meaningful alternative to the politics he decried.

Instead, *Them* is on the dulling edge of political thought, a book that can safely be omitted from the syllabus of any University of Florida seminar unless Sasse himself teaches it. "Genuine wisdom will require not just acknowledging the disruption of our ways of making a living, but also our way of thinking about ourselves, our identities and our places in the world," Sasse offers in a typically vapid sentence. He cautions us not to tackle America's troubles with a "formula" or a "silver bullet" or a "one-size-fits-all solution," an impressive trifecta of triteness.

Sasse, who was against Trump before he supported him before he was against him once again, is disappointed by both Fox News and MSNBC. (Same here.) At the end of the book, after lamenting how a politics-obsessed country has split into us-versus-them factions, he urges Americans to resist partisan tribalism, deemphasize politics, and spend more time with their families. That's fine, except the inverse of your problem is not its solution. It's just another way of phrasing the same problem.

Books, like politicians, can impress on their own merits, or they can just sound good compared to the competition. No doubt, Sasse is more intellectually stimulating than the election-denying conspiracists who have overrun his Republican Party. But shouldn't the bar remain higher than that?

Them is that familiar type of book, one that serves only to affirm the author's rep as a Washington intellectual or—what journalists call people with *Master of the Senate* in their Skype backgrounds—a "student of history." Sasse, who wrote his doctoral dissertation on Cold War debates over religion in American public life, requires no such validation. But he is committed to the bit.

Them followed the senator's 2017 volume, *The Vanishing American Adult*, which extols the value of hard work, self-reliance, and adversity for young people—listen up here, Gators—lest their passivity torpedo the nation's freedoms and entrepreneurialism. The links between greater individualism (book one) and greater community (book two) as the cures to America's ills seem intriguing enough to explore, but the author takes a pass. Maybe he'll write another book on campus.

In hindsight, *Them* hinted at Sasse's discontent with the world's greatest nondeliberative body. "It was not Washington, D.C., that gave America its vitality," he writes, one of many times he dings the capital and his role in it. "Deep, enduring change does not come through legislation or elections," Sasse writes, but from "the tight bonds that give our lives meaning, happiness, and hope."

In a Q and A at the University of Florida on Monday, Sasse said that he looks forward to "the opportunity to step back from politics." That opportunity seems unlikely to materialize. Ron DeSantis, the governor of Florida, whose office issued a statement calling Sasse a "deep thinker" and a "good candidate" for university president, has made a culture war out of the state's education system at multiple levels, and Sasse must now take sides in those battles.

Former president Trump reacted in his usual measured tones, predicting that the university would "soon regret" hiring "Liddle" Ben Sasse, calling him a "lightweight" and a "weak and ineffective RINO." And the students who protested during Sasse's visit denounced the opacity of the university's selection process and the senator's past positions on same-sex marriage. (Sasse has stated that though he disagrees with the protesters, he "intellectually and constitutionally" welcomes them.)

Based on a Twitter statement from the senator, *Them*-style ideas may be on their way to Gainesville. "The University of Florida is uniquely positioned to lead this country through an era of disruption," Sasse wrote. (Disruption: check.) "Technology is changing everything about where, when, why, what and how Americans work." (Tech: check.) "Washington partisanship isn't going to solve these work force challenges." (Washington bad: check.) And

Sasse is "delighted to be in conversation with the leadership of this special community about how we might together build a vision."

If having conversations about maybe building visions is the job on offer here, Sasse is the right guy for it, and *Them* the right blueprint.

And I could have reviewed the book after all.

October 2022

THE SPEECHWRITER

YOU DON'T NEED TO BE a speechwriter to know that the phrase "I won't begin in any particular spot" is a poor way to start a public address. Yet those were the opening words of one of the more remarkable political spectacles in recent years: Mark Sanford's rambling and teary news conference of June 24, 2009, in which South Carolina's then-governor confessed that rather than hiking the Appalachian Trail, he'd been hooking up with his Argentine mistress.

In the crowd that afternoon at the statehouse rotunda in Columbia, South Carolina, was the man responsible for crafting Sanford's speeches. People still ask Barton Swaim, "Did you write that speech?" He can't even answer. "I just chuckle miserably," he explains.

No, Swaim didn't write that speech, but now he has authored something just as revealing and unusual: a political memoir that traffics in neither score-settling nor self-importance but that shares, in spare, delightful prose, what the author saw and learned. *The Speechwriter* feels like *Veep* meets *All the King's Men*—an entertaining and engrossing book not just about the absurdities of working in the press shop of a southern governor but also about the meaning of words in public life.

"For a long time the job of the speechwriter had sounded romantic to me," writes Swaim, who came to the position from the academic world. "The speechwriter, I felt, was a person whose job it was to put words in the mouths of the powerful, who understood the import and varieties of political language and guided his master through its perils. . . . A speechwriter has all the gratification of being a writer but has political power too."

Swaim would soon be unburdened of those misapprehensions. He quickly learned that his job was not to compose soaring rhetoric but to cobble together the kind of speeches the governor would write for himself if he had the time. And this governor couldn't write. At all.

When Swaim waded through his new boss's old op-eds, looking for the "voice" and "cadence" Sanford wanted him to capture, he couldn't find it. "What I heard was more like a cough," he writes. "Or the humming of a bad melody, with most of the notes sharp. One sentence stands out in my memory: 'This is important not only because I think it ought to be a first order of business, but because it makes common sense.'"

He learned the boss's tics. Sanford liked to have three points in a speech, never two. Never. "I'm not getting out there to talk about two stupid points," the governor said when presented with a pair of rebuttals to a bill. "I need three points, first, second, third. Got that?" He loved referring to an amorphous "larger notion" in his remarks. Larger than what? It didn't matter. "When we drafted a release or a press statement and weren't sure if he would approve it, someone would say, 'Stick a "larger notion" in there and it should be fine.'" The governor would often deploy an "indeed" when trying to rescue a trite phrase, as in "we're indeed mortgaging our children's future." Also, Sanford always looked for chances to mention Rosa Parks in a speech. He just really wanted to do that.

At the urging of his wife, Swaim gave in and started writing poorly. He assembled a list of Sanford-friendly lines (such as "given the fact that," "speaks volumes," "very considerable," "the way you live your life"). They were awkward and lazy, but the boss liked them.

The term "speechwriter" is misleading. Swaim spent much time crafting news releases, composing thank-you missives, and drafting scathing statements and op-eds about whatever the legislature was pushing. "We did a lot of scathing," he recalls. He also wrote "surrogate letters," that is, letters to the editor ostensibly from supporters but actually written by the governor's staff. "There was something slightly but definitely dishonest" about them, Swaim admits, but they were also an art form: start off with some generic sass ("Which constitution is Senator So-and-so reading?"), and then make an argument that doesn't reflect too much insight, or otherwise editors would see through the ruse.

Swaim consoled himself that such tricks served a good cause, but he has enough self-awareness to know that his incentives were off. "One of the melancholy facts of political life is that your convictions tend to align with your paycheck," he writes.

The nature of politics is to subtract meaning from language, Swaim understands, but he develops a relatively benign philosophy about political speech: "Using vague, slippery, or just meaningless language is not the same as lying: it's not intended to deceive so much as to preserve options, buy time, distance oneself from others, or just to sound like you're saying something instead of nothing." And politicians resort to such devices not out of deviousness but because every day they must weigh in "on things of which they have little or no reliable knowledge or about which they just don't care."

Take that, George Orwell.

The Speechwriter should become a classic on political communication, because it goes beyond the contortions of public statements to explore how politicians speak to their staffers when no cameras are around. In this case, the governor demeaned and humiliated them at every turn, usually as a way of coping with anxiety or working through ideas. "Being belittled was part of the job," explains Swaim, who often drove to work nervous to the point of vomiting, bracing for whatever mood might grip the boss. When the governor noticed that a whiteboard hadn't been updated with his latest goals, he collapsed "into a fit of angry inarticulacy." And in a petty breach of office etiquette, Sanford sliced off a piece of a subordinate's birthday cake and took it into his office, before they'd even celebrated. Later, Swaim recalls, staffers sang "Happy Birthday" to their colleague while gathered around a cake with a corner missing.

It wasn't malice. It was indifference. "The governor wasn't trying to hurt you," Swaim concluded. "For him to try to hurt you would have required him to acknowledge your significance." His attitude fostered perverse camaraderie among staffers, but also undercut any loyalty. He was the same with state lawmakers. The governor barely remembered their names, and that enraged them. He didn't care.

And just as Sanford became a national figure in the stimulus battle against the Obama administration, just "when veep speculation was at its not very considerable height," came the fall. The governor's conversations with the staff shortly after his infidelity speech were exquisite in their inanity. "I just wanted to say the obvious, which is the obvious," the boss began. "I mean, the obvious—which is that I caused the storm we're in now." He also mentioned reading *Man's Search for Meaning*, the Holocaust memoir by Viktor Frankl. "You can find beauty, you can find reasons to keep going, in the most appalling circumstances," Sanford lectured. "We're not in a concentration camp. So let's not stay in the dumps."

Swaim was tasked with rewriting the governor's form letters to scrub terms such as "integrity" or "honesty" that would remind recipients of the scandal. The boss also told him to "come up with a few examples from the Bible—or from history, or from whatever—that kind of show, you know, how when you've made a mess, you can do the best you can to clean it up, you make it right the best you can, and you keep going."

Sanford did keep going. Despite impeachment calls, he served out his second term and now represents South Carolina's First Congressional District after winning a 2013 special election. Swaim left the governor's office in 2010, but not before delivering one last time for his boss.

The governor was about to address an electric-bus company, and he'd rejected every idea for the speech. Suddenly, Swaim found the answer: it was Rosa Parks's birthday. "Rosa Parks thought about buses in a new way," he explained to the governor. "What she did on a bus changed the world. What [the company] is doing with an old idea—the bus idea—has the potential to change the world. Both take courage. The one changed society for the better and made us a better nation. The other is improving our quality of life . . . Something like that."

The boss approved. "It was absolutely ridiculous," the speechwriter writes. "But it was perfect."

July 2015

VI. IMAGINING

WHY REACTIONARY NOSTALGIA BEATS LIBERAL HOPE

On the ninth of September 2001, Mark Lilla published *The Reckless Mind*, an inquiry into why notable twentieth-century European philosophers and intellectuals—Martin Heidegger, Carl Schmitt, Walter Benjamin, and Michel Foucault, among others—had at times succumbed to what he calls "philotyranny," a narcissistic embrace of totalitarian politics, assuming that tyrants would put their big ideas into action. It was very much a book of the interwar, postwar, and Cold War era. Its heroes were thinkers, its raw material was found in books, lectures, and correspondence, and the sirens luring its subjects were Nazism, Marxism, and the Iranian revolution.

Two days later, the twentieth century came to a close. Hitler, Stalin, and other ghosts gave way to Osama bin Laden and, eventually, the Islamic State. World wars and cold ones yielded to drone wars and GWOTs. Reckless minds grew even more so.

Now, Lilla, a professor of humanities at Columbia University, has produced a new work that is inseparable from the first—*The Shipwrecked Mind* can be read as a detour through the tributaries of the first volume— yet by focusing on the rise of reactionary thinkers and movements, it feels timelier than its predecessor. Lilla's publisher, New York Review Books, has reissued *The Reckless Mind* as well, with a new afterword as grafting tissue between the two books and the two moments.

"We have theories about why revolution happens, what makes it succeed, and why, eventually, it consumes its young," Lilla writes. "We have no such theories about reaction, just the self-satisfied conviction that it is rooted in ignorance and intransigence, if not darker motives." With *The Shipwrecked Mind*, Lilla is rescuing reaction, or at least arguing that "one simply cannot

understand modern history without understanding how the reactionary's political nostalgia helped to shape it."

The term first acquired its negative moral connotations in postrevolution-
ary France, Lilla explains. "The river of time flows in one direction only. ...
During the Jacobin period anyone who resisted the river's flow or displayed
insufficient enthusiasm about reaching the destination was labeled a 'reactionary,'" he writes.

Today's reactionaries, Lilla contends, are found among the American
right, longing for the strength and uniformity of the early postwar years;
European nationalists, blaming Enlightenment values for the continent's ills;
and political Islamists, animated by visions of a caliphate restored. Their nostalgia is more powerful than liberal hope. "Hopes can be disappointed," Lilla
writes. "Nostalgia is irrefutable."

The battles between reason and religion—between "Athens and Jeru-
salem," Lilla writes—propel many of Lilla's thinkers. Franz Rosenzweig, a
German philosopher of the early twentieth century, sought to renew his Jewish faith in the face of a Europe where bourgeois culture and the scientific
outlook were "extinguishing something essential," Lilla writes, something
previously captured in religious belief. "The battle against history in the
nineteenth-century sense," Rosenzweig wrote in his diaries, "becomes for us
the battle for religion in the twentieth-century sense."

Lilla dwells on Eric Voegelin, another German philosopher, who in
dense, ambitious, and often unfinished works of political theory concluded
that the Enlightenment, by banishing God, had pushed people "to the creation of grotesque secular deities like Hitler, Stalin, and Mussolini"; and on
Leo Strauss, who from his perch at the University of Chicago during the
1950s and 1960s argued that "modern liberalism has declined into relativism
... indistinguishable from the kind of nihilism that gave rise to the political
disasters of the twentieth century." It was a philosophy that, after Strauss's
death, would inspire disciples—not in ivory towers but in Washington think
tanks and bureaucracies—to believe in a "redemptive historical mission" for
America to promote liberal democracy in an increasingly illiberal world, an
argument, Lilla notes, that was "nowhere articulated by Strauss himself."

In the reactionary mind, the arc of history is long, and it bends toward ever greater horrors.

Though *The Reckless Mind* remains the more compelling work in its writing and scope and in the fullness of its characters, *The Shipwrecked Mind* showcases Lilla's gift for sketching out such long histories—and historical mythologies—with a few artful brushstrokes, covering centuries of thought and politics in a few pages. (His chapter titled "From Luther to Walmart," channeling academics such as Alasdair MacIntyre and Brad Gregory to describe the post-Reformation descent into today's rapacious capitalism, is a minor classic all on its own.) So the book's concluding chapter is jarring in a good way; after one-hundred-plus pages plumbing essays and letters, Lilla places us in France on January 7, 2015—another 9/11, of a sort.

Lilla was living in Paris on the morning of the *Charlie Hebdo* massacre, and he reflects on the longing for a lost golden age that grips the minds of Islamist extremists. "Once the butchery ends, as it eventually must, through exhaustion or defeat, the pathos of political Islam will deserve as much reflection as its monstrosity," he writes. "One almost blushes to think of the historical ignorance, the misplaced piety, the impotent adolescent posturing, the blindness to reality, and fear of it, that lay behind the murderous fever."

Yet Lilla seems even more interested in the reaction—in every sense—of contemporary French intellectuals who seized upon that day. He explores the works of journalist Éric Zemmour, who writes of France's cultural and political suicide, and of Michel Houellebecq, who writes of its submission. They speak to the shipwrecked, those who see the chasm between past and present and become "obsessed with taking revenge on whatever demiurge caused it to open up," Lilla writes. "Their nostalgia is revolutionary. Since the continuity of time has already been broken, they begin to dream of making a second break and escaping from the present." For them, that present is multiculturalism, it is demographic decline, it is freedom gone too far.

"We are so accustomed to the old opposition of reason versus passion, spirit versus life," Hannah Arendt wrote, "that the idea of a passionate thinking, in which thinking and aliveness become one, takes us somewhat aback." Both *The Reckless Mind* and *The Shipwrecked Mind* wade deep into passionate thought, sometimes with admiration, usually with judgment. Lilla distinguishes real thinkers from pretenders; the latter are often political leaders "passionate about the life of the mind, but unlike the philosopher [they] cannot master that passion." Such leaders are "sunburned" by ideas, imagining themselves independent thinkers, when in fact they are "a herd driven by their inner demons and thirsty for the approval of a fickle public."

Plato once traveled to Syracuse in Sicily, hoping to tutor Dionysius, the ruler whose intellectual pretensions barely masked his tyrannical ones. He failed. "Dionysius is our contemporary," Lilla writes in *The Reckless Mind.* "Over the last century he has assumed many names: Lenin and Stalin, Hitler and Mussolini, Mao and Ho, Castro and Trujillo, Amin and Bokassa, Saddam and Khomeini, Ceaușescu and Milosevic—one's pen runs dry." And each had intellectual enablers, lured to Syracuse.

Lilla suggests that the years between the fall of the Berlin Wall and the destruction of the World Trade Center were a time of "introspection and self-satisfaction," when intellectuals began to ask themselves big questions, such as whether history had reached its end. But after September 11, "our thinking became small again," and now "a cloud of willful unknowing seems to have settled on our intellectual life."

In that environment, nostalgia reasserts itself. On this side of the Atlantic, we see it in slogans yearning for lost American greatness—with a wink to those conflating such greatness with a throwback cultural conformity—and politicians promising a new era of robust growth. "The lure of tyranny is not the only force that pulls intellectuals off course," Lilla concludes. "Self-deception has countless forms." Nostalgia is one of them, and it offers its own kind of tyranny.

September 2016

SAMUEL HUNTINGTON,
A PROPHET FOR THE TRUMP ERA

SOMETIMES A PROPHET CAN BE right about what will come, yet torn about whether it should.

President Trump's recent speech in Warsaw, in which he urged Europeans and Americans to defend Western civilization against violent extremists and barbarian hordes, inevitably evoked Samuel P. Huntington's "clash of civilizations"—the notion that superpower rivalry would give way to battles among Western universalism, Islamic militance, and Chinese assertiveness. In a book expanded from his famous 1993 essay, Huntington described civilizations as the broadest and most crucial level of identity, encompassing religion, values, culture, and history. Rather than "which side are you on?" he wrote, the overriding question in the post–Cold War world would be "who are you?"

So when the president calls on the nations of the West to "summon the courage and the will to defend our civilization," when he insists that we accept only migrants who "share our values and love our people," and when he urges the transatlantic alliance to "never forget who we are" and cling to the "bonds of history, culture and memory," I imagine Huntington, who passed away in late 2008 after a long career teaching at Harvard University, nodding from beyond.

It would be a nod of vindication, perhaps, but mainly one of grim recognition. Trump's civilizational rhetoric is just one reason Huntington resonates today, and it's not even the most interesting one. Huntington's work, spanning the mid-twentieth century through the early twenty-first, reads as a long argument about America's meaning and purpose, one that explains the tensions of the Trump era as well as anything can. Huntington both chronicles and anticipates America's fights over its founding premises, fights that Trump's ascent has aggravated. Huntington foresees the rise of white nativism in response to Hispanic immigration. He captures the dissonance between working classes and elites, between nationalism and cosmopolitanism, that played out in the 2016 campaign. And he warns how populist demagogues appeal to alienated masses and then break faith with them.

This is Trump's presidency, but even more so, it is Huntington's America.

Huntington's books speak to one another across the decades; you find the origins of one in the unanswered questions of another. But they also reveal deep contradictions. As much as a clash of civilizations, a clash of Huntingtons is evident, too. One Huntington regards Americans as an exceptional people united by nothing but a creed. Another favors an America that finds its essence in faith, language, culture, and borders. One Huntington views new groups and identities entering the political arena as a revitalization of American democracy. Another considers such identities pernicious, anti-American.

These works embody the intellectual and political challenges for the United States in the Trump years and beyond them. In Huntington's writings, idealistic visions of the United States mingle with the country's baser impulses, and eloquent defenses of American values betray a fear of the pluralism at the nation's core. Which vision wins out will determine what country we become.

To understand our current turmoil, the most relevant of Huntington's books is not *The Clash of Civilizations and the Remaking of World Order* (1996) or *Who Are We? The Challenges to America's National Identity* (2004). It is the lesser-known and remarkably prescient *American Politics: The Promise of Disharmony*, published in 1981.

In that work, Huntington points to the gap between the values of the American creed—liberty, equality, individualism, democracy, constitutionalism—and the government's efforts to live up to those values as the central tension of American life. "At times, this dissonance is latent; at other times, when creedal passion runs high, it is brutally manifest, and at such times, the promise of American politics becomes its central agony."

Whether debating health care, taxes, immigration, or war, Americans invariably invoke the founding values to challenge perceived injustices. Reforms cannot merely be necessary or sensible; they must be articulated and defended in terms of the creed. This is why Trump's opponents attack his policies by declaring not only that they are wrong but that "that's not who we are." As Huntington puts it, "Americans divide most sharply over what brings them together."

The book looks back to the Revolutionary War, the Jacksonian age, the Progressive era, and the 1960s as moments of high creedal passions, and Huntington's descriptions capture America today. In such moments, he writes, discontent is widespread, and authority and expertise are questioned; traditional values of liberty, individualism, equality, and popular control of government dominate public debates; politics is characterized by high polarization and constant protest; hostility toward power, wealth, and inequality grows intense; social movements focused on causes such as women's rights and criminal justice flourish; and new forms of media emerge devoted to advocacy and adversarial journalism.

Huntington even predicts the timing of America's next fight: "If the periodicity of the past prevails," he writes, "a major sustained creedal passion period will occur in the second and third decades of the twenty-first century."

We're right on schedule.

There is a cyclical nature to our passions, Huntington argues. Indignation cannot endure long, so cynicism supplants it, a belief that all are corrupt, and we learn to tolerate the gap between ideals and reality. (Today we might call this the "lol nothing matters" stage.) Eventually hypocrisy takes over and we deny the gap altogether—until the next wave of moralizing. In the Trump era, moralism, cynicism, and hypocrisy coexist. Not peacefully.

The creed is relevant not just because it produces America's divisions and aspirations but because it provides a spare, elegant definition of what it means to be American. It is not about ethnic identity or religious faith, Huntington writes, but about political belief. "We hold these truths to be self-evident," begins the second paragraph of the Declaration of Independence, and Huntington uses the line to define us. "Who holds these truths? Americans hold these truths. Who are Americans? People who adhere to these truths. National identity and political principle were inseparable."

In this telling, the American dream matters most because it is never fulfilled, the reconciliation of liberty and inequality never complete. Even so, *American Politics* is not an entirely pessimistic book. "Critics say that America is a lie because its reality falls so short of its ideals," Huntington writes in its final lines. "They are wrong. America is not a lie; it is a disappointment. But it can be a disappointment only because it is also a hope."

Over the subsequent two decades, Huntington lost hope. In his final book, *Who Are We?*—which, he emphasizes, reflects his views not just as a scholar but also as a patriot—he revises his definitions of America and Americans. Whereas once the creed was paramount, here it is merely a by-product of Anglo-Protestant culture—with its English language, Christian faith, work ethic, and values of individualism and dissent—that he now says forms the true core of American identity.

Threatening that core, Huntington writes, is the ideology of multiculturalism; the new waves of immigrants from Latin America, especially Mexico, who Huntington believes are less able to assimilate than past immigrants; and the spread of the Spanish language, which undercuts the cultural and political integrity of the United States. "There is no Americano dream," he asserts. "There is only the American dream created by an Anglo-Protestant society. Mexican-Americans will share in that dream and in that society only if they dream in English."

The Huntington of 1981, apparently, was just wrong. When listing academics who had—inaccurately, he contends in *Who Are We?*—defined Americans by their political beliefs, Huntington quotes an unnamed scholar who once eloquently described Americans as inseparable from those self-evident truths of the Declaration. Unless you recognize the passage from *American Politics* or bother to check the endnotes, you have no idea he is quoting himself. It's as close to a wink as you'll find in Huntington's angriest book.

The principles of the creed are merely "markers of how to organize a society," Huntington decides. "They do not define the extent, boundaries, or composition of that society." For that, he contends, you need kin and culture; you must belong. He claims that Latin American immigrants and their offspring do not disperse throughout the country as thoroughly as past immigrants, worries they seek only welfare benefits, and warns they'll leave behind fewer opportunities for native workers. Huntington also traffics in stereotypes, even citing Mexico's supposed "mañana syndrome."

I don't know why Huntington changed his mind. Perhaps he felt the abstractions of the creed could no longer withstand the din of America's multiplicity, or maybe mixing scholarship and patriotism does a disservice to both. Either way, anyone arguing for border walls and deportation forces will find much to like in this new incarnation, because Huntington describes the Hispanic threat with militaristic imagery. "Mexican immigration is leading toward the demographic reconquista of areas Americans took from Mexico by force in the 1830s and 1840s," he writes, stating that the United States is experiencing an "illegal demographic invasion."

Huntington blames pliant politicians and intellectual elites who uphold diversity as the premier American value, largely because of their misguided guilt toward victims of alleged oppression. So they encourage multiculturalism over a more traditional American identity, he says, and they embrace free trade and porous borders despite the public's protectionist preferences. It is an uncanny preview of the battles of 2016. Denouncing multiculturalism as "anti-European civilization," Huntington calls for a renewed nationalism devoted to preserving and enhancing "those qualities that have defined America since its founding."

Little wonder that, long before Trump cultivated the alt-right and Hillary Clinton denounced "deplorables" in our midst, Huntington foresaw a backlash against multiculturalism from white Americans. "One very plausible reaction would be the emergence of exclusivist sociopolitical movements," he writes, "composed largely but not only of white males, primarily working-class and middle-class, protesting and attempting to stop or reverse these changes and what they believe, accurately or not, to be the diminution of their social and economic status, their loss of jobs to immigrants and foreign countries, the perversion of their culture, the displacement of their language,

CARLOS LOZADA

and the erosion or even evaporation of the historical identity of their country. Such movements would be both racially and culturally inspired and could be anti-Hispanic, anti-black, and anti-immigration." The more extreme elements in such movements, Huntington notes, fear "the replacement of the white culture that made America great by black or brown cultures that are ... in their view, intellectually and morally inferior."

Yes, in 2004, Huntington warned of a racist tide focused on protecting that which makes America great.

Having redefined the substance of American identity, Huntington ties its continued salience to war. "The Revolution produced the American people, the Civil War the American nation, and World War II the epiphany of Americans' identification with their country," he writes in *Who Are We?* Born in principle, American identity now survives by steel. When the Soviet threat receded, the United States needed a new foe, and "on September 11, 2001," Huntington declares, "Osama bin Laden ended America's search."

This is a conflict he had long anticipated. In his 1996 book proclaiming a clash of civilizations, he writes that the West will continue its slow decline relative to Asia and the Islamic world. While economic dynamism drives Asia's rise, population growth in Muslim nations "provides recruits for fundamentalism, terrorism, insurgency, and migration." Much as Trump mocks politicians who refuse to decry "radical Islamic terrorism," Huntington criticizes American leaders such as Bill Clinton who argued that the West had no quarrel with Islam, only with violent extremists. "Fourteen hundred years of history demonstrate otherwise," he remarks.

Huntington's clash has been caricatured as a single-minded call to arms against Muslims, and certainly his argument is neither so narrow nor so simple. He is probably more concerned with China and fears a "major war" if Washington challenges Beijing's rise as Asia's hegemon. Yet the threat Huntington sees from the Muslim world goes far beyond terrorism or religious extremism. He worries about a broader Islamic resurgence, with political Islam as only one part of "the much more extensive revival of Islamic ideas, practices, and rhetoric and the rededication to Islam by Muslim populations." Huntington cites scholars warning of the spread of Islamic legal concepts in the West, decries the "inhospitable nature of Islamic culture" for democracy, and suggests that Islam will prevail in the numbers game against Christianity. In the long run, "Mohammed wins out," he states. "Christianity spreads primarily by conversion, Islam by conversion and reproduction."

The vision evokes the zero-sum rhetoric of Trump political strategist Stephen K. Bannon, who was a force behind the administration's travel ban targeting Muslim-majority countries, and of former national security adviser Michael Flynn, who authored a 2016 book heralding a multigenerational US conflict against Islam's "failed civilization." Huntington, at least, has the grace to consider two sides of the clash.

"The underlying problem for the West is not Islamic fundamentalism," he writes. "It is Islam, a different civilization whose people are convinced of the superiority of their culture and are obsessed with the inferiority of their power. The problem for Islam is not the CIA or the US Department of Defense. It is the West, a different civilization whose people are convinced of the universality of their culture and believe that their superior, if declining, power imposes on them the obligation to extend that culture throughout the world."

He does not regard Western values as universal. They are ours alone.

While Huntington foresees an America roiled by self-doubt, white nationalism, and enmity against Islam, he does not predict the rise of a Trump-like leader in the United States. But he would have recognized the type.

Consider his earliest books. In *Political Order in Changing Societies* (1968), Huntington examines how Latin American, African, and Asian countries in the throes of economic modernization struggled to adapt their politics and incorporate new groups with new demands. The result, Huntington explains, was not political development but "political decay."

And what sort of authorities personify this decay? Across the developing world, Huntington saw "the dominance of unstable personalistic leaders," their governments rife with "blatant corruption ... arbitrary infringement of the rights and liberties of citizens, declining standards of bureaucratic efficiency and performance, the pervasive alienation of urban political groups, the loss of authority by legislatures and courts, and the fragmentation and at times complete disintegration of broadly based political parties."

These self-styled revolutionaries thrive on divisiveness. "The aim of the revolutionary is to polarize politics," Huntington explains, "and hence he attempts to simplify, to dramatize, and to amalgamate political issues into a single, clear-cut dichotomy." Such leaders attract new rural voters via "ethnic and religious appeals" as well as economic arguments, only to quickly betray their aspirations.

"A popular demagogue may emerge," Huntington writes, "develop a widespread but poorly organized following, threaten the established interests of the rich and aristocrats, be voted into political office, and then be bought off by the very interests which he has attacked." Such interests include those of the leaders' close relatives, he explains, because for them "no distinction existed between obligations to the state and obligation to the family."

Huntington's *The Soldier and the State* (1957), a study of civilian-military relations, is instructive on the self-regard of such leaders, especially when the author contrasts the professionalism of military officers with the imperiousness of fascist strongmen. "Fascism emphasizes the supreme power and ability of the leader, and the absolute duty of subordination to his will," Huntington writes. The fascist is intuitive, with "little use or need for ordered knowledge and practical, empirical realism. He celebrates the triumph of the Will over external obstacles."

Such obstacles take the form of popular protests against unpopular leaders. Today, some writers even find solace in our national upheaval, arguing that the activism and energy Trump's election has wrought will strengthen US democracy. But in a book titled *The Crisis of Democracy* (1975), Huntington examines a time of similar civic resurgence, and is not encouraged by the outcome.

"The 1960s witnessed a dramatic renewal of the democratic spirit in America," Huntington writes. Not yet dismissive of identity politics, he praises the "markedly higher levels of self-consciousness" and mobilization on the part of African Americans, Latinos, students, and women in that era, noting that "the spirit of equality [and] the impulse to expose and correct inequities were abroad in the land." The problem, he explains, is that the political system also became weighed down by popular mistrust, however deserved, of American institutions. "The vitality of democracy in the 1960s," he writes, "raised questions about the governability of democracy in the 1970s."

The biggest questions involved the highest office. "Probably no development of the 1960s and 1970s has greater import for the future of American politics than the decline in the authority, status, influence, and effectiveness of the presidency," Huntington writes. He fears that a delegitimized executive threatened not just national cohesion but national security. "If American citizens don't trust their government, why should friendly foreigners? If American citizens challenge the authority of American government, why shouldn't unfriendly governments?"

Huntington was writing in the aftermath of the Watergate scandal, and now the current White House faces its own crisis of credibility. Trump, so obsessed with his electoral victory that a framed map of the 2016 results has been spotted in the White House, would do well to heed warnings about governability.

"Once he is elected president," Huntington writes, "the president's electoral coalition has, in a sense, served its purpose. The day after his election the size of his majority is almost—if not entirely—irrelevant to his ability to govern the country. ... What counts then is his ability to mobilize support from the leaders of the key institutions in society and government."

It feels odd to write of Trump as a Huntingtonian figure. One is instinctual and anti-intellectual; the other was deliberate and theoretical. One communicates via inarticulate bursts; the other wrote books for the ages. I imagine Huntington would be apprehensive about a commander in chief so indifferent to a foreign power's assault on the US electoral system, and one displaying so little of the work ethic and reverence for the rule of law that Huntington admired.

What makes the professor a prophet for our time is not just that his vision is partially reflected in Trump's message and appeal but that he understood well the dangers of the style of politics Trump practices.

Where they come together, I believe, is in their nostalgic and narrow view of American uniqueness. Huntington, like Trump, wanted America to be great, and came to long for a restoration of values and identity that he believed made the country not just great but a nation apart. However, if that path involves closing ourselves off, demonizing newcomers, and demanding cultural fealty, then how different are we, really, from anywhere else? How exceptional?

That's not a clash of civilizations. It's a civilization crashing.

July 2017

AMERICA NEEDS A FEW
GOOD MYTHS

IN THE REALM OF FOLKLORE and ancient traditions, myths are tales forever retold for their wisdom and underlying truths. Their impossibility is part of their appeal; few would pause to debunk the physics of Icarus's wings before warning against flying too close to the sun.

In the worlds of journalism and history, however, myths are viewed as pernicious creatures that obscure more than they illuminate. They must be hunted and destroyed so that the real story can assume its proper perch. Puncturing these myths is a matter of duty and an assertion of expertise. "Actually" abounds.

I can claim some experience in this effort, not as a debunker of myths but as a clearinghouse for them. When I served as the editor of the *Washington Post*'s Sunday Outlook section several years ago, I assigned and edited dozens of "5 Myths" articles in which experts tackled the most common fallacies surrounding subjects in the news. This regular exercise forced me to wrestle with the form's basic challenges: How entrenched and widespread must a misconception be to count as an honest-to-badness myth? What is the difference between a conclusive debunking and a conflicting interpretation? And who is qualified to upend a myth or disqualified from doing so?

These questions came up frequently as I read *Myth America: Historians Take On the Biggest Legends and Lies About Our Past*, a new collection edited by Kevin M. Kruse and Julian E. Zelizer, historians at Princeton. The book, which the editors describe as an "intervention" in long-running public discussions on American politics, economics, and culture, is an authoritative and fitting contribution to the myth-busting genre—authoritative for the quality of the contributions and the scope of its enterprise, fitting because it captures in one volume the possibilities and pitfalls of the form. When you face down so many myths in quick succession, the values that underpin the effort grow sharper, even if the value of myths themselves grows murkier. All of our national delusions should be exposed, but I'm not sure all should be excised. Do not some myths serve a valid purpose?

Several contributors to *Myth America* successfully eviscerate tired assumptions about their subjects. Carol Anderson of Emory University discredits the persistent notion of extensive voter fraud in US elections, showing how the politicians and activists who claim to defend election integrity are often seeking to exclude some voters from the democratic process. Daniel Immerwahr of Northwestern University puts the lie to the idea that the United States historically has lacked imperial ambitions; with its territories and tribal nations and foreign bases, he contends, the country is very much an empire today and has been so from the start. And after reading Lawrence B. Glickman's essay "White Backlash," I will be wary of writing that a civil rights protest or movement sparked or fomented or provoked a white backlash, as if such a response is instinctive and unavoidable. "Backlashers are rarely treated as agents of history, the people who participate in them seen as bit players rather than catalysts of the story, reactors rather than actors," Glickman, a historian at Cornell, writes. Sometimes the best myth-busting is the kind that makes you want to rewrite old sentences.

The collection raises worthy arguments about the use of history in the nation's political discourse, foremost among them that the term "revisionist history" should not be a slur. "All good historical work is at heart 'revisionist' in that it uses new findings from the archives or new perspectives from historians to improve, to perfect—and yes, to revise—our understanding of the past," Kruse and Zelizer write. Yet this revisionist imperative at times makes the myths framework feel forced, an excuse to cover topics of interest to the authors.

Sarah Churchwell's enlightening chapter on the evolution of "America First" as a slogan and worldview, for instance, builds on her 2018 book on the subject. But to address the topic as a myth, Churchwell, a historian at the University of London, asserts that Donald Trump's invocation of "America First" in the 2016 presidential race was "widely defended as a reasonable foreign policy doctrine." (Her evidence is a pair of pieces by the conservative commentators Michael Barone and Michael Anton.)

In his essay defending the accomplishments of the New Deal, Eric Rauchway of the University of California, Davis, admits that the policy program's alleged failure "is not a tale tightly woven into the national story" and that "perhaps 'myth' seems an inappropriate term." He does believe the New Deal's failure is a myth worth exploding, of course, but acknowledges that there are "many analytical categories of falsehood." The admission deserves some kudos, but it also might just be right.

In Kruse's chapter on the history of the southern strategy—the Republican Party's deliberate effort to bring white southerners to its side as the Democratic Party grew more active in support of civil rights—the author allows that "only recently have conservative partisans challenged this well-established history." This singling out of conservatives is not accidental. In their introduction, Kruse and Zelizer argue that the growth of right-wing media platforms and the Republican Party's declining "commitment to truth" have fostered a boom in mythmaking. "Efforts to reshape narratives about the U.S. past thus became a central theme of the conservative movement in general and the Trump administration in particular," they write.

The editors note the existence of some bipartisan myths that transcend party or ideology, but overwhelmingly, the myths covered in *Myth America* originate or live on the right. In an analysis that spans twenty chapters, more than three hundred pages, and centuries of American history and public discourse, this emphasis is striking. Do left-wing activists and politicians in the United States never construct and propagate their own self-affirming versions of the American story? If such liberal innocence is real, let's hear more about it. If not, it might require its own debunking.

One of those bipartisan myths, typically upheld by politicians of both major parties, is the ur-myth of the nation: American exceptionalism. In his essay on the subject, David A. Bell, another Princeton historian, can be dismissive of the term. "Most nations can be considered exceptional in one sense or another," he writes. Today, the phrase is typically deployed as a "cudgel" in the country's culture wars, Bell contends, a practice popularized by politicians like Newt Gingrich, who has long hailed the United States as "the most unique civilization in history" and assails anyone who does not bow before the concept. "For Gingrich, demonstrating America's exceptionality has always mattered less than denouncing the Left for not believing in it," Bell writes.

When exploring earlier arguments about America's unique nature, Bell touches on John Winthrop's seventeenth-century sermon "A Model of Christian Charity," in which the future governor of the Massachusetts Bay Colony declared that the Puritan community would be "as a city on a hill" (a line that President Ronald Reagan expanded centuries later to a "shining city upon a hill"). The reference is obligatory in any discussion of American exceptionalism, though Bell minimizes the relevance of the lay sermon to the exceptionalism debates, both because the text "breathed with agonized doubt" about whether the colonists could meet the challenge and because the sermon "remained virtually unknown until the nineteenth century."

It is an intriguing assumption, at least to this non-historian, that the initial obscurity of a speech (or a book or an argument or a work of any kind) would render it irrelevant, no matter how significant it became to later generations. It is the same attitude that Akhil Reed Amar, a law professor at Yale and the author of a chapter on myths surrounding the Constitution, takes toward Federalist No. 10. James Madison's essay "foreshadowed much of post-Civil War American history," Amar writes, in part for its argument that the federal government would protect minority rights more effectively than the states, "but in 1787–1788, almost no one paid attention to Madison's masterpiece." Unlike other Federalist essays that resonated widely during the debates over constitutional ratification, Amar writes, No. 10 "failed to make a deep impression in American coffeehouses and taverns where patrons read aloud and discussed both local and out-of-town newspapers."

Alas, Mr. Madison, your piece was not trending, so we're taking it off history's home page.

To his credit, Amar is consistent in privileging immediate popular reactions in his historical assessments. He criticizes the argument of Charles Beard's *An Economic Interpretation of the Constitution* (1913), that the Constitution was an antidemocratic document. "If the document was truly antidemocratic, why did the people vote for it?" Amar asks. "Why did tens of thousands of ordinary working men enthusiastically join massive pro-constitutional rallies in Philadelphia and Manhattan?" Even just in the aftermath of the 2020 election and the Capitol assault of January 6, however, it seems clear that people in a free society can be rallied to antidemocratic causes, with great enthusiasm, if they come to believe such causes are righteous.

Other contributors to *Myth America* are more willing to squint at the first impressions of the past. In a chapter minimizing the transformational impact of the Reagan presidency, Zelizer laments how "the trope that a 'Reagan Revolution' remade American politics has remained central to the national discourse," even though it "has been more of a political talking point than a description of reality." (Reminder: calling them talking points is an effective shorthand way to dismiss opposing views.) When Zelizer looks back on a collection of historians' essays published in 1989, just months after Reagan left office, and which argued that Reagan's 1980 victory was "the end of the New Deal era," he does not hesitate to pass judgment on his professional colleagues. "Even a group of historians was swept up by the moment," he writes.

Here, proximity to an earlier historical era renders observers susceptible to transient passions, not possessors of superior insights. If so, perhaps an essay collection of American myths that is published shortly after the Trump presidency also risks being swept up by its own moment. (Incidentally, that 1989 book, edited by the historians Steve Fraser and Gary Gerstle and titled *The Rise and Fall of the New Deal Order, 1930–1980*, shares one contributor with *Myth America*. Michael Kazin, take a bow.)

Zelizer writes that the notion of a revolutionary Reagan era did not emerge spontaneously but was "born out of an explicit political strategy" aimed at exaggerating both conservative strength and liberal weakness. This is another conclusion of *Myth America*—that many of our national mythologies are the product not of simple misunderstandings or organically divergent viewpoints that become entrenched over time but rather of deliberate efforts at mythmaking. The notions that free enterprise is inseparable from broader American freedoms, that voting fraud is ubiquitous, that the feminist movement is anti-family—in this telling, they are myths peddled or exaggerated, for nefarious purposes, by the right.

But in his essay on American exceptionalism, Bell adds in passing an idea somewhat subversive to the project of *Myth America*, and it separates this book from standard myth-quashing practices. After writing that narratives about America's exceptional character were long deployed to justify US aggression abroad and at home, Bell posits that notions of exceptionalism "also highlighted what Americans saw as their best qualities and moral duties, giving them a standard to live up to."

Bell does not suggest that the belief in American exceptionalism fulfills this latter role today; to the contrary, its politicization has rendered the term vacuous and meaningless. "The mere notion of being exceptional can do very little to inspire Americans actually to be exceptional," he writes. Still, Bell has opened a door here, even if just a crack. National myths can be more than conspiratorial, self-serving lies spread for low, partisan aims. They can also be aspirational.

American aspiration, idealism, and mythology have mingled together from the start. In her 2018 one-volume American history, *These Truths*, Jill Lepore wrote eloquently of those self-evident truths of the Declaration of Independence—political equality, natural rights, popular sovereignty—that the country never ceases to claim yet always struggles to uphold. It is the argument, often made by former president Barack Obama, that America becomes a more perfect union when it attempts to live up to its ideals and mythologies, even if it often fails. The tension between myth and reality does not undermine America. It defines it.

January 2023

WHEN AMERICA THOUGHT
FOR ITSELF

Louis Menand is a chronicler of the American mind, particularly in those moments when America is having second thoughts.

In *The Metaphysical Club* (2001), Menand told the story of the nation in the decades after the Civil War, as it groped for "a set of ideas, and a way of thinking, that would help people cope with the conditions of modern life." He identified those concepts in the works of Charles Pierce, William James, Oliver Wendell Holmes Jr., and John Dewey, who saw ideas as contingent and fallible, believed they develop in social contexts, and regarded them as adaptable tools more than immutable principles.

In the epilogue of that book, Menand hinted at his next stop. The pragmatists' thinking, he wrote, came to be seen as naive in post–World War II America, a shift he linked to "the difference between the intellectual climate after the Civil War and the intellectual climate of the Cold War." After all, the Cold War was a time of irreconcilable principles, a period, as Harry Truman put it in a 1947 speech declaring the standoff, when nations had to "choose between alternative ways of life." Hardly the time for a worldview stressing tolerance and fallibility.

Now, with *The Free World*, Menand charts the transformations of cultural and intellectual life, primarily in the United States and Europe, during those early Cold War years. He examines and interprets the lives and works of scholars, essayists, painters, poets, novelists, dancers, singers, filmmakers, and critics active in the mid-1940s through the mid-1960s. It is an engrossing and impossibly wide-ranging project—as idiosyncratic as it is systematic—written by an author confident that the things that interest him will interest his readers, too. And he's right.

The Cold War–era cultural world prized freedom, Menand argues, in the most elastic sense of the word. Writers warned of the lurking dangers of totalitarianism and oppression—George Orwell and Hannah Arendt get plenty of attention here—and artists came to value the forms of their art over its social content, and authenticity over political obligations. The most vital freedom of this world was the freedom to experiment, to cast off old commitments "that had previously seemed sacrosanct or indispensable." In an era of containment, the American mind was suddenly uncontainable.

The exercise of this freedom catapulted American creators to the center of mid-century artistic and intellectual life, even as the US government, a superpower still trying out its new abilities, followed up a successful war of liberation in World War II with a failed war of domination in Vietnam. In *The Free World*, America simultaneously builds up enormous cultural capital and squanders vast political capital. It's still not clear how such accounts have been settled.

One of the most memorable moments in *The Free World* is Menand's retelling of *Theater Piece No. 1*, a multimedia creation by composer John Cage, which featured dance, lectures, piano, film projections, and poetry readings, performed all at once at North Carolina's Black Mountain College in 1952. A true description of the event is difficult. There was no real stage—the audience sat in chairs facing one another while the performers occupied the aisles—so witness accounts differ dramatically. This effect was deliberate. The seating arrangement "de-centered the performance," Menand explains. "The experience of each member of the audience was a function of the direction in which they were looking and the actions to which they elected to pay attention." Cage was amused when an audience member arrived early, hoping for the best seat. "There was no best seat," Menand writes, just different ones from which to choose and absorb some portion of the endless variations. Merce Cunningham was among the dancers, while Robert Rauschenberg's *White Paintings* hung overhead, the canvases white, uninflected, changing only depending on the light, the environment, the context, and, above all, the spectator. The burdens and possibilities fell on the audience, as with so much of the art and thought Menand assesses.

The Free World feels like *Theater Piece No. 1* at times. There are so many different people to watch and works to consider—readers can skip from George Kennan to George Orwell, from the Beats to the Beatles, from Richard Wright to Betty Friedan—and so much is changing all at once that everything competes for attention. If it feels that way reading it, how must the era have felt living it?

This was a period when artists radically challenged the subject, style, and meaning of their work. It was when Jackson Pollock confronted the "essential attributes" of painting, posing, as Menand writes, the "persistent and unanswerable question of where the optimal viewing point might be." (Again, no best seat.) Pollock did not just answer the challenge of surrealism—"the problem of rendering in visual form things that are supposed to be unconscious and intangible"—but also transformed the act of painting into an integral part of the art. With the artist dancing and flinging and dripping in and around a canvas laid upon the ground, the art became inseparable from the manner of its creation. Or as Menand puts it in one of his many memorable précis, "The idea of a 'Pollock painting' includes Pollock painting."

Menand regards Andy Warhol and pop art as far more than a response to Pollock and abstract expressionism; the movement was an effort to question the nature of art itself, portraying it as one more commodity, or recognizing it as such. There is a market for soup cans, and a market for a painting of soup cans, too. "At that moment, art could be anything it wanted," Menand writes. "The illusion/reality barrier had been broken."

Pop's commercial and critical success owes not just to the art itself but also to what Menand calls the "art-world infrastructure"—the galleries and dealers and collectors and critics, not to mention the audience—that had built up around the American art scene by the early 1960s. In *The Free World*, this broader cultural marketplace is as integral to the story as any painter or musician.

In particular, artists are inextricable from the critics assessing them. Menand cannot consider Pollock without noting the work of Clement Greenberg, whose landmark *Partisan Review* essay "Avant-Garde and Kitsch" made clear that art had become about art-making itself. He cannot explain the Beatles without considering the influence of Jann Wenner, cofounder of *Rolling Stone*, which featured John Lennon on the magazine's first cover. And he cannot describe the resonance of films such as *Bonnie and Clyde* without exploring the role of critic Pauline Kael, whose seven-thousand-word defense of the movie in *The New Yorker* embodied her argument that even so-called serious movies should meet the popular standard of, well, providing entertainment. "The critics let us know which angels are worth wrestling with," Menand writes.

Those wrestling matches could become intramural. Menand, who is an English professor at Harvard University and a staff writer at *The New Yorker*, devotes great attention to mid-century debates in literary criticism. Lionel Trilling's 1950 essay collection, *The Liberal Imagination*, is a particular fascination of his (Menand wrote an admiring introduction to the 2008 edition), in part because Trilling was unapologetic about using literature to understand politics, a tendency that his colleagues in Columbia University's English Department abhorred as excessively sociological. Yet Menand also hails New Criticism, the movement that professionalized literary criticism as an academic discipline—"a field in which professors write only for other professors"— for focusing solely on, say, the poem on the page and not any personal or political context, let alone the intentions of the poet or the emotional responses of the reader. Menand mitigates such differences by contending that the two approaches share a "cerebral" character and arguing that the theory-laden practice of criticism is really "an effort to figure out why we create such things, what they mean, and why we care so much about them."

But such tensions reveal a deeper breach cutting through *The Free World*. The Cold War was a conflict over ideals as well as ideas, yet the art and thought of the era were as often apolitical as they were politically engaged. Was America's global ascent to the heights of high culture, its ability to scurry out from under Europe's jagged shadow, a function of the politics of American art—or art's distance from politics? "The War in Vietnam disrupted the artistic and critical avant-garde of its time," Menand writes. "Preoccupations changed from formal and aesthetic questions to political ones." If culture is what happens when you keep politics at a safe remove, if World War II and Vietnam form the bookends of your cultural moment, then the price of that art creeps ever higher.

Menand acknowledges in his prologue that this book is "a little like a novel with a hundred characters," and that's lowballing it. Each chapter introduces a whole new cast with numerous supporting roles, and the names to remember multiply. This proliferation flows from Menand's tendency to explore not only influential artists and writers of the era but also their influences, and their influences' influences.

What underground movie affected Susan Sontag's thinking when she wrote "Notes on Camp" and "Against Interpretation," her two most famous essays? Which nonfiction treatise was Orwell freaking out about as he crafted *Nineteen Eighty-Four* to the point that he parodied it in the novel? And what translated bestseller on women's "lived experience" prompted Betty Friedan to take seventy pages of notes and jot the words " 'Mystique of femininity'— why women believe it" next to the page number of a particularly memorable passage? (Jack Smith's *Flaming Creatures*, James Burnham's *The Managerial Revolution*, and Simone de Beauvoir's *The Second Sex*, respectively.) Art can begin with a blank canvas, but artists themselves are never blank slates. Menand's digressions hardly digress; they are essential to the story.

Menand shows how art is invariably interconnected, co-created, appropriated, reinterpreted. Parisians' reception of twentieth-century American literature, for instance, was as rapturous as it was funny: Hemingway wrote like that because that's just the way Americans are, French critics concluded, or maybe because American novelists like to imitate American movies. White American teenagers embraced R&B music because black teens made it cool to do so, and soon, Menand writes, "a style of music identified with Black musicians ... was taken up and eventually dominated by white performers and producers." And the varied ancestry of Elvis Presley's "Hound Dog" reveals it to be a quintessentially American mutt. "The song's chain of custody extended from the Jewish twenty-year-olds who wrote it for a fee, to the African American singer who had to be instructed how to sing it, to the white lounge act that spoofed it, to the hillbilly singer who performed it as a burlesque number," Menand recounts. "Presley's version of 'Hound Dog' isn't inauthentic, because nothing about the song was ever authentic."

For all the detail he offers and detours he cannot resist, Menand is also good at pithily summing up movements and people. "The Beats were men who wrote about their feelings," he writes, picking apart the vulnerability in Jack Kerouac's prose. Of James Baldwin: "He wanted to be respected for making it clear that he didn't need anyone's respect." Of Kennan's foreign policy views: "He thought that Americans needed to be realists because they could not trust themselves to be moralists." These are the seemingly throw-away lines that become possible only after deep reading and careful synthesis.

The Free World is lengthy—857 pages does require some commitment from both reader and writer—yet I was sad to reach the end. Even Menand's footnotes are delightful. It is a book that compels you to buy other ones (Sontag's *Against Interpretation and Other Essays* now sits on the shelf above my writing desk) and to scour the internet for old essays that seem entirely relevant once again ("Everybody's Protest Novel" by Baldwin tops that list).

Still, I wanted one more chapter. *The Metaphysical Club* features an epilogue that ties things together nicely. This book ends abruptly, with Kennan, the father of anticommunist containment, testifying before a Senate committee in 1966 and basically my-badding the Vietnam War: "I did not mean to convey ... the belief that we could necessarily stop communism at every point on the world's surface." (Good to know!) I wanted Menand to be more explicit, to tell me what it all meant. I wanted more interpretation, not less.

Then again, if the art and thought of the Cold War placed that burden on the viewer, Menand has earned the right to do the same. And in *The Free World*, every seat is a good one.

April 2021

HOW TO STRANGLE DEMOCRACY
WHILE PRETENDING TO
ENGAGE IN IT

It was during my senior year of college that I received a comment from a professor, scribbled at the bottom of one of my papers, that would transform how I think and write, how I read books, and how I try to read the world. So rare to possess written proof of an epiphany.

"Carlos—this is just great! Nice job. You have a fine Hirschmanian mind."

Hirschmanian? I don't recall, at age twenty, knowing much about the social scientist Albert O. Hirschman—at least I hope I didn't—but this nudge sent me deep into his writings on economic growth, political change, and ideological temptation. Three decades later and almost ten years after his death, I've yet to come up for air. Hirschman imbued me with skepticism of all-encompassing worldviews, which he dismissed as "shortcuts to the understanding of multifarious reality." He warned against experts peddling self-serving agendas but also displayed "a bias for hope," as one of his book titles has it, a caution against seductive fatalism at the prospect of political renewal. And particularly valuable for a time, like today, when polarization and demagoguery are overtaking American politics, Hirschman bequeathed us a slim and vital book identifying the slippery arguments that pretend to engage in democratic deliberation, even as they strangle it.

Published in 1991, Hirschman's *The Rhetoric of Reaction* may have once read like thoughtful musings on conservative responses to the French Revolution, the Great Society, and much in between. (A *New York Times* reviewer called it a "handbook for bemused liberals.") Today it is a siren blast for a US political system that has lost the ability to reconcile differences and the desire to try. Long before America was cleaved into red versus blue, deplorable versus woke, or MAGA versus everybody else, Hirschman argued that political factions were cementing into extreme, unyielding stances and that their arguments, with a nod toward Clausewitz, had become little more than "the continuation of civil war with other means."

Hirschman devoted the bulk of the book to the rhetoric of the right, a prescient choice. When conservatives decry calls for progressive reform, he wrote, they often deploy one of three theses: perversity, futility, and jeopardy. The first warns of unintended consequences: you may think a new social welfare program will mitigate economic inequality, for instance, but perversely, it will only entrench disparity. The second is even more pessimistic: your policy proposal cannot make a dent in the status quo, and your repeated futile efforts only make me question your motives. The third is most ominous: your agenda will have devastating effects on many other arenas that you may have not even considered and is therefore too dangerous or foolish to carry out.

Once you have Hirschman's categories in mind, they appear everywhere. The battles over the minimum wage have long featured the perversity argument—that setting an artificial floor for wages will backfire by reducing employment. (Hirschman recalled Milton Friedman's assertion that "minimum wage laws are about as clear a case as one can find of a measure the effects of which are precisely the opposite of those intended.") Debates over the availability of firearms in America include all three arguments: curtailing lawful access to guns would mean that only criminals will have them and will be freer to wield them (perversity); America is too awash in guns already for restrictions to make much difference (futility); gun control is a threat to the constitutional rights that are vital to the preservation of a free people (jeopardy).

That the three theses can be deployed in illogical combinations—your antipoverty program won't reach those most in need, and it will also destroy their incentive to work!—does little to lessen their appeal. They reflect what Sam Tanenhaus, a dedicated observer of conservatism, has called the right's "unity of certitude," the belief that a liberal agenda necessarily equals an assault on American values. With such an enemy, any mix of arguments will do.

But the German-born Hirschman—who in addition to being an academic economist was a US Army veteran, an antifascist resister, an adviser on the Marshall Plan, and a consultant to the Colombian government—was too intellectually honest, or simply had seen too much of the world, to stop with the right. The left displays its own unity of certitude, he suggested in the penultimate chapter of *The Rhetoric of Reaction*, and its habit of rationalization is "richer in maneuvers, largely of exaggeration and obfuscation, than it is ordinarily given credit for."

So, credit where it is due. The first progressive argument Hirschman pinpoints is the mutual support thesis: Rather than coming into conflict, new and old progressive reforms will produce a "happy, positive interaction." In this world, the law of unintended consequences delivers only happy surprises. Next is the imminent danger thesis, contending that a particular policy is urgently needed to fend off a looming disaster, whether real or just really scary. Finally, the right-side-of-history thesis, a sort of reverse futility argument, revels in the inevitability of righteous progress, so comforting to politicians, activists, and assorted true believers. "People enjoy and feel empowered by the confidence, however vague, that they 'have history on their side,'" Hirschman wrote.

This right-side-of-history argument is rarely about history at all. It is a preemptive assertion of one side's virtue and another's wickedness; it is not about interpreting the past but about scoring points in the present to shape the future. Hirschman likened this argument to "the earlier assurance, much sought after by all combatants, that God was on their side." The comparison is apt: God on your side will help you win, and history on your side will say you did.

The Rhetoric of Reaction emerged in part from lectures and essays Hirschman gave and wrote during the mid- to late 1980s. At the time, he saw the perversity thesis as the most common argument on the right and the imminent danger thesis as the most powerful on the left. Today, though, two others seem ubiquitous: the jeopardy thesis and the right-side-of-history argument. So much so, in fact, that they've broken free of the ideological silos Hirschman assigned to them. On virtually any debate, every side now proclaims dire jeopardy from their opponents while basking in history's certain vindication.

With disagreements involving historical commemoration, the position has a certain logic, as when, in June 2020, a bipartisan group of US senators urged Donald Trump to "stand on the right side of history" and support the renaming of army installations named after Confederate officers. But frequently history is enlisted to defend more ambiguous terrain. Would a federal abortion ban starting at twenty weeks of pregnancy place America on the "right side of history," as Sen. Lindsey Graham declared when reintroducing the proposal in 2021? If so, why has Graham, in a post-*Dobbs* world, called for a ban after fifteen weeks instead? (History must be losing patience.)

Jeopardy and history mix in the arguments over the fate of American democracy. Recall how, in his speech outside the White House on January 6, Trump warned of the greatest jeopardy a nation-state can face. "If you don't fight like hell, you're not going to have a country anymore," he said. He proffered the same line in a rally last month: if the Democrats prevail in the midterm elections, "you won't have a country left." The former president proposed to fight "left-wing sickos" by restoring patriotism to the nation's schools, thus ensuring that future generations would "honor our history." President Biden embraced the jeopardy thesis in a speech in Philadelphia last month, warning that "the MAGA Republicans represent an extremism that threatens the very foundations of our Republic." He expressed confidence that "together, we can choose a different path," because, as he explained, "I know our history." We all know, of course, where history stands.

These positions are not equivalent in their moral aspirations, in their reliance on truth, or in the risks they pose. They are nevertheless rhetorically similar, staking out immovable and irreconcilable positions. Believing that your opponents are extreme and destructive whereas you have history on your side renders dialogue not just impossible but unfathomable. Perhaps that is where the country already stands. In an August 2022 poll, the same high proportion of Democrats and Republicans (69 percent) considered American democracy to be verging on collapse, while identifying entirely different culprits (namely, the opposition) for that danger.

Even in 1991, Hirschman seemed to anticipate a both-sides-ism critique of his book. "My purpose is not to cast 'a plague on both your houses,'" he assured readers. I mostly believe him. It is no accident that the book focuses overwhelmingly on right-wing transgressions. But even if he did not intend to cast a plague on both houses, he understood that both houses can help spread one. Hirschman examined rhetoric across a range of political beliefs because he longed "to move public discourse beyond extreme, intransigent postures of either kind, with the hope that in the process our debates will become more 'democracy friendly.' "

That "friendly" is not squishy; Hirschman was not merely wishing for a more civil public square. He viewed democratic pluralism as a shaky bargain, based not on a consensus over shared political values but on a recognition by competing sides that none could achieve political dominance. "Tolerance and acceptance of pluralism resulted eventually from a standoff between bitterly hostile opposing groups," Hirschman wrote. Democracy is not what partisans believe in; it is what they settle for.

When one group feels it can dominate by disregarding the terms of that democratic bargain, as many Republicans do today, what will compel them to remain a party to it? When those on the left see their opponents becoming incoherent and dangerous, what prevents them from developing the self-enclosed self-assurance that their way is the only way, that any complicating critique is simply bad faith and therefore easily disregarded, that they are not just history's participants but ultimately its masters?

Chroniclers of the American story love to describe the country's democratic system as an experiment, a term often uttered with the pride of the exceptional, with that last-best-hope swagger. But experiments can falter, and that confidence has morphed into anxiety and, in some quarters, indifference. Hirschman's book identifies one reason. Democracy's legitimacy and durability depend on dialogue and deliberation—on process as much as on outcomes—but the arguments commonly invoked on various sides "are in effect contraptions specifically designed to make dialogue and deliberation impossible." Hirschman did not despair of this fact, though he foresaw a "long and difficult road" to a less facile public debate.

To call my mind "Hirschmanian" was undeserved praise, in college and certainly now. Experiencing Hirschman's mind is more than enough.

The Rhetoric of Reaction has been described as the most characteristic of his books, with its "delight in paradox" and "insistence on the creative power of doubt," as Cass Sunstein put it in the *New York Review of Books*. I read it as a good faith examination of bad faith and, with my own bias for hope, as an affirmation that even if the American experiment can go wrong, there is no reason to stop experimenting with America.

October 2022

ORIGINAL PUBLICATION
INFORMATION

"The Memoir George H. W. Bush Could Have Written" was published as "The memoir I wish George H. W. Bush had written" in the *Washington Post*, December 1, 2018.

"The Self-Referential Presidency of Barack Obama" was published in the *Washington Post*, December 15, 2016.

"The Choices of Barack Obama" was originally published as "Before Michelle, Barack Obama asked another woman to marry him. Then politics got in the way" in the *Washington Post*, May 2, 2017.

"The Examined Life of Barack Obama" was published in the *Washington Post*, November 17, 2020.

"The Last Throes of Dick Cheney" was published in the *Washington Post*, September 3, 2015.

"Hillary Clinton's Only Manifesto" was published as "This is the closest thing we've ever had to a Hillary Clinton political manifesto" in the *Washington Post*, February 25, 2016.

"The Evergreen Hillary Clinton" was published as "To understand Hillary Clinton, don't watch the convention. Read her memoirs" in the *Washington Post*, July 22, 2016.

"How to Hate Hillary Clinton, Especially If You Already Do" was published as "These books will help you hate Hillary Clinton. But only if you already do" in the *Washington Post*, October 7, 2016.

"The Collected Works of Donald Trump" was published as "I just binge-read eight books by Donald Trump. Here's what I learned" in the *Washington Post*, July 30, 2015.

"Donald Trump and the Fictional American Dictator" was published as "How does Donald Trump stack up against American literature's fictional dictators? Pretty well, actually" in the *Washington Post*, June 9, 2016.

"American Presidents Get the Scandals They Deserve" was published as "The presidency survived the Watergate, Iran-contra and Clinton scandals. Trump will exact a higher toll" in the *Washington Post*, December 21, 2017.

"Meet the Trumps" was published as "The real villain of Mary Trump's family tell-all isn't Donald. It's Fred" in the *Washington Post*, July 9, 2020.

"Three Ways to Write About Donald Trump" was published as "How the House of Trump Was Built" in the *New York Times*, December 28, 2022.

"The Premature Redemption of Mike Pence" was published as "Mike Pence is Having a Moment He Doesn't Deserve" in the *New York Times*, November 29, 2022.

"The Luck of Joe Biden" was published as "Joe Biden won the presidency by making the most of his lucky breaks" in the *Washington Post*, February 28, 2021.

"The False Choices of Kamala Harris" was published as "In her memoir, Kamala Harris calls for social change, but plays the inside game" in the *Washington Post*, August 14, 2020.

"Ron DeSantis and His Enemies" was published as "Ron DeSantis Has a Secret Theory of Trump" in the *New York Times*, March 19, 2023.

"Biden's 'Still' versus Trump's 'Again' " was published as "In One Word, Biden and Trump Tell Us Exactly Who They Are" in the *New York Times*, August 8, 2023.

"9/11 Was a Test, and We Failed" was published as "9/11 was a test. The books of the last two decades show how America failed" in the *Washington Post*, September 3, 2021.

"The Cautionary Tale of H. R. McMaster" was published as "20 years ago, H. R. McMaster wrote a cautionary tale. Now he risks becoming one" in the *Washington Post*, May 19, 2017.

"How to Read Vladimir Putin" was originally published in the *Washington Post*, March 3, 2022.

"Liberals versus Authoritarians" was published as "Authoritarianism is surging. Can liberal democracy fight back?" in the *Washington Post*, May 13, 2022.

"A History of America's Coming War with China" was published as "A Look Back at Our Future War With China" in the *New York Times*, July 18, 2023.

"Reading Tocqueville at Just the Right Time" was published as "The book every new citizen—and every old one, too—should read" in the *Washington Post*, December 17, 2015.

"The Radical Chic of Ta-Nehisi Coates" was published in the *Washington Post*, July 16, 2015.

"The Project of the 1619 Project" was published as "The 1619 Project started as history. Now it's also a political program" in the *Washington Post*, November 19, 2021.

"Always Columbine" was published as "17 years after Columbine, the mother of one of the killers finally tells her story" in the *Washington Post*, February 13, 2016.

"Josh Hawley and the Problem with Men" was published as "Men Have Lost Their Way. Josh Hawley Has Thoughts About How to Save Them" in the *New York Times*, June 1, 2023.

"The Challenges of Impeachment" was published as "What It Would Take: Can impeachment appear legitimate in a hyper-partisan environment?" in the *Washington Post*, January 25, 2019.

"Stacey Abrams's Leap of Faith" was published as "Stacey Abrams wants to be Biden's veep. But her new book is about bigger hopes" in the *Washington Post*, June 4, 2020.

"Of Scandals and Warnings" was published as "Every report on past presidential scandal was a warning. Why didn't we listen?" in the *Washington Post*, March 22, 2019.

"The United Hates of America" was published in the *Washington Post*, October 30, 2020.

"The Big Lie and the Big Joke" was published as "The Inside Joke That Became Trump's Big Lie" in the *New York Times*, September 22, 2022.

"Mueller, Ukraine, and January 6" was published as "This Is What Happened When the Authorities Put Trump Under a Microscope" in the *New York Times*, February 9, 2023.

"*Roe, Casey*, and *Dobbs*" was published as "How three major abortion rulings reveal a fractured culture" in the *Washington Post*, July 1, 2022.

"How Far Will the Justices Go?" was published as "In Which Conservative Justices Ponder Just How Far They Will Go" in the *New York Times*, April 13, 2023.

"The Next Civil War" was published as "A new book imagines a looming civil war over the very meaning of America" in the *Washington Post*, January 6, 2022.

"Making It in This Town" was published as "Review of Mark Leibovich's 'This Town'" in the *Washington Post*, July 3, 2013.

"When Politicians Acknowledge" was published as "God, family and donors: Inside the book acknowledgments of the 2016 GOP field" in the *Washington Post*, August 27, 2015.

"Critical Carlos Reads Healthy Holly" was published in the *Washington Post* on April 5, 2019.

"The Self-Regard of James Comey" was published as "In his new book, James Comey calls for 'ethical leadership.' But does he live up to it?" in the *Washington Post*, April 14, 2018.

"Profiles in Thinking About Courage" was published as "Profiles in Thinking About Courage: inside 'A Warning' by Anonymous" in the *Washington Post*, November 13, 2019.

"Down and Out in Trump World" was published as "An aide dishes on the Trump White House. But what does she say for herself?" in the *Washington Post*, October 1, 2021.

"The Generic Intellectualism of Ben Sasse" was published as "What Exactly is Ben Sasse the Right Guy For?" in the *New York Times*, October 13, 2022.

"The Speechwriter" was published as "What it's like to write speeches for a rude, rambling and disgraced politician" in the *Washington Post*, July 8, 2015.

"Why Reactionary Nostalgia Beats Liberal Hope" was published as "Why reactionary nostalgia is stronger than liberal hope" in the *Washington Post*, September 9, 2016.

"Samuel Huntington, a Prophet for the Trump Era" was published in the *Washington Post*, July 18, 2017.

"America Needs a Few Good Myths" was published as "I Looked Behind the Curtain of American History, and This Is What I Found" in the *New York Times*, January 6, 2023.

"When America Thought for Itself" was published as "How Americans re-learned to think after World War II" in the *Washington Post*, April 16, 2021.

"How to Strangle Democracy While Pretending to Engage in It" was published in the *New York Times*, October 20, 2022.

ACKNOWLEDGMENTS

BEHIND EVERY ESSAY IN THIS book there is an editor who sharpened my thoughts, improved my prose, and commanded my trust. Special thanks to Adam Kushner and Aaron Retica, as well as to Steven Levingston, Jennifer Morehead, Janet Byrne, Marisa Bellack, Tracy Grant, Cameron Barr, Sally Buzbee, Marty Baron, and Katie Kingsbury.

It is a lucky journalist who has worked for either the *Washington Post* or the *New York Times*; it is a blessed one who has worked for both. I am grateful to the *Post* and the *Times* for allowing me to reproduce the essays, columns, and reviews that appear in *The Washington Book* but even more so for letting me write them at all. It is a privilege to work in institutions with a culture of ambition, collaboration, and independence.

This is my second book with Priscilla Painton and Jonathan Karp of Simon & Schuster and with Gail Ross of WME. I am honored by your confidence and grateful for your patience.

Jason Kelly of the University of Notre Dame's Gallivan program in journalism, ethics, and democracy invited me to deliver the 2023 Red Smith Lecture, a wonderful experience that inspired this book. My thanks as well to Meghan Sullivan, Angie Appleby Purcell, and everyone at the Notre Dame Institute for Advanced Study for your intellectual fellowship (plus drinks at Rohr's), and to my *Matter of Opinion* podcast comrades Michelle Cottle, Ross Douthat, and Lydia Polgreen, for making me smarter on just about everything.

My endless gratitude to my mother, Maya, and my sister Rosi for your love and lessons; and to my late father, Elias, and my departed sister, Marilu, for your loving memories.

Jamie, Fiona, and Finn, you are the reason for everything I do. Thanks for letting me still read with you, even as you grow older.

Kathleen McBride, this book is for you. You've always wanted it, and you gave it its title. With love, here it is.

INDEX

ABOUT THE AUTHOR

Carlos Lozada is a *New York Times* opinion columnist and winner of the Pulitzer Prize for Criticism. He is the author of *What Were We Thinking: A Brief Intellectual History of the Trump Era* and cohost of the weekly *Matter of Opinion* podcast. Previously, Lozada was a senior editor and book critic at the *Washington Post* and managing editor of *Foreign Policy* magazine. He has been a Knight-Bagehot fellow at Columbia University and a professor of political journalism at the University of Notre Dame. A native of Lima, Peru, he became a US citizen in 2014.